CORTE
AND THE INTERIOR
See pp130–151

**AJACCIO AND
THE WEST COAST**

Ajaccio

*Îles
Sanguinaires*

**BONIFACIO AND
THE SOUTH**

Bonifacio

Île Cavallo

Îles Lavezzi

BONIFACIO
AND THE SOUTH
See pp106–129

0 kilometre

0 miles

15

D0993640

EYEWITNESS TRAVEL GUIDES

CORSICA

EYEWITNESS TRAVEL GUIDES

CORSICA

LONDON, NEW YORK,
MELBOURNE, MUNICH AND DELHI
www.dk.com

PRODUCED BY Fabio Ratti Editoria Srl, Milan, Italy

PROJECT EDITOR Donatella Ceriani

ART EDITOR Oriana Bianchetti

EDITORS Marina Beretta, Angela Magrì

DESIGNER Elisabetta Mancini

CONTRIBUTORS Fabrizio Ardito, Cristina Gambaro, Angela Magrì

PHOTOGRAPHERS Fabrizio Ardito, Adriano Bacchella,
Cristina Gambaro, Lucio Rossi, Marco Stoppato

CARTOGRAPHERS Grafema Cartografia Srl, Novara

ILLUSTRATORS Modi Artistici, Anna Mucciarelli, Tiziano Perotto

ENGLISH TRANSLATION Richard Pierce

Dorling Kindersley Limited
EDITORS Sylvia and David Tombesi-Walton (Sands
Publishing Solutions); Lauren Robertson
CONSULTANT David Abram
SENIOR DTP DESIGNER Jason Little
PRODUCTION Melanie Dowland

Reproduced by Fabio Ratti Editoria Srl, Milan
and in Singapore by Colourscan
Printed and bound in China by
Toppan Printing Co. (Shenzhen Ltd)

First published in Great Britain in 2003
by Dorling Kindersley Limited,
80 Strand, London WC2R 0RL

Reprinted with revisions 2006

Copyright © 2003, 2006 Dorling Kindersley Limited, London
A Penguin Company

ALL RIGHTS RESERVED. NO PART OF THIS PUBLICATION MAY
BE REPRODUCED, STORED IN A RETRIEVAL SYSTEM, OR TRANSMITTED
IN ANY FORM OR BY ANY MEANS, ELECTRONIC, MECHANICAL,
PHOTOCOPYING, RECORDING OR OTHERWISE WITHOUT THE
PRIOR WRITTEN PERMISSION OF THE COPYRIGHT OWNER.

A CIP CATALOGUE RECORD IS AVAILABLE FROM THE BRITISH LIBRARY.

ISBN 13: 978 1 40531 185 4
ISBN 10: 1 40531 185 1

**The information in this
Eyewitness Travel Guide is checked annually**.
Every effort has been made to ensure that this book is as up-to-date
as possible at the time of going to press. Some details, however,
such as telephone numbers, opening hours, prices, gallery hanging
arrangements and travel information are liable to change. The
publishers cannot accept responsibility for any consequences arising
from the use of this book, nor for any material on third party
websites, and cannot guarantee that any website address in this
book will be a suitable source of travel information. We value the
views and suggestions of our readers very highly. Please write to:
Publisher, DK Eyewitness Travel Guides,
Dorling Kindersley, 80 Strand, London WC2R 0RL, Great Britain.

◁ The white limestone cliffs at Bonifacio, with the famous Grain de Sable

CONTENTS

The Romanesque church
of San Michele de Murato

Laricio pines in the beautiful
Forêt d'Aïtone

Cheese and charcuterie – two of
the many specialities of Corsica

OUTDOOR
ACTIVITIES *180*

SURVIVAL GUIDE

PRACTICAL
INFORMATION *188*

TRAVEL
INFORMATION *196*

GENERAL INDEX
200

A crystal-clear sea and white rocks in a cove in front of Îles Lavezzi

A typical maquis plant,
Euphorbia dendroides, in bloom

Snow-capped mountains near
Monte Cinto

The "Moor's
Head", symbol of
Independent Corsica

The citadel in Corte, with
Musée de la Corse and the University

HOW TO USE THIS GUIDE

THIS GUIDE helps visitors to get the most out of their stay in Corsica by providing detailed descriptions, practical information and expert advice. *Introducing Corsica* sets the island in its geographical, historical and cultural context. *Corsica Area by Area* describes the main sights in detail, with maps, photographs and illustrations. *Travellers' Needs* offers recommendations on hotels, restaurants, local food, bars, shopping, sports and entertainment, while the *Survival Guide* provides useful information on safety, health, transport and local currency.

CORSICA AREA BY AREA

Corsica has been divided into four main areas, each coded with a coloured thumb tab *(see the front flap and inside front cover)*. The sights described in the regions are plotted and numbered on a *Pictorial Map*. The key to symbols and a *Road Map* can be found on the back flap and inside back cover.

1 Corsica at a Glance
This presents the island divided into four areas, whose colours correspond to those on the colour-coded thumb tabs.

The drawings illustrate the main sights in each area.

2 Introduction
The history, landscape and character of each area are described here, showing how the region has developed over time and what it has to offer visitors.

The area colour code is in the top margin of each page.

A locator map shows the colour of each area in relation to the island of Corsica for quick reference.

3 Pictorial Map
This gives an illustrated overview of the area. All the sights covered in the chapter are numbered and there is useful information on getting around by car and public transport.

4 Major Towns
All major towns are described on two or more pages, with the most interesting sights described individually.

The Town Map shows the main streets. The key sights are plotted, along with the parking areas, churches and tourist-information offices.

Practical Information
includes the location of the towns and villages on the *Road Map*.

5 Detailed Information
All important places to visit are described individually, and also have detailed practical information. The entries are listed in order, following the numbering on the Pictorial Map.

Boxes highlight special or unique aspects of an area or sight.

6 Tours
These features provide useful tips on interesting artistic or nature tours. The stages of each tour are numbered, and information is given on refuges and where to buy provisions.

A Visitors' Checklist provides a summary of the practical information necessary for planning a visit.

The scale gives an idea of the distances and a wind rose indicates north.

7 Corsica's Top Sights
In two or more pages, historic buildings or fortifications are dissected to reveal their interiors, while photographs highlight the most interesting features.

Stars indicate sights that visitors should not miss.

INTRODUCING
CORSICA

Putting Corsica on the Map

CORSICA IS A REGION of France, but geographically it lies closer to Italy, between the Ligurian and Tyrrhenian seas, separated from Sardinia by the wind-swept Straits of Bonifacio, and only a few nautical miles from the coast of Tuscany. The island has an area of 8,680 sq km (3,350 sq miles) and a population of around 260,000, which increases considerably in the summer, when tourists arrive. The administrative capital is Ajaccio, while Corte is referred to as the historical capital and Bastia as the economic capital.

F R A N C E

Turin

Monaco
Nice

Marseille

Toulon

Mediterranean Sea

NORWAY
FINLAND
SWEDEN
ESTONIA
UNITED
KINGDOM
IRELAND
DENMARK
LATVIA
LITHUANIA
RUSSIA
THE NETHERLANDS
BELARUS
ATLANTIC
OCEAN
BELGIUM GERMANY
POLAND
LUXEMBOURG
CZECH REP.
UKRAINE
SLOVAKIA
FRANCE
SWITZERLAND AUSTRIA
HUNGARY
SLOVENIA
MOLDOVA
PORTUGAL
ANDORRA
CROATIA
BOS-HERZ
ROMANIA
SERBIA AND
MONTENEGRO
BULGARIA
SPAIN
CORSICA
Ajaccio
ITALY
MAC.
ALBANIA
SARDINIA
GREECE

Porto
Torres

Sassari

0 kilometres   50

0 miles   50

◁ **A Corsican village depicted by Xiaoyang Galas in her oil painting *Sea, Sun and Village***

A satellite image of Corsica

Lago d'Iseo

Milan

E64

E70

E35

E62

E70

Po

I T A L Y

E25

E33

E70

Genoa

E80

Ligurian Sea

E76

Arno

Florence

Livorno

E78

Perugia

Piombino

E35

E45

Tevere

D80

Porto S. Stefano

alvi N197

Bastia

Civitavecchia

E80

ROME

N193

Corte

N200

CORSICA

accio N196 *Taravo* N198

Tyrrhenian Sea

Bonifacio

200

Olbia

Cagliari

Cagliari

Palermo

SARDINIA

597

KEY

✈	International airport
⚓	Ferry port or service
▭	Motorway
▬	Major road
═	Minor road
---	National border
----	Ferry route

A PORTRAIT OF CORSICA

THE LIGHT-REFLECTING GRANITE ROCKS, *the dense, dark forests, the sandy coves, the expansive panoramas of Cap Corse or the compressed Bozio valley – Corsica is an enigmatic island with many and varied facets. Despite its large number of visitors, the island remains a wild and fascinating place.*

A long, slow continental drift moved Corsica from the coast of Provence to its present position, in the northernmost waters of the Tyrrhenian Sea, with the Côte d'Azur and the Tuscan archipelago only a stone's throw away. A central chain of tall mountains culminating in Monte Cinto (2,706 m/8,878 ft) descends from Calvi, in the northwest, towards Porto-Vecchio, in the southeast corner of the island, separating it into two distinct regions. Pisan and Genoan rulers called the northeastern part *Diqua dei monti* ("Hither the mountains") while the for them inaccessible, untamed southwestern part was known as *Dila dei monti* ("Beyond

A brotherhood member

the mountains"). Geologically, the divide separates the schist regions to the east from the predominantly granite areas descending towards the west coast. The exceptions to this rule are the extraordinary landscapes along the coasts of the Scandola Nature Reserve, the result of ancient volcanic eruptions, and the bright limestone rich in fossils on the cliffs of the south coast, especially around Bonifacio. Inland, mountains, gorges and torrents make Corsica a hiker's paradise. "Imagine a world still in the midst of chaos, a tempest of mountains separating narrow gorges in which torrents flow," wrote the French author Guy de Maupassant.

A fishmonger's stall at the Ajaccio marina

◁ **The crowded Vieux Port of Bastia, with the characteristic façade of the church of St-Jean-Baptiste**

Traditional Corsican products

He continues "No plains, but rather immense waves of granite and colossal undulations of earth covered with maquis or tall chestnut and pine forests." Much of Corsica's fascination is due to this lush interior cut through by wild torrents, a sign that it receives a heavier rainfall than the other Mediterranean islands. Corsica also has a splendid sea that is much admired by travellers from all over the world. This means, of course, that the coastline is often crowded, but it is still possibly to find secluded coves, only accessible by foot or boat.

A local handmade marionette

AN AGE-OLD CULTURE

Archaeologists say that the first humans arrived in Corsica around 9,000 years ago, probably after dangerous, but short, sea journeys from the Tuscan coast. The first Corsicans owed their survival to the breeding of livestock and hunting, which later gave rise to their own unique

Sheep on their way to a pasture – an age-old Corsican scene

megalithic culture. The best examples of this can be found in the southwest region of the island: the menhirs of Filitosa, the dolmens at Sartène and the *castelli* at Cucuruzzu and Capula. Agricultural products were introduced by Greek colonists and then spread when the Romans conquered the island and made the principal city, Aléria, their capital. With the grim and chaotic Middle Ages came invaders, pirates, preachers and, above all, merchants. A bone of contention between the agile ships of Pisa and Genoa, Corsica became a Genoese colony in the 13th century and was to remain so, amid revolts and battles, up to the 18th century.

THE "CORSICAN NATION"

The Corsicans were fierce opponents already of the Roman legions and have always felt they were a separate people with their own language (still a hallmark of the "Corsican nation") and ancient traditions. The downfall of Genoese power paved the way for the French and, at the same time, for the brief but crucial period of independence, linked to the figure of Pascal Paoli, the "Father of the Nation" (*see pp46–7*). Renowned as the birthplace of Napoleon Bonaparte – who was born in Ajaccio on 15 August 1769 – Corsica has been part of France for over two centuries.

The Corsicans' continued demands for independence from France are a sign of their national pride, which is rooted in the distant past. Although there is still an ardent yearning for the "Corsican nation", support for the violent paramilitary groups so active in the 1970s is no longer very strong. Since the

Starting a sailing trip from a Corsican beach

Matignon Agreement, finally reached in 2001, France has been investing heavily in both economy and infrastructure on the island, a fact that perhaps has made total autonomy less tempting. The wish for cultural independence and identity, however, is still deeply felt, with manifestations centred at the University of Corte, and through an abundance of websites relating to the island's language, history and traditions *(see also pp30–31).*

THE PEOPLE AND THE LAND

There are only about 260,000 Corsicans on the island; three times as many work in mainland France. During the winter, as less jobs are available in the tourism sector, many leave for temporary work on the continent. The majority of the population live along the coast, mostly near the main towns such as

Ajaccio and Bastia. Apart from Corte, the interior is sparsley inhabited – a fact that makes it appealing to the many visitors who come here to experience wilderness, leaving behind the hustle and bustle of modern life. Paradoxically, what leads to a diminishing population and lack of conventional work opportunities, is in some way still beneficial since it attracts tourists.

Luckily tourism, despite being a major source of income, has not been allowed to take over the island, not even along the coasts. So far, the natural environment and local traditions have been respected, thanks to projects such as the Parc Régional de la Corse *(see p99),* and there are no sprawling highrise resorts on the island.

Corsicans are generally quite traditional, and family comes first – a reflection of the old clan values *(see p31).* Women might no longer be the cause of vendettas, but the attitude towards them is very conservative and, compared to northern Europe, equality is a very remote goal. On the other hand, no one receives more respect than a Corsican mother.

The locals' reputation of aloofness or suspiciousness towards strangers is not altogether an exaggeration, but visitors who show respect and admiration for this captivating island will be welcome and treated with Mediterranean warmth.

One of Corsica's many beaches

Corsica's Landscape and Fauna

CORSICA IS ESSENTIALLY a tall, craggy peak descending to the sea, with valleys furrowed by mountain torrents and small plains around the river estuaries. As well as the coastline and the sea, the mountains also offer spectacular natural scenery, with summits over 2,500 m (8,200 ft) high and the large Corsican pine forests that cover the central zone of the island. Many rivers, mostly along the east coast, create coastal lakes called *étangs* near their outlets. There is an abundance of flora, with almost 3,000 species of plants, 80 of which are endemic, providing a marvellous carpet of Mediterranean maquis (*see p73*).

A river along the route to the Col de Bavella

THE COASTLINE

The maquis undergrowth dominates the coastline up to the first hill ranges. In the eastern plain around Porto-Vecchio and in the peninsula of Cap Corse there are cork oaks and holm oaks. In the inhabited coastal areas, the century plants (Mexican agave), palm trees, prickly pears and aloes create an exotic atmosphere. The large umbrella pine woods are particularly thick around Porto-Vecchio and Calvi.

THE HILLS

Maquis shrubs cover the first hill ranges and are present up to 1,000 m (3,300 ft). Olive trees grow to an altitude of 600 m (2,000 ft). At a lower level, vineyards cover the seaward slopes of Cap Corse, the Nebbio area, and the eastern and southern coastal plains. The numerous citrus-fruit orchards boast fine oranges, lemons, mandarins, limes and clementines. There are also many eucalyptus trees, introduced in 1868 to drain the swampy coasts and eradicate malaria.

The aloe *is a succulent plant with spinous leaves that, from January to April, has lovely red or yellow tubular flowers that bloom in thick clusters.*

Woodpeckers *live in the woods of Corsica. Visitors may hear their characteristic pecking and glimpse their bright plumage among the pine and cork oak trees.*

Myrtle *is a fragrant evergreen shrub that thrives in sunny areas. Its lovely white flowers bloom in spring, while the berries mature in the autumn.*

Olive trees *are among the trees that live longest, becoming gnarled with time. Olives are harvested by hanging large nets under each tree.*

WILDLIFE

As well as the wild boar and the rarely seen moufflon, which is the symbol of the island, the Corsican deer has also recently returned to the area, thanks to a reintroduction project. The rocky coasts are the habitat of such marine birds as seagulls, ospreys and cormorants. In the

Tyrrhenian wall lizard

A family of boars, common in Corsica

maquis, the Hermann's tortoise can be found, which is closely related to a species now extinct on the European continent. There are no vipers in Corsica, but there are two endemic species of lizard, the Tyrrhenian wall lizard and the Bedriaga's wall lizard, as well as the harmless Aesculapian snake. The sea is rich in fish, including groupers and breams, and also provides tasty molluscs and crustaceans.

THE FORESTS

The central zone of the island is an immense forest, except for the valley floors and the areas destroyed by fire. At an altitude of 500–800 m (1,600–2,600 ft) there are chestnut trees, planted by the Genoese. Chestnuts were a staple in the diet of the mountain population. Further up, at 700–1,500 m (2,300–5,000 ft), are the conifers, with the marvellous Valdu-Niellu, Aïtone and Vizzavona forests, dominated by giant Laricio pines.

Mushrooms thrive in the damp underbrush of the forests, at the foot of conifers and beech trees. They are gathered from late summer onwards.

Chestnuts mature in early autumn. As the prickly burs fall to the ground, they break, showing the nuts inside. September and October are the ideal times for hikes among the chestnut orchards.

THE MOUNTAINS

Covered by snow from autumn to late spring, the mountains in Corsica are tall and solitary, inhabited only by a few shepherds. At 1,500 m (5,000 ft), the woods give way to alders, junipers and barberries. Higher up, just before the rocky peaks, are the grassy mountain pastures. The tallest peaks are Monte Cinto (2,706 m/8,878 ft), Monte Rotondo (2,622 m/8,602 ft), Monte Padro (2,393 m/ 7,851 ft) and Monte d'Oro (2,389 m/7,838 ft).

The golden eagle is a formidable raptor that lives on the tallest peaks. It can catch large prey, such as lambs, in its powerful talons.

The juniper is one of the characteristic and most fragrant plants of the high mountain zones. It can be recognized by its silver-green needles and almost black berries.

The Corsican Coastline

Maritime pine cones

FROM THE SMALL ISOLATED BAYS among granite rocks on the west coast, to the long sandy beaches between Bastia and Bonifacio that are ideal for family holidays, Corsica is a paradise for sunbathers. The island's 1,000 km (620 miles) of coastline offer visitors the chance to lie in the sun from May to October, and it is possible to find secluded spots even in July and August. Except for the major beaches near towns such as Calvi, Porto-Vecchio and Ajaccio, most have no lifeguards, so it is advisable to be cautious when bathing, especially when the wind is strong and the sea is rough.

From St-Florent to L'Île Rousse, small bays with fine sand alternate with cliffs covered in maquis.

From Calvi to Ajaccio, steep cliffs line the coast and many beaches can be reached only by sea. Landing is not possible along the red cliffs of the Scandola Nature Reserve.

0 kilometres 25

0 miles 15

Golfe d'Ajaccio has many beaches and rocky areas. The Pointe de la Parata peninsula extends into the sea towards the Îles Sanguinaires, where the sea is crystal clear.

The white cliffs along the southern coast around Bonifacio are among the best known in Corsica. Some of the large rocks even have a name, such as the famous Grain de Sable ("grain of sand"), seen here in the background.

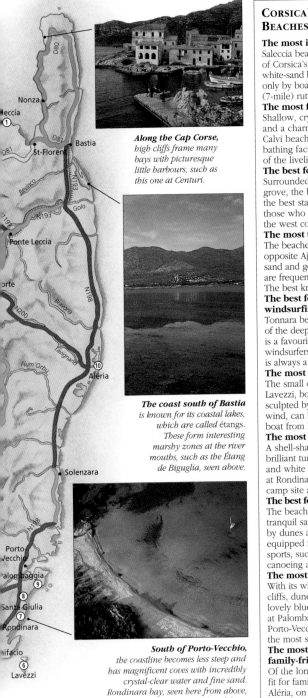

Along the Cap Corse, high cliffs frame many bays with picturesque little harbours, such as this one at Centuri.

The coast south of Bastia is known for its coastal lakes, which are called étangs. These form interesting marshy zones at the river mouths, such as the Étang de Biguglia, seen above.

South of Porto-Vecchio, the coastline becomes less steep and has magnificent coves with incredibly crystal-clear water and fine sand. Rondinara bay, seen here from above, is one of the best examples of these.

CORSICA'S TEN BEST BEACHES

The most inaccessible ①
Saleccia beach *(see p72)*, one of Corsica's most arresting white-sand bays, is accessible only by boat or via an 11-km (7-mile) rutted track.

The most fashionable ②
Shallow, crystal-clear water and a charming harbour: Calvi beach, with fine bathing facilities, is one of the liveliest in Corsica.

The best for diving ③
Surrounded by a eucalyptus grove, the beach at Porto is the best starting point for those who want to explore the west coast's sea floor.

The most urban ④
The beaches at Porticcio, opposite Ajaccio, have white sand and good facilities and are frequented by the locals. The best known is La Viva.

The best for windsurfing ⑤
Tonnara beach, at the end of the deep Golfe de Figari, is a favourite with expert windsurfers because there is always a stiff breeze.

The most sheltered ⑥
The small coves of the Îles Lavezzi, bordered by rocks sculpted by the sand and wind, can be reached by boat from Bonifacio.

The most tropical ⑦
A shell-shaped cove with brilliant turquoise water and white sand, the beach at Rondinara also has a camp site and a restaurant.

The best for watersports ⑧
The beach at Santa Giulia, a tranquil sandy bay bordered by dunes and pine trees, is equipped for all aquatic sports, such as windsurfing, canoeing and sailing.

The most photogenic ⑨
With its white sand, pink cliffs, dunes, pines and a lovely blue sea, the beach at Palombaggia, south of Porto-Vecchio, is perhaps the most spectacular.

The most family-friendly ⑩
Of the long, sandy beaches fit for families, the best is at Aléria, on the east coast.

GR20: Stages 1–5

CROSSING CORSICA from northwest to southeast, the GR20 (Grande Randonnée 20) is 200 km (124 miles) long. The path runs at an average altitude of 1,000–2,000 m (3,300–6,600 ft), linking Calenzana, in the Balagne region, with Conca, in the Porto-Vecchio hinterland. Every year several thousand hikers try this tour, which is only for those in very good condition. The GR20 is divided into 15 stages, and the hikes last from 8am–5pm on terrain with altitude differences as much as 800 m (2,600 ft). Stages 1 to 5 have spectacular but difficult stretches, the most notorious being Cirque de la Solitude, a route fitted with fixed ladders, chains and cables.

The Sentier de Spasimata *is a path that skirts the slopes of the Cirque de Bonifatu. It is famous for the recently restored footbridge suspended over a torrent.*

The refuges *along the route are small stone constructions built in the local mountain architectural style, so that they blend in well with the natural setting. The Carozzu refuge is immersed in the surrounding vegetation; other refuges are in open meadows.*

The alpine asphodel *is a species of plant that blooms between late May and June.*

WARNING

The GR20 route is recommended only for persons in good physical condition, with some experience in hiking and climbing. Hikers must be equipped with mountain boots, waterproof jackets, fleece wear, sun hats and first-aid kits. From June to September expensive food is available at some refuges, but it is safest to bring your own provisions. You can restock (on food and drink) at points where the trail descends to road level.

CALVI

Calenzan
tiny village in
Balagne region
where the G
begins. The
stage has a ste
ascent an
quite challeng

Ortu di u Piob

Stage 1
Start: *Calenzana (275 m/902 ft)*
Finish: *Ortu di u Piobbu refuge (1,570 m/5,151 ft)*
Length: *10 km (6 miles)*
Degree of difficulty: *hard*
Average duration: *7 hours*
Maximum altitude: *1,570 m (5,151 ft)*
Stopover: *Ortu di u Piobbu refuge (bed space for 30)*

CIRQUE DE BONIFATU

Carozzu

Stage 2
Start: *Ortu di u Piobbu refuge (1,570 m/5,151 ft)*
Finish: *Carozzu refuge (1,270 m/4,167 ft)*
Length: *8 km (5 miles)*
Degree of difficulty: *hard*
Average duration: *6 1/2 hours*
Maximum altitude: *1,950 m (6,400 ft)*
Stopover: *Carozzu refuge (bed space for 26)*

CIRQUE

Stage 5
Start: *Bergeries de Ballone (1,440 m/4,724 ft)*
Finish: *Castel de Verghio (1,404 m/4,606 ft)*
Length: *13 km (8 miles)*
Degree of difficulty: *average*
Average duration: *7 hours*
Maximum altitude: *2,000 m (6,562 ft)*
Stopover: *Castel de Verghio hotel (29 rooms and restaurant)*

Col de Verghio

Castel de Verg

EVISA

D84

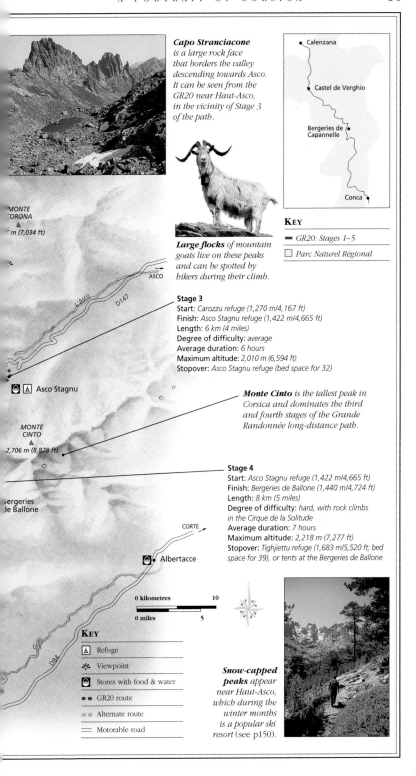

Capo Stranciacone *is a large rock face that borders the valley descending towards Asco. It can be seen from the GR20 near Haut-Asco, in the vicinity of Stage 3 of the path.*

Calenzana

Castel de Verghio

Bergeries de Capannelle

Conca

KEY

▬ *GR20: Stages 1–5*

☐ *Parc Naturel Régional*

Large flocks *of mountain goats live on these peaks and can be spotted by hikers during their climb.*

MONTE CORONA
▲
m (7,034 ft)

ASCO

L'Asco   D147

🏪 🛆 Asco Stagnu

MONTE CINTO
▲
2,706 m (8,878 ft)

ergeries de Ballone

CORTE

🏪 Albertacce

G30   D84

Stage 3
Start: *Carozzu refuge (1,270 m/4,167 ft)*
Finish: *Asco Stagnu refuge (1,422 m/4,665 ft)*
Length: *6 km (4 miles)*
Degree of difficulty: *average*
Average duration: *6 hours*
Maximum altitude: *2,010 m (6,594 ft)*
Stopover: *Asco Stagnu refuge (bed space for 32)*

Monte Cinto *is the tallest peak in Corsica and dominates the third and fourth stages of the Grande Randonnée long-distance path.*

Stage 4
Start: *Asco Stagnu refuge (1,422 m/4,665 ft)*
Finish: *Bergeries de Ballone (1,440 m/4,724 ft)*
Length: *8 km (5 miles)*
Degree of difficulty: *hard, with rock climbs in the Cirque de la Solitude*
Average duration: *7 hours*
Maximum altitude: *2,218 m (7,277 ft)*
Stopover: *Tighjiettu refuge (1,683 m/5,520 ft; bed space for 39), or tents at the Bergeries de Ballone*

0 kilometres   10

0 miles   5

KEY

🛆 Refuge

☆ Viewpoint

🏪 Stores with food & water

▪▪ GR20 route

▪ ▪ Alternate route

═ Motorable road

Snow-capped peaks *appear near Haut-Asco, which during the winter months is a popular ski resort (see p150).*

GR20: Stages 6–10

Stage 7 of the GR20 offers the best views but is one of the toughest stretches. It does not climb any peaks, but it crosses the GR20's highest pass, the Brêche de Castillo, at 2,225 m (7,300 ft). The easiest part is the eighth stage, a shaded route without steep slopes.

At the Col de Verghio the view opens on to a pass crossed by a motorable road. This is the edge of the Valdu-Niellu woods. A little further up are the alpine meadows and rocky zones.

Lac de Nino (Lake Nino) is a glacial lake that feeds the Tavignano river. It forms a marshy area called Pozzine ("the wells") that from above looks like lace work.

KEY

⚠	Refuge
❀	Viewpoint
⬢	Stores with food & water
■ ■	GR20 route
▪ ▪	Alternate route
=	Motorable road
■ ■	Other paths

Stage 6

Start: *Castel de Verghio (1,404 m/4,606 ft)*
Finish: *Manganu refuge (1,601 m/5,253 ft)*
Length: *14 km (9 miles)*
Degree of difficulty: *average*
Average duration: *5 1/2 hours*
Maximum altitude: *1,760 m (5,774 ft)*
Stopover: *Manganu refuge (bed space for 31)*

Lac de Capitello is surrounded by rocky scenery. The Punta dei Sette Laghi (Seven Lakes Peak) is so named because it affords an excellent view of a series of glacial lakes.

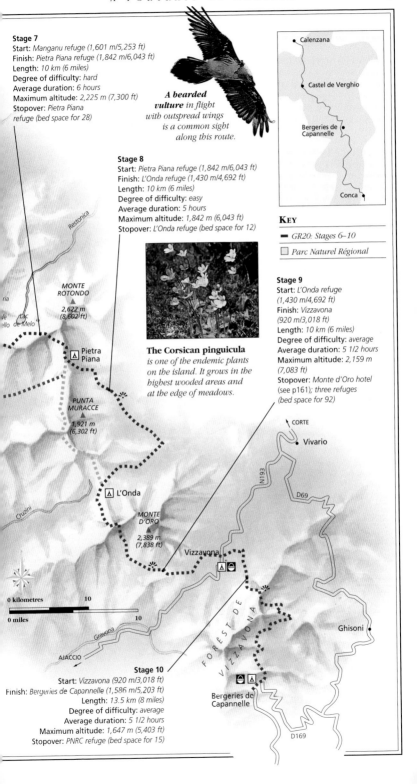

Stage 7
Start: *Manganu refuge (1,601 m/5,253 ft)*
Finish: *Pietra Piana refuge (1,842 m/6,043 ft)*
Length: *10 km (6 miles)*
Degree of difficulty: *hard*
Average duration: *6 hours*
Maximum altitude: *2,225 m (7,300 ft)*
Stopover: *Pietra Piana refuge (bed space for 28)*

A bearded vulture in flight with outspread wings is a common sight along this route.

Stage 8
Start: *Pietra Piana refuge (1,842 m/6,043 ft)*
Finish: *L'Onda refuge (1,430 m/4,692 ft)*
Length: *10 km (6 miles)*
Degree of difficulty: *easy*
Average duration: *5 hours*
Maximum altitude: *1,842 m (6,043 ft)*
Stopover: *L'Onda refuge (bed space for 12)*

KEY

— *GR20: Stages 6–10*

☐ *Parc Naturel Régional*

The Corsican pinguicula
is one of the endemic plants on the island. It grows in the highest wooded areas and at the edge of meadows.

Stage 9
Start: *L'Onda refuge (1,430 m/4,692 ft)*
Finish: *Vizzavona (920 m/3,018 ft)*
Length: *10 km (6 miles)*
Degree of difficulty: *average*
Average duration: *5 1/2 hours*
Maximum altitude: *2,159 m (7,083 ft)*
Stopover: *Monte d'Oro hotel (see p161); three refuges (bed space for 92)*

MONTE ROTONDO
2,622 m (8,602 ft)

Pietra Piana

PUNTA MURACCE
1,921 m (6,302 ft)

L'Onda

MONTE D'ORO
2,389 m (7,838 ft)

Vizzavona

CORTE
Vivario

N193
D69

Ghisoni

0 kilometres   10
0 miles   10

FOREST DE VIZZAVONA

AJACCIO

Bergeries de Capannelle

D169

Stage 10
Start: *Vizzavona (920 m/3,018 ft)*
Finish: *Bergeries de Capannelle (1,586 m/5,203 ft)*
Length: *13.5 km (8 miles)*
Degree of difficulty: *average*
Average duration: *5 1/2 hours*
Maximum altitude: *1,647 m (5,403 ft)*
Stopover: *PNRC refuge (bed space for 15)*

Calenzana
Castel de Verghio
Bergeries de Capannelle
Conca

GR20: Stages 11–15

THE LAST STAGES of the GR20 path offer no respite to those who have come this far without descending to the valley. Almost all stages have difficult stretches but make up for this with spectacular views, especially in the Aiguilles de Bavella area. Two weeks should be enough to walk the entire GR20, finishing at Conca.

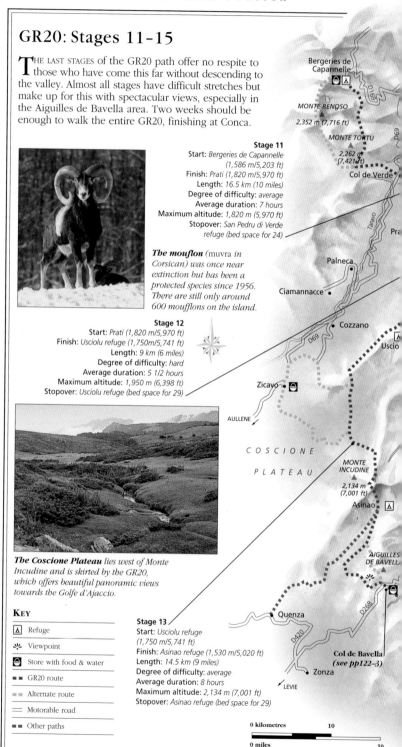

Stage 11
Start: *Bergeries de Capannelle (1,586 m/5,203 ft)*
Finish: *Prati (1,820 m/5,970 ft)*
Length: *16.5 km (10 miles)*
Degree of difficulty: *average*
Average duration: *7 hours*
Maximum altitude: *1,820 m (5,970 ft)*
Stopover: *San Pedru di Verde refuge (bed space for 24)*

The mouflon (muvra in
Corsican) was once near
extinction but has been a
protected species since 1956.
There are still only around
600 moufflons on the island.

Stage 12
Start: *Prati (1,820 m/5,970 ft)*
Finish: *Usciolu refuge (1,750m/5,741 ft)*
Length: *9 km (6 miles)*
Degree of difficulty: *hard*
Average duration: *5 1/2 hours*
Maximum altitude: *1,950 m (6,398 ft)*
Stopover: *Usciolu refuge (bed space for 29)*

The Coscione Plateau lies west of Monte
Incudine and is skirted by the GR20,
which offers beautiful panoramic views
towards the Golfe d'Ajaccio.

KEY

△	Refuge
�½	Viewpoint
⬟	Store with food & water
■ ■	GR20 route
▪ ▪	Alternate route
=	Motorable road
■ ■	Other paths

Stage 13
Start: *Usciolu refuge (1,750 m/5,741 ft)*
Finish: *Asinao refuge (1,530 m/5,020 ft)*
Length: *14.5 km (9 miles)*
Degree of difficulty: *average*
Average duration: *8 hours*
Maximum altitude: *2,134 m (7,001 ft)*
Stopover: *Asinao refuge (bed space for 29)*

Bergeries de
Capannelle

MONTE RENOSO
2,352 m (7,716 ft)

MONTE TORTU
2,262 m
(7,421 ft)

Col de Verde

Palneca

Ciamannacce

Cozzano

Uscio

Zicavo

AULLENE

COSCIONE
PLATEAU

MONTE
INCUDINE
2,134 m
(7,001 ft)

Asinao

AIGUILLES
DE BAVELL

Quenza

Col de Bavella
(see pp122–3)

Zonza

LEVIE

0 kilometres 10

0 miles 10

The kite is commonly seen in the Parc Naturel Régional (Regional Park). Kites can be recognized by their distinctive forked tail.

Calenzana

Castel de Verghio

Bergeries de Capannelle

Conca

KEY

━ *GR20: Stages 11–15*

□ *Parc Naturel Régional*

The martagon lily *is one of the most spectacular alpine bulbous plants, with large flowers that are easy to recognize because of their warm orange colour.*

Stage 14
Start: *Asinao refuge (1,530 m/5,020 ft)*
Finish: *Paliri refuge (1,040 m/3,412 ft)*
Length: *13 km (8 miles)*
Degree of difficulty: *hard*
Average duration: *6 1/4 hours*
Maximum altitude: *1,530 m (5,020 ft)*
Stopover: *Paliri refuge (bed space for 20)*

Punta Paliri *dominates the Bavella forest and rises up behind the Bavella refuge, which is the last high-altitude stage in the GR20 route before it descends back to "civilization".*

THE "SEA AND MOUNTAINS" AND "SEA TO SEA" PATHS

A hiker halfway between the mountains and the sea

The GR20 is not the only long hiking route in Corsica. There are two *Mare e Monti* (between sea and mountains) paths: the first links Calenzana to Cargèse in ten easy stages and the second goes from Porticcio to Propriano in five stages overlooking the sea. There are also three *Mare a Mare* (from sea to sea) paths: the northern one stretches from Moriani to Cargèse in 12 stages, the central one from Ghisonaccia to Porticcio in seven stages, and the southern path goes from Porto-Vecchio to Propriano in five stages. These paths are relatively easy to walk, although in the central zone they intersect with the GR20. *Gîtes d'étape* (hikers' hostels) along these routes offer half-board stopovers. See also page 180.

PUNTA D'ORTU
695 m (2,280 ft)

Conca

PORTO-VECCHIO

Stage 15
Start: *Paliri refuge (1,055 m/3,461 ft)*
Finish: *Conca (252 m/827 ft)*
Length: *12 km (7 miles)*
Degree of difficulty: *average*
Average duration: *5 hours*
Maximum altitude: *1,055 m (3,461 ft)*
Stopover: *Gîte La Tonnelle (bed space for 30)*

SONACCIA
Fium'Orbo

Asinao

SOLENZARA

Solenzara

Paliri

Architecture in Corsica

The various peoples that have ruled Corsica have left their imprint in the cities and around the island. The Pisans built the Romanesque churches, while the Genoese built almost all the splendid Baroque ones as well as the defensive structures indispensable for an island: the watchtowers along the coastline and the citadels. In the field of domestic architecture, the mortuary chapels, which were often constructed along the sides of roads, are particularly interesting. They were a mark of distinction of the rich families, especially those that had made their fortunes abroad.

Polychrome marble on the façade of a Romanesque church

ROMANESQUE

Corsica has some splendid examples of Romanesque church architecture, mostly dating from the late 11th century onwards, during Pisan rule. These churches often have an aisle-less nave with a semicircular apse, while the façade is decorated with blind arches and panels that continue along the sides. Polychrome marble is also a characteristic feature.

Greek cross

The striation is orange, light green and light blue.

Gilded grey marble reflects the sunlight.

Bas-relief with the Lamb of God above the portal.

Half-pilasters with simple lines

Single portal

La Canonica Church (see p148) has extremely simple lines and an interior with two aisles. The only other church with this feature is Santa Maria Assunta at St-Florent (see p70).

BAROQUE

In the 17th and 18th centuries, the Genoese imported a northern Italian Baroque style to Corsica. In the rich areas, such as Castagniccia, Balagne and Bastia, large churches were built, the linear façades of which were animated by cornices, pilasters, pediments and volutes. The interiors feature spectacular stucco work, multicoloured marble and trompe l'oeil.

Wrought-iron railing

Lantern

Belfry, usually with four bells.

The bell tower of a Baroque church, such as St-Jean-Baptiste in Porta, is next to the church but not adjacent to its main body.

Base

St-Jean-Baptiste in Porta (see p147) is the best-known example of Baroque architecture in Corsica. Like many other churches, it has an aisle-less nave and central plan.

Curved pediment

Rinceau

Overhanging courses consisting of the frieze and cornice.

Volute

Cartouche

Pilaster

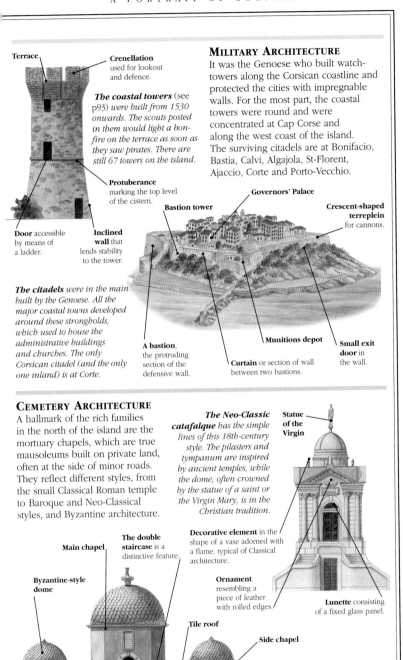

MILITARY ARCHITECTURE

It was the Genoese who built watch-towers along the Corsican coastline and protected the cities with impregnable walls. For the most part, the coastal towers were round and were concentrated at Cap Corse and along the west coast of the island. The surviving citadels are at Bonifacio, Bastia, Calvi, Algajola, St-Florent, Ajaccio, Corte and Porto-Vecchio.

Terrace

Crenellation used for lookout and defence.

The coastal towers (see p93) were built from 1530 onwards. The scouts posted in them would light a bon-fire on the terrace as soon as they saw pirates. There are still 67 towers on the island.

Protuberance marking the top level of the cistern.

Door accessible by means of a ladder.

Inclined wall that lends stability to the tower.

Governors' Palace

Bastion tower

Crescent-shaped terreplein for cannons.

The citadels were in the main built by the Genoese. All the major coastal towns developed around these strongholds, which used to house the administrative buildings and churches. The only Corsican citadel (and the only one inland) is at Corte.

A bastion, the protruding section of the defensive wall.

Munitions depot

Curtain or section of wall between two bastions.

Small exit door in the wall.

CEMETERY ARCHITECTURE

A hallmark of the rich families in the north of the island are the mortuary chapels, which are true mausoleums built on private land, often at the side of minor roads. They reflect different styles, from the small Classical Roman temple to Baroque and Neo-Classical styles, and Byzantine architecture.

The Neo-Classic catafalque has the simple lines of this 18th-century style. The pilasters and tympanum are inspired by ancient temples, while the dome, often crowned by the statue of a saint or the Virgin Mary, is in the Christian tradition.

Statue of the Virgin

Decorative element in the shape of a vase adorned with a flame, typical of Classical architecture.

Main chapel

The double staircase is a distinctive feature.

Byzantine-style dome

Ornament resembling a piece of leather with rolled edges.

Lunette consisting of a fixed glass panel.

Tile roof

Side chapel

Byzantine taste is often visible in the mausoleums of merchant families, who often travelled widely to carry out their trade. The superimposed tile domes were inspired by those on mosques, although the material (schist, a local slate) is less precious.

Houses in Corsica

A GREAT VARIETY OF HOUSES can be seen across the island. Many of them, especially in the more isolated areas, were built not only to afford shelter, but also to defend the families that lived in them. Others were designed to facilitate all aspects of farm life, and a few were constructed as holiday homes for rich families. Corsicans have a strong, deeply felt attachment to their land, and many of the houses have belonged to the same families since they were first constructed.

The windows in northern towns are framed by a shield motif

MOUNTAIN HOMES

The mountain villages lie on the slopes exposed to the sun *(solanu)*, while the shaded areas *(umbriccia)* are mostly wooded. There are two types of houses: the permanent homes, mostly of the "box-shape" style, found in the towns halfway up the slopes, and the seasonal dwellings built near summer grazing land that house the family members who take care of the livestock.

The "maison bloc" is a simple "box" house, commonly seen in the Niolo region. It is used only as living quarters.

Curved terracotta tiles cover the roof.

Main wall made of granite

A sloping roof extends over the walls.

Entrance

Stone slabs cover the roof.

Small windows insulate the house from heat and cold.

The mountain hut is the home of the shepherds in the bergeries *and is used only in summer. It has a central room with a fireplace for cooking and sleeping, and two annexes for storing farm tools and making cheese.*

Sloping roof covered with tiles *(teghie)*.

Communal room with a central fireplace *(fucone)* on the top floor.

The tower house is one of the most successful defensive domestic structures. It was lived in by several related families and was built to protect their common interests.

Cellar-stable

One family lived on each intermediate floor.

Masonry made of crude shale slabs.

HILLSIDE HOUSES

The hilly regions such as Castagniccia used to be densely populated because of their fertile soil and good climate. The houses in these areas were built to hold several families. This was because large numbers of people could defend themselves more effectively against pirates attracted by the produce of this rich land.

Masonry made of plastered bricks.

The patriarchal houses in the Castagniccia region were also used by families that were related, but they had no defensive function.

HOUSES ON THE PLAINS

The few plains in Corsica are concentrated along the east coast. On the plains, the permanent settlements were built only when there was less risk of pirate raids. There are many types of houses, depending on the social status and activities of the owners.

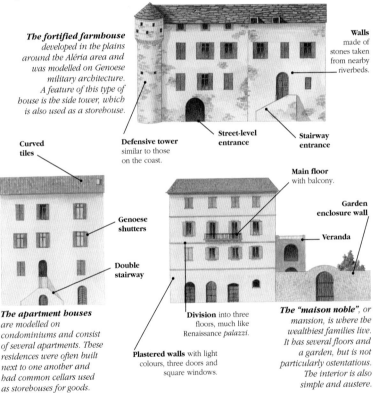

Tile roof

Stable with cane roofing.

The farmsteads on the plains include the farmhouse and the adjacent stable. There is no need for seasonal migration, since there is plenty of local grazing land for the livestock all year round.

Walls made of bricks and mud.

The fortified farmhouse developed in the plains around the Aléria area and was modelled on Genoese military architecture. A feature of this type of house is the side tower, which is also used as a storehouse.

Walls made of stones taken from nearby riverbeds.

Defensive tower similar to those on the coast.

Street-level entrance

Stairway entrance

Curved tiles

Genoese shutters

Double stairway

Main floor with balcony.

Garden enclosure wall

Veranda

The apartment houses are modelled on condominiums and consist of several apartments. These residences were often built next to one another and had common cellars used as storehouses for goods.

Division into three floors, much like Renaissance *palazzi*.

Plastered walls with light colours, three doors and square windows.

The "maison noble", or mansion, is where the wealthiest families live. It has several floors and a garden, but is not particularly ostentatious. The interior is also simple and austere.

THE *BERGERIES*

The word *bergerie* is used for the seasonal settlements of wandering shepherds. The *bergeries* are rather small complexes with a house for the shepherds, the sheepfolds (pens) and the structures used for cheese-making. Nowadays, the *bergeries* are protected as part of the Parc Naturel Régional (*see p99*) because they are a fundamental part of the island's traditional way of life.

Sheepfold

House

Oven

Storehouse for cheese

Trees for firewood

Courtyard

Language, Literature, Music and Traditions

ORSICA IS A BILINGUAL region, and all road signs are written in Corsican and French. The Corsican language is similar to Italian and is still spoken and written everywhere, though less by young people. The island's literary tradition is mostly oral, based on legends that were handed down during cold winter months around the hearth, or in the songs describing the salient events in the lives of the locals. The ancient melodies are now being performed by music groups that sing in the local language and are also famous outside of Corsica.

Local costume

An allegory of Corsica in an 18th-century print

Page from an old encyclopedia with the entry "Corsica"

THE CORSICAN LANGUAGE

IN THE NORTHEAST, the Corsican language *(Corsu)* is soft and musical, with an inflection and many words that are similar to Tuscan dialects. It is harsher and more crisp in the southwest, bearing influences of neighbouring Sardinia. The "double d" is used a lot in the southwest. For example, the word for "beautiful" in Bastia is *bellu*, while in Ajaccio it becomes *beddu*.

The Corsican language derived from Latin and, over the centuries, has been influenced by the various populations that ruled the island, mainly Tuscan – and not only because of Pisan dominion. In fact, Genoa,

which ruled Corsica for five centuries, used Tuscan as the official and written language. The few Genoese words that have remained exist mostly in maritime and technical terminology. Influences also came from southern Italy, especially Calabria and Sardinia, and from French, which determined the spread of generic terms such as *cammi di ferru*, or railway, *(chemin de fer* in French).

The French language was first used in Corsica in 1769, when the island was annexed by France. It began to spread in the late 19th century, with the introduction of compulsory education.

Two ancient "foreign" dialects have remained on the island, but are disappearing due to the predominance of French. In Bonifacio, the Ligurian dialect of the 13th-century Genoese colonists can still be heard, while at Cargèse, Greek, imported by refugees from the Peloponnese in the 17th and 18th centuries, is virtually extinct. As for books, all the texts printed before the 18th century are in Italian. After that time, French became widespread, even though Italian was still used.

Recognized as a regional language in 1974, Corsican

is now enjoying a revival thanks to the courses at the University of Corsica *(see p137)*, where a vast data bank on the language has been created. Although most children on the island learn Corsican at home, the language is also taught at school, and many schools offer bilingual education.

Many associations and periodicals have also promoted Corsican, and there are several radio stations broadcasting in Corsican. The first newspaper in Corsican, *A Tramuntana*, was published in 1896, followed by others, especially in the period between the two World Wars.

The phrasebook on page 214 gives some examples of Corsican words.

CORSICAN LITERATURE

CORSICAN HAS ALWAYS been a spoken language and the local literary production was passed on orally, expressed as stories *(stabato-ghji)* and legends *(fole)* that were handed down from generation to generation. Then there were poems and songs that narrated life experiences: the *lamentu* for a death or a departure, and the *voceri*, the cries

Honoré de Balzac (1799–1850)

of black-clad women for a violent death.

Written literature made its appearance around the 17th century, with the establishment of the first literary circles, most of which were linked to liberation movements. The literature of this period dealt mainly with history and politics. Only at the end of the 19th century were the first poems, short stories and novels published in the Corsican language.

Between the World Wars, *A Muvra* became the newspaper of the Partitu Corsu d'Azione (Corsican Action Party), the main independence-movement party.

In the 19th century, many prominent French authors wrote works inspired by the island: Honoré de Balzac's *The Vendetta*; Guy de Maupassant's *The Corsican Bandit*, *A Vendetta* and *Histoire Corse*; and Alexandre Dumas' *Corsican Brothers*.

Among contemporary authors, Angelo Rinaldi paints a ruthless portrait of his home town, Bastia, in the novels *La Dernière Fête de l'Empire* and *Les Roses de Pline*, and Marie Susini deals with the Corsican family and provinciality in novels such as *L'Île sans Rivage* and *La Renfermée*. Sisters Hélène and Jeanne Bresciani, both authors in their own right, together wrote *2, rue de la Marine*, a poetic account of coming to terms with the death of their father, reflected through Corsican culture.

MUSIC

SONGS ARE undoubtedly the best expression of Corsican musicality. An excellent example of this discipline is the *paghjella*,

Cetera, a 16-string cittern

a traditional polyphonic song for three male voices that may have been imported from the Balearic Islands and is still sung during mass and other religious ceremonies in some towns and villages. Each voice has a specific function: the first, a tenor, provides the melodic and tonal base; the second, which is lower, provides the background; and the third, the highest, adds improvised embellishments. According to tradition, the singers must all be dressed in black. All Corsican songs express an emotion, a state of mind, or retell a joyful or painful event. In the past, they were used to hand down traditions orally.

A particularly sorrowful song, the *voceru*, is sung by women dressed in black on the occasion of a wake: they weep and sing while rocking their bodies back and forth to mourn the deceased. A more playful genre is the *chjama e rispondi*, a form of choral competition in which two contestants improvise insults in verse.

Instruments in Corsica are traditionally wind-based, and typical of a pastoral society: flutes and fifes made of wood or animal horns (*a ciallamella, u liscarolu, a caramusa, u fischju*). Jew's harps (*ghjerbula*) and castanets (*chjoche*) are also used, as well as violins and guitars. Some instruments have recently been revived – for example, the 16-string *cetera*, a sort of cittern; the *pifane*, a goat horn used in the past by local shepherds; and the *pirula*, another wind instrument.

Some local groups – such as I Muvrini, A Filetta, Canta U Populu Corsu and Donasulana – have specialized in polyphonic music and have become famous on and off the island.

LOCAL TRADITIONS

Almost all Corsicans are Catholic and the local traditions that have been preserved are mostly of a religious nature. The most fascinating are the processions held during Easter Week, for example in Bonifacio, Calvi, Sartène and Erbalunga. Local saints' days are well celebrated in the cities and villages, as are ceremonies for the dead, accompanied by solemn processions to the cemeteries or to the unusual and impressive mortuary chapels *(see p27)* along the roads of Cap Corse and the west coast. However, the best-known "custom" in Corsica is the vendetta, which was common practice up to the mid-19th century. The physical distance and perceived indifference of Genoese justice led Corsican families to take the law into their own hands and seek revenge for offences. Rivalry for love, the division of a plot of land or any other dispute, even the most futile, could trigger a chain of murders – or even wars – that would carry on for generations. The feud would end only if the parish priest managed to broker an agreement between the families. Avengers going into hiding in the maquis were known as *bandits d'honneur* ("bandits of honour") to differentiate them from common highway robbers.

Scene of a vendetta between Corsican clans in a period print

CORSICA THROUGH THE YEAR

HE BEST MONTHS to visit Corsica are May, June and September: the climate is mild, the prices are lower, and the beaches are not crowded. In addition, the risk of fires is low. In the summer, the island is filled with tourists and it is more difficult to find convenient and comfortable accommodation. Hikers and cyclists especially should

Mural at Solenzara

avoid July and August because of the heat. From November to April, Corsica comes to a halt, and only a few hotels are open in the cities and main tourist locations along the coast. In these colder months, transport connections with the island are reduced to a minimum, and the sea can be quite rough.

Rockrose and lavender in bloom in the spring months

SPRING

HE BLOSSOMING MAQUIS fills the air with its sweet scent. This begins in March with rosemary and lavender and continues in April with the pink and white rockrose flowers that cover entire areas. In mid-May, myrtle begins to blossom. The air is mild and visitors can enjoy a swim in the clear waters. At high altitudes, the snow may last until June and some paths and roads are closed.

MARCH

Our Lady of Mercy Feast *(18 Mar)*, Ajaccio, with a procession and solemn mass.
Bastia Film Festival *(Mar)*. A celebration of international film production.

Olive Festival *(mid-Mar)*, Santa Lucia di Tallano.
Greek Orthodox Procession *(Easter Mon)*, Cargèse. Traditional ceremonies and songs among the Greek community.
Procession de la Cerca *(Maundy Thu, Good Fri)*, Erbalunga. A 21-km (13-mile) procession that begins at 7am and goes through all the towns in the Brando region. At 8pm there is the *Granitula* procession, with hooded penitents.
Good Friday Procession, Bonifacio. The five city confraternities carry wooden sculptures and walk to the church of Ste-Marie-Majeure to worship the relics of the Holy Cross.
Good Friday Procession, Sartène. At 9:30pm, in the city illuminated by candles, there is the *Catenacciu* (Great Penitent) procession.

APRIL

Salon de la Bande Dessinée *(early Apr)*, Bastia. Comic books and strips.
Brocciu Day *(date depending on cheese production)*, Piana. Festival dedicated to *brocciu* (traditional sheep's-milk cheese).

MAY

May 1 Fair, Ucciani. Trade show of Corsican handicrafts.
Festimare *(early May)*, L'Île Rousse. A sea festival for young people.
Ste-Restitute's Feast Day *(late May)*, Calenzana. Pilgrimage, procession.
Île Danse *(late May)*, Ajaccio. Dance festival with leading European companies.
Nautival *(end of May)*, Macinaggio. Sea festival with stalls, performances, fish tastings and a procession.

The Orthodox Easter procession at Cargèse

AVERAGE DAILY HOURS OF SUNSHINE

HOURS

Sunshine Hours
Corsica is well-known as a sunny island, even in autumn and spring, when the weather is still mild due to the many daily hours of sunshine. Along the coast, the warm sun makes swimming possible even into the early autumn.

SUMMER

DURING THE SUMMER, the number of visitors to Corsica triples. The hotels, residences and camp sites are all booked up and charge high-season rates. The beaches are packed with bathers, and the harbours are filled with sailing boats and motorboats. At this time the island also offers many festivals to enjoy.

JUNE

St Erasmus's Feast Day
(2 Jun), Bonifacio. The feast day of the patron saint of fishermen includes a procession in the sea.
Cavall'in Festa *(early Jun)*, Corte. Horse festival. Among the events are horse parades in period costumes, shows, contests, exhibitions and displays.
Exposition d'Art Contemporain
(Jun–Sep), Calvi. Exhibition of contemporary painters and sculptors, held in the citadel.
La Nuit du Conte *(Jun)*, Vero. Celebrations for the arrival of summer.
Fête de St-Jean
(24 Jun), Bastia. A traditional celebration held in honour of St John.
Jazz Festival *(last week of Jun)*, Calvi. Concerts and jam sessions are held along the quayside.

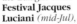

The Guitar
Nights festival

JULY

La Relève de la Garde
(every Thu throughout Jul), Ajaccio. Changing of the Guard ceremony, in costume.
Wine Fair *(first weekend of Jul)*, Luri.
La Relève des Gouverneurs
(11 July), Bastia. Commemoration of an historical event with a procession in the citadel.
Book Fair *(Jul)*, L'Île Rousse. Corsican books and authors.
Music in the Village *(Jul)*, Corbara. Concerts and shows.
Estivoce *(early Jul)*, Pigna. Corsican polyphonic music: folk music, medieval religious songs, theatre.
Blues Festival "Nuits du Blues"
(first two weeks of Jul), Ajaccio. National and international musicians, exhibitions and films.
Olive Festival *(first weekend after 14 Jul)*, Montemaggiore. Trade show featuring olive oil produced in the Balagne area.
Festival Jacques Luciani *(mid-Jul)*, Corte. Festival of folk dances with international groups.
Guitar Nights *(third week of Jul)*, Patrimonio. Folk, jazz and gypsy musicians.
Mediterranean Trophy *(last ten days of Jul)*. Regatta in three stages. It starts from Bastia and stops at Ajaccio, Maddalena and Elba.
Les Estivales *(Jul–Sep)*, Ajaccio. A traditional music festival also featuring dance performances.

Participants in the Mediterranean Trophy regatta

AUGUST

Film Festival *(late Jul–early Aug)*, Lama. European films and meetings with directors.
Music Festival *(first week of Aug)*, Erbalunga. Outdoor concerts.
Ancient Rome Festival *(first week of Aug)*, Aléria. Festival dedicated to ancient Rome, featuring costume processions, guided tours, Olympic contests, ancient-handicraft stalls and food.
Celebrations in Honour of Napoleon *(mid-Aug)*, Ajaccio. Ceremonies for the birth of Napoleon Bonaparte. Exhibitions and parades in period costumes.
Calvi Allegria *(mid-Aug)*, Calvi. Sound-and-light spectacle narrating the history of Calvi's citadel.
Porto Latino *(mid-Aug)*, St-Florent. Lively festival of Latin-American music.
St Bartholomew Procession *(24 Aug)*, held in Bonifacio.

AVERAGE MONTHLY RAINFALL

Rainfall
Autumn and winter are the wettest periods of the year in Corsica, with intense rainfall that may last several days. At the end of the summer there are often violent thunderstorms, but it is still the driest season on the island.

AUTUMN

THE SKY IS CLEAR, the climate is mild, and until October the temperature of the sea is warm enough for bathing. On the coastline, the maquis begins to blossom again after the summer drought, and the strawberries and black myrtle berries ripen. In the valleys and mountains, the trees take on the colours of the autumn. In the chestnut-grove regions, Castagniccia and Evisa, the earth is carpeted with prickly chestnut burs, and the first rainfall encourages mushrooms to grow.

SEPTEMBER

Settembrinu di Tavagna *(end of Aug–early Sep)*, Tavagna. Festival of international music –
including Cuban, Corsican, African and Romany.

Procession of the Virgin Mary *(7–10 Sep)*, Casamaccioli. This celebration of the Virgin Mary is the oldest pilgrimage on the island.

8 September Procession, Lavasina. A torch-lit procession and midnight mass.

Fête de Notre Dame *(8 Sep)*, Bonifacio. The Festival of the Virgin Mary, during which a special dish of stuffed aubergines (eggplant) is prepared and eaten.

European Diving Film Festival *(early Sep)*, different location each year. Festival of films on underwater diving by leading directors in this genre.

Porto-Vecchio Fair *(second week of Sep)*, Porto-Vecchio. This annual trade fair features a complete range of Corsican handicrafts.

The Procession of the Virgin Mary at Casamaccioli

Polyphonic Music Week *(3rd week of Sep)*, Calvi. Traditional Corsican music.

Festi'Acqua *(mid-Sep)*, Propriano. Water festival featuring boat races, floats, marine exhibitions and seafood tastings.

Honey Festival *(Sep)*, Murzo. A traditional festival to celebrate a Corsican speciality.

One of the public events honouring Napoleon Bonaparte at Ajaccio *(see p33)*

AVERAGE MONTHLY TEMPERATURE

Temperature
Thanks to the sea, the temperature along the coast is mild even in winter, the annual average being 15° C (59° F). Inland, however, the winter is harsh, with heavy snowfall and frequent frost, while the summers are cool, even if the sun is very hot.

OCTOBER

Rally de France *(late Sep–early Oct)*. Great auto-rally champions compete on the winding roads of Corsica – one of the most interesting stages of this race.
Les Musicales de Bastia *(Oct)*, Bastia. Jazz, dance, theatre and music.
Le Tour de Corse à la Voile *(late Oct)*. Regatta with start and finish at Bonifacio.
Festiventu *(last week of Oct)*, Calvi. A festival of model-aeroplane contests and hot-air balloon flights.

NOVEMBER

Chestnut Festival *(Nov)*, Evisa. Harvest celebrations.
Mediterranean Cultures Film Festival "Arte Mare" *(Nov)*, Bastia. Film productions, art and literature from Mediterranean countries.
Journées de la Pomme *(first weekend of Nov)*, Bastelica. Apple festival. Preserves, juices and dried fruits can be sampled and purchased. Also available are charcuterie and handicrafts.

WINTER

THE WEATHER becomes colder, partly due to the mistral wind. The mountain tops are covered with snow and the ski-lift facilities are sporadically in operation. At Christmas Corsican cities

Chestnuts, harvested in late autumn

are decorated with holiday illuminations, and in Ajaccio games are organized and stalls display their wares. At this time of the year, many hotels and restaurants are closed, and accommodation can be difficult to find outside the cities and main tourist localities.

However, this can be a very pleasant season; the coastline is green, the streets are lined with flowers, the maquis vegetation retains its foliage, and on sunny days it is possible to forget that it is winter.

In December, the olives are gathered and taken to the presses, and in February the almond trees begin to blossom, allowing for the first taste of spring.

DECEMBER

Chestnut Festival *(mid-Dec)*, Bocognano. A popular festival featuring dishes and desserts made from chestnut flour.
Animation de Noël *(Dec)*, Ajaccio. Christmas entertainment in the streets of the capital: bingo contests, games and gig rides.

JANUARY

Italian Film Festival *(late Jan)*, Bastia. Popular festival featuring screenings of Italian films, themed by director and/or actor, exhibitions, conferences, and Italian cuisine.

The polyphonic music group A Filetta performing at a festival

St Anthony Procession *(first Sun after 17 Jan)*, Corbara and Aregno. Procession in honour of St Anthony.

FEBRUARY

A Tumbera *(second week of Feb)*, Renno. This festival is organized around a type of Corsican pig and offers competitions and food stalls.

PUBLIC HOLIDAYS

New Year's Day *(1 Jan)*
Easter Sunday and Monday *(Mar or Apr)*
Labour Day *(1 May)*
1945 Victory Day *(8 May)*
Ascension Day *(40 days after Easter)*
Pentecost Sunday and Monday *(mid-May–mid-Jun)*
Bastille Day *(14 Jul)*
Assumption Day *(15 Aug)*
All Saints' Day *(1 Nov)*
Armistice Day *(11 Nov)*
Christmas Day *(25 Dec)*

THE HISTORY OF CORSICA

S ITUATED NEAR THE TUSCAN *and Provençal coasts, Corsica has been occupied, colonized and fought over for millennia. Its history and culture are the results of the convergence of different civilizations, from the Carthaginians and Romans to the Pisans, Genoese and French. These experiences have given rise to the unique identity of the Corsican nation.*

The rock massif that includes the island of Corsica reached its present position in the Tyrrhenian Sea about 18 million years ago.

Drinking vessel in the shape of a horse's head (480 BC)

The exact date of the arrival of people on the island is still shrouded in mystery, but there is evidence that humans settled in Corsica 9,000–10,000 years ago. The most ancient sites excavated are at Macinaggio, Cap Corse and Araguina, not far from Bonifacio. Here archaeologists found the skeleton of the Dame de Bonifacio, a 40-year-old woman who was buried in 6570 BC; her remains are now kept in the Levie museum.

In the 6th millennium BC, Corsica experienced a considerable influx of migrant populations. The Neolithic inhabitants of this period bred livestock and practised weaving. This growth in population was followed by ever-increasing trade. The mid-4th millennium was the age of megalithic monuments *(see p129)*, the most impressive ruins of ancient Corsica *(see pp38–9)*. During this period, the

Corsicans traded mostly with people on the Italian coast: digs have brought to light Etruscan vases and other items from Magna Graecia.

Around 1500 BC, with the advent of the Bronze Age, the south of Corsica was invaded by a population known as the Torréens, after the towers *(torri)* they erected in several parts of the island. The Torréens ruled the south until about 600 BC, when infighting between tribes prompted another migration, this time to Sardinia.

In 565 BC, colonists from Phocaea founded the city of Alalia. After Etruscan and Carthaginian rule, the city was conquered by the Romans when Scipio's legions landed in 259 BC and renamed Aléria. During the Pax Romana, the city was developed, first by Caesar and then by the emperors Hadrian, Caracalla and Diocletian. It became the capital of the province of Corsica and remained so until the Barbarian invasions in AD 455. In 100 BC, the Roman general and consul Marius founded the colony of Mariana, just south of present-day Bastia.

TIMELINE

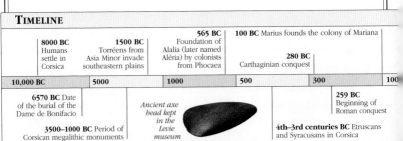

			565 BC	100 BC Marius founds the colony of Mariana
8000 BC	**1500 BC**	Foundation of		
Humans	Torréens from	Alalia (later named		**280 BC**
settle in	Asia Minor invade	Aléria) by colonists		Carthaginian conquest
Corsica	southeastern plains	from Phocaea		

10,000 BC	**5000**	**1000**	**500**	**300**	**100**

| **6570 BC** Date of the burial of the Dame de Bonifacio | | *Ancient axe head kept in the Levie museum* | | **259 BC** Beginning of Roman conquest |
| **3500–1000 BC** Period of Corsican megalithic monuments | | | | **4th–3rd centuries BC** Etruscans and Syracusans in Corsica |

◁ **"Father of the Nation" Pascal Paoli, portrayed by Richard Cosway**

From Megaliths to Romans

**Attic crater,
5th century BC**

ANCIENT CORSICA was an island whose prehistoric populations were extremely dynamic. The most active period of these ancestral cultures began in the Neolithic era, roughly 6000 BC, an epoch when cardial ware was produced. During this time, these populations became more settled, lived on livestock raising, and began to build their dwellings with dry walls, often fortifying them. Towards the end of this period, the megalithic monuments *(see p129)* first appeared. There soon followed invasions, first by the Torréens and then by the Phocaeans and the Etruscans. Lastly, the Romans settled in Alalia, founded by the Phocaeans, renaming it Aléria. Their hegemony extended over most of the island, remaining until the Barbarian invasions.

*Anthropomorphic menhirs,
with facial features and
sometimes warriors'
weapons, are unique to
Corsican culture.*

*The alignments
of menhirs are
a distinguishing
element of
Neolithic Corsican
culture. Many of
the arrangements
were probably
connected to
prehistoric
religious rituals.*

Filitosa has one of the most important alignments of anthropomorphic menhirs on the island *(see p129).*

• Filitosa

THE REMAINS OF THE PAST

Most of the menhir alignments and dolmens that are still standing date from the period between the 2nd and 1st millennia BC. They are mainly located in southwest Corsica, while fortified castles can be found on the hills in the eastern sector. The most important Roman ruins lie at the site of Aléria, where the original plan of this ancient city can still be seen.

• Cauria

*Cardial ware is
a type of pottery
dating from the 5th
or 6th millennium BC.
The name derives from
the Cardium, or
cockle shell, whose
jagged lips were
used to fashion
the characteristic
patterns on each piece.*

The Cauria plateau has many of the best-preserved menhirs and dolmens, which miraculously avoided destruction by the Christians. Stantari, Pagliaju, Renaggiu and Fontanaccia are the sites to visit *(see p127).*

The city of Aléria, the ancient Roman capital, was uncovered during the digs that were begun in 1920 but mostly carried out after 1955 *(see p144)*.

• Aléria

LOCATOR MAP

☐ *Archaeological area described*

The Roman plaques in Corsica narrate wars and victories in a land where the population has always been fiercely proud and very hard to dominate.

The *castellu* of Cucuruzzu stood on a rocky spur, 700 m (2,300 ft) above sea level, that dominates the valley below. Its ruins provide an insight into its massive structure and defensive capabilities *(see p125)*.

Cucuruzzu

Arraggio

rraggio is one of e fortified megalithic mplexes used to defend e local population. It ates from the 16th–12th enturies BC and its ucture, which must have een impregnable, can ill be admired *(see p121)*.

PREHISTORIC MONUMENTS IN CORSICA

There are many constructions and monuments in Corsica that demonstrate the nature of its prehistoric cultures, only partly shared with other Mediterranean islands. Among the most significant legacies of the oldest culture on the island are the anthropomorphic menhirs – which are called *stantari* in the Corsican language *(see p129)* – sculpted for ritual purposes, mostly connected to the cult of the dead. The same is true of the dolmens (*stazzoni*), tombs covered with large stone slabs symbolizing the body of the deceased. The *castelli* (castles) and *torri* (towers) are cyclopean dwellings that resemble the *nuraghi* of Sardinia and the *talayot* on the Balearic Islands. These are fortified structures that, in dangerous circumstances, afforded shelter to the population of a village. In peacetime they were used as storehouses for the village's provisions and possessions. The most interesting examples are in Arraggio, Tappa and Cucuruzzu.

The ruins of the *castellu* of Arraggio

BARBARIAN INVASIONS

The fall of the Roman Empire had immediate repercussions for the island, which was soon overrun by Barbarian populations. The Vandals landed in Corsica in AD 455 and were probably the cause of the final abandonment of Aléria.

After conquering the North African coastline, the Vandals sent bishops from the conquered cities into exile in Corsica. This was probably a key factor in the evangelization

A Vandal warrior, shield decoration

of the island, which had begun a century earlier. In 534 the Byzantines, under Emperor Justinian, took over, but the island remained at the mercy of repeated Barbaric invasions, including those of the Lombards and the Saracens. The Lombards ruled until 774, when they were defeated by the Franks, who had initially been called to support the papacy in Rome against the Lombard threat. The Frankish king, Pepin the Short, donated Corsica to Pope Stephen, a deal that was confirmed by his son Charlemagne 20 years later.

However, a new threat was looming on the horizon for the inhabitants of Corsica. The Arab expansion across the Mediterranean was extensive during this period. A series of landings along the entire coastline of Corsica, particularly in the fertile region of Balagne, was so overwhelming that a 15th-century chronicler, Giovanni della Grossa, talked of a mass conversion to Islam.

The many Carolingian expeditions did very little to lessen the pressure of the Saracens, and many Corsicans fled from the island to settle on the nearby Italian coast. Historians mention a flourishing Corsican community in the Roman port of Ostia, the town of Pope Formosus (891–896), who had been born in the Corsican town of Porto.

FEUDALISM IN THE MIDDLE AGES

After the year 1000, the influence of the mainland increased, and feudalism developed in Corsica with a structure similar to that prevailing throughout Europe. On the island, however, this political configuration was strongly influenced by the power of the various clans that fought among themselves. These feuds led to the division of the territory into two geographical areas: the *Deçà des Monts*, the northeastern half of the island, which was more developed and receptive to trade; and the *Delà des Monts*, the pastoral and "backwards" southwestern sector. Internal struggles prevented the island from strengthening its military force, so the papacy was forced to request that the republics of Pisa and Genoa should step in to defeat the Arabs and bring stability to the island of Corsica.

A 16th-century painting depicting the Arab invasion of Corsica

TIMELINE

Pisan Romanesque bas-relief, San Giovanni Battista, Carbini *(see p125)*

THE PISAN PERIOD

In 1077, the Church granted Corsican rule to Bishop Landolfe of Pisa, thus initiating the period of Pisan domination. There were interesting cultural developments during this time, but it was troubled from a political standpoint. The rivalry with Genoa was at first handled well, thanks to the Holy See, but soon degenerated so much that, in 1133, Pope Innocent II had to divide the island's six bishoprics between Pisa (Ajaccio, Aléria and Sagone) and Genoa (Accia, Mariana and Nebbio).

By 1187, the Genoese, who were becoming increasingly powerful in the Mediterranean, took possession of the harbour of Bonifacio and, in 1268, founded Calvi. The Genoese took control of Corsica in 1284 with the naval battle of Meloria *(see pp42–3)* near the Tuscan coast. There are many traces of Pisan rule on the island, including Romanesque architecture,

such as the beautiful churches of La Canonica and San Michele de Murato, and the development of Cap Corse, where the Pisans created vineyards, small ports and emporia.

EARLY GENOESE RULE

After defeating Pisa, the Republic of Genoa worked swiftly to consolidate its grip on the island by laying out a series of defensive systems along the coastline and creating an administrative structure. However, this proved to be a difficult task. Genoese rule was opposed by some of the local lords, in particular those in Cinarca, who were still faithful to Pisa. With the aim of setting up a Corsican government ruled by the towns (perhaps in the wake of the rise of the Italian city republics), the lords stirred up popular insurrections. In addition, there were repeated attacks by other European nations, often with the backing of the Church. For example, in 1297, Pope Boniface VIII, asserting the rights of the Holy See in the Mediterranean, granted Corsican and Sardinian rule to the Aragonese kings, who sided with the Cinarca lords and remained a thorn in the side of the Genoese republic until the French took over in the mid-18th century.

Boniface VIII (1294–1303)

Relief at La Canonica, a church built in the Pisan period

The citadel of Bonifacio

891–896 Papacy of Formosus, born in Porto

1000

1077 Pope Gregory VII grants Corsica to Pisa

1100

1133 Pope Innocent II divides bishoprics between Pisa and Genoa

1195 Genoese colony is established in Bonifacio

1200

1268 The Genoese found Calvi

6 August 1284 Battle of Meloria

1297 Boniface VIII gives Corsica in fee to kingdom of Aragon

The Battle of Meloria

I N THE COURSE OF ITS HISTORY, Corsica was subject to the rule of two Italian maritime republics, Pisa and Genoa. The event that marked the passage from one ruler to the other was the Battle of Meloria (1284).

The coat of arms of Pisa

Both republics had previously helped to free the Mediterranean from the Saracens and the pirates that had been plaguing the region, after which they vied for control of Corsica. In 1077, Pope Gregory VII granted Corsican rule to Landolfe, the bishop of Pisa. This led to an increase in friction: skirmishes, confrontations and treaties became the norm, until the battle. During the first two centuries of Genoese rule, the island continued to be torn by war, pirate attacks and vendettas. Only in the late 1500s did Genoa manage to impose some kind of order.

The coat of arms of the Republic of Pisa displays a ship that is also found on the Leaning Tower in Campo dei Miracoli. It is one of the many iconographic symbols of the city's maritime supremacy.

Oberto Doria

The commander Albertino Morosini was, with Ugolino della Gherardesca and Andreotto Saraceno, the head of the Pisan fleet, which was helpless against the two Genoese fleets.

The Saracens set fire to the towns and massacred the inhabitants or made them their slaves. Pisa in particular was devoted to freeing the island from this scourge.

The Pisan fleet comprised 72 galleys and its defeat was total: 5,000 Pisans died and 11,000 were taken to Genoa in chains.

THE FATE OF COUNT UGOLINO

After the defeat of Meloria, Ugolino della Gherardesca gave castles and land to the enemy to avoid a siege by the Florentines and Luccans, who were allies of Genoa and therefore enemies of Pisa. Accused of betrayal, he was imprisoned with his sons and grandsons in a tower, where he died. Dante considered him a traitor to his country, and in the *Divine Comedy* had him put in Hell, a curse that accompanied the count for centuries: "Ah, Pisa, scandal to the people / of the beauteous land where the 'yes' is heard, / since thy neighbours are slow to punish thee / let the Caprara and Gorgona move."

Illustration of the *Divine Comedy*

Benedetto Zaccaria *led a second group of Genoese ships that arrived by surprise at Meloria at a later stage in the battle, when the Pisans felt they were almost out of danger. His intervention was a key factor in the Ligurian republic's victory.*

__The chains__ of the anchors of the Pisan ships were impounded by the Genoese at the end of the battle. Considered a sort of war booty, they were on exhibit in Genoa as a sign of the city's supremacy. Only in the 19th century were they given back to Pisa, where they hang under the loggia of the Camposanto.

The cliffs of Meloria are about 7 km (4 miles) off the coast of Livorno, facing Corsica.

Meloria was the scene of an earlier battle, in 1241, in which the Pisans, aided by the emperor Frederick II, defeated the Genoese.

__The wealth__ of Genoa, which stemmed from commercial trading, made it a political power that dominated the Mediterranean for a long time.

IN THE THICK OF THE BATTLE

In August 1284, a Genoese fleet led by Oberto Doria sailed into the waters opposite Porto Pisano. Startled by this move, the Pisans attacked from the cliffs of Meloria. The battle was violent and the outcome uncertain, until the arrival of a second group of Genoese galleys, which caught their enemies by surprise and decided the outcome of the fight. Giovanni David's *The Battle of Meloria* (left) hangs in the Palazzo Ducale in Genoa.

The Genoese fleet consisted of 93 galleys.

__The Genoese galleys__ were fast ships, suitable for both cargo transport and naval battles. Largely because of these vessels and their commanders, Genoa prospered and became a power able to defeat its enemies and rivals.

The Genoese fleet near the coast of Corsica on a print kept at the Musée de la Corse

THE END OF THE MIDDLE AGES

The 14th century was a troubled time for Corsica. In 1348, the population was decimated by the Black Death, and difficult living conditions triggered a series of revolts among the islanders. On the one hand, there were the landowners who were keen to maintain the feudal system, and on the other there were the commoners, who wanted to get rid of the aristocrats.

One of the members of the feudal faction was Arrigo della Rocca, who in 1376 asked the Aragonese to come to his aid. The commoners also boasted legendary figures, such as Sambucuccio d'Alando, a peasant whose famous exploits shook the foundations of local feudalism. The common people established the *Terres des Communes*, a confederation of villages favouring the common use of local land, in opposition to the feudal powers.

Sambucuccio d'Alando

GENOESE POLICY

Occasionally, the Genoese Republic gave control of the island over to private organizations that, as well as administering it, also safeguarded Genoa's interests. The first such commercial company to have this assignment was the Maona, in 1378, but it soon went bankrupt, prompting some of the nobles to ask the Aragonese throne for help. One of these nobles was Vincentello d'Istria, a soldier, estate owner and pirate who, in 1420, led a Spanish fleet of 400 ships to the island. Bonifacio resisted, but almost all of Corsica fell into Vincentello's hands. A few years later, Genoa had an opportunity to subdue the feudal landowners but did not make the most of it. The Genoese chose instead to ignore the *Terres des Communes*' request to protect the interests of the people. This refusal only increased the gap between the coastal town populations and those in the interior; it was the latter who were to cause the biggest problems in the future.

THE BANK OF ST GEORGE

In 1453, Genoa delegated control of Corsica to the Bank of St George, whose power was sanctioned by the *Capitula Corsorum*, the statute of the Genoese government of the island.

TIMELINE

1348 The plague decimates the island population	**1376** Arrigo della Rocca asks the Aragonese to support the rebellion	**1453** *Capitula Corsorum*: Corsica governed by the Bank of St George

1300	1350	1400	1450	1500

Victims of the plague

1378 Corsica governed by the Maona organization

1358 Revolt of Sambucuccio d'Alando

1420 Revolt of Vincentello d'Istria, who founds Corte

1498 Sampiero Corso is born in Bastelica

This Genoese bank ruled Corsica with special powers. It had the right to collect taxes, mint coins and to administer justice, and it had its own army. The bank's activities were many and varied, and were controlled by a series of basic guidelines. One of its primary objectives was to guarantee political control of the land by curbing the powers of the feudal lords. In addition to this, the Genoese promised to make the coastal plains productive in the hope of overcoming the scourge of malaria.

Royal Corsican artillery (1740)

SAMPIERO AND THE END OF GENOA

Born in 1498 in a hamlet near Bastelica, Sampiero Corso was one of the many islanders forced by poverty and tradition to enlist as a mercenary in the French Army. In 1553, after the momentous clash between France and Spain, the French decided to land on Corsica to gain a solid foothold in the Mediterranean. Sampiero Corso also took part in the French expedition, which was backed by the ships of the renowned pirate Dragut.

The Genoese strongholds fell one after the other – Bastia, St-Florent, Corte, and even the impregnable Bonifacio – until a peace treaty obliged the French to withdraw. Sampiero refused, however, and continued his struggle against the Genoese, even going so far as to ask various European courts to come to his aid. In 1563, a few months after landing once again in Corsica with the hope of stoking the fire of popular rebellion, Sampiero was assassinated. Genoese rule was reinstated in 1569, and for the next 200 years the island swung between insurrections on the one hand and normal colonial administration on the other. Genoa's power was in decline, however, and widespread dissatisfaction smouldered among the Corsicans. In the early 18th century, a series of revolts led first to independence for the island, and then to annexation by France. The only traces of the troubled Genoese rule that future islanders would note would be the chain of coastal towers and some cities with massive walls – the citadels.

Monserrato Fort, in Bastia, in a 1761 drawing

Sampiero Corso   **1640–70** Religious revival

1676 Foundation of a Greek colony at Sagone

1729 Revolt of Corte and peasants

| 1550 | 1600 | 1650 | 1700 | 1750 |

1569 Genoa reconquers Corsica

The citadel of Corte

1755–69 Pascal Paoli's government

1553 Sampiero Corso's landing with a French expedition

Revolt and Independence

ONE KEY EVENT TRIGGERED the Corsicans' fight for independence – the imposition of new taxes by the Genoese rulers in 1729. Many Corsicans refused to pay the taxes and several years of revolts followed. In 1735 in Corte, the Corsicans first drafted a constitution for an independent sovereign state. The following year, Corsica elected a king, Baron Theodor von Neuhof, but he abandoned the throne after only eight months. In 1745, Jean-Pierre Gaffori became the leader of a major insurrection, followed by the 30-year-old Pascal Paoli in 1755. Paoli succeeded in establishing a constitutional state, founded the University of Corte, and created an army. For 14 years the island was independent, but on 8 May 1769, Paoli lost the battle of Ponte-Novo, and French rule began.

***Theodor von Neuhof**, a German baron who had taken up the island's cause, was elected king by the Corsicans in 1736 but was forced to flee only a few months later.*

The hills of Castagniccia

French army

***Jean-Pierre Gaffori** was one of the leaders of the 1745–55 revolts and was a member of the triumvirate during that period. He was assassinated in a street in Corte in 1753.*

***Faustina**, Gaffori's wife, also took part in the clashes. She is portrayed in the bas-reliefs on the pedestal of the monument to her husband in Corte (see p134).*

*A **combatant** for Corsican independence wrote in a letter: "General, I entrust my old father to your care, as in two hours I shall be among those who have died for their country."*

THE END OF A DREAM

On 8 May 1769, near the bridge at Ponte-Novo, the nationalist Corsican troops led by Pascal Paoli suffered a decisive defeat at the hands of the French army. This event brought to an end 14 years of independence, the only period to date during which the island was free from domination by other peoples or nations.

The Moor's Head *has been the symbol of Independent Corsica for three centuries. Used by the Aragonese kings to celebrate the victory over the Moors in the 13th century, it was ceded to local clan leaders, taken up by Neuhof and then adopted by Paoli.*

JAMES BOSWELL AND CORSICA

The British author James Boswell went to Corsica in 1765 and published his travel journal, *Account of Corsica*, in England three years later, thus spreading the image of Pascal Paoli's democratic government throughout Europe. During the period of the French Revolution, the still-fresh memory of French intervention on the island made the revolutionary politician Comte de Mirabeau express his "regret and sorrow" for having helped to suppress the freedom of such a proud people.

Two thousand Corsican patriots led by Paoli took part in the battle.

Ponte-Novo was named after a new stone bridge built by the Genoese over the Golo river.

The French army surrounding the Corsicans on the bridge

Pascal Paoli *was not only a fine military strategist, he was also an educated, enlightened and cultured man. He drafted the only constitution that Corsica ever had and founded the University of Corte, which was reopened in 1981 (see p137).*

The bridge was a typical Genoese construction, much like those that still be found on the island.

The Golo river

(see p137)

TIMELINE

1720	1730	1740	1750	1760

1729 First revolt against Genoa; start of the War of Independence

1735 Declaration of Independence

1748 Second French intervention

1755 Pascal Paoli is elected General of the Nation

8 May 1769 Corsicans defeated at Ponte-Novo

1765 The University of Corte opened

1733 Second revolt headed by Hyacinthe Paoli, Pascal's father

1738 France intervenes on request by the Genoese

1745 Third revolt led by Jean-Pierre Gaffori

1753 French troops leave the island

1762 The Moor's Head becomes the national symbol

FRENCH DOMINION

During Corsica's years of revolt and brief period of independence, France had kept a close eye on the island, intervening on the side of Genoa against the Corsicans. In 1768, the weakened Genoese ceded the island to France, but French rule only started after a final attempt of resistance at the Battle of Ponte-Novo in 1769 *(see pp46–47)*. Corsica

Napoleon Crossing the St Bernard Pass,
Jacques-Louis David, 1800

was now governed by a provincial administrator and a military governor, one of whose duties was to repress popular revolts, which from then on were labelled as banditry.

Corsica was divided into provinces, each of which had its own law court. The cities gradually lost the privileges conferred on them by the Genoese, and efforts were made to establish clear-cut limits between private property and the municipalities.

Supporters of French rule were granted a series of benefits, including land, which stirred discontent among the people. Corsican nationalism was by no means dead, as proved by a rebellion that broke out in Niolo in 1774 and by the constant support given to General Paoli during his exile by the French. At the first signs of revolutionary activity in France, Corsicans made it quite clear that they would not be mere spectators to these events. There were differences, however, between the demands made by the French and those of the

Corsicans. The latter were not interested in the struggle against the noble class, but fought for equal rights for French people and Corsicans. In 1790, the people disarmed the garrison in Bastia and political exiles such as Paoli could return to the island.

Sentenced to death by radical French revolutionaries, the Jacobins, Paoli appealed to the English for help. Their intervention led to the birth of the Anglo-Corsican kingdom (1794–96), with Sir George Elliott as viceroy. The sidelined Paoli left for London, where he died in 1807. In 1796 French troops were sent out to retake the island. They were led by a young Corsican-born officer – Napoleon Bonaparte. He would always have close ties with his motherland, and Ajaccio in particular *(see p87)*.

THE 19TH AND 20TH CENTURIES

After Napoleon's fall in 1815, the 19th century in Corsica was fairly calm, and the presence of France took on ever-increasing importance. The decrease in banditry and vendettas, alongside a relatively stable economic and political scene, lent a certain credibility to French rule.

Efforts were made to create a middle class that would support and promote the island's growth. One of the most successful initiatives was the development of an infrastructure on the island, which vastly

TIMELINE

Napoleonic crest

1790 Paoli returns from exile

1830 First maritime service to Corsica established

	1775	1800	1825	1850	1875

1769 Birth of Napoleon Bonaparte in Ajaccio

1794–96 Anglo-Corsican kingdom

1827 Opening of Ajaccio–Bastia road

1855–70 Repression of banditry and blood feuds

Corsican emigrants waiting to embark

improved communications. The Ajaccio–Bastia road was constructed in 1827 and the railway in 1894, and a permanent ferry service was established in 1830. All this led to an unprecedented population increase, from 150,000 people in 1790 to 300,000 in 1890. There was a parallel development in agriculture, even in the hills and mountain areas inland, and the centralized administration tried to curb the free circulation of transhumance shepherds. Around the mid-19th century a liberal Corsican middle class was on the rise.

However, a short time later, during the Industrial Revolution, Corsica was affected by decline. The mainly rural and, in comparison, non-modernized society could not compete with agricultural products from the mainland and the French colonies. Despite improvements in living standards, dire poverty once again afflicted the island, forcing thousands of Corsicans to emigrate. Corsica paid a high toll in World War I (20,000 dead), then lost an average of 5–6,000 people annually to emigration. In

A Corsican Nationalist Party rally

1942, Italian troops occupied Corsica. After the rise of a strong Resistance movement known as the "Maquis", Corsica was the first French *département* to be liberated, in 1943.

THE INDEPENDENCE MOVEMENT

At the end of World War II, the many Corsicans who had gone abroad were repatriated, and in the 1960s there was a new presence in the elections, the Front Régionaliste Corse (FRC). In 1973, the FRC, together with the Action Régionaliste Corse (ARC), demanded autonomy for Corsica, a decentralized government and protection for Corsican land against tourist developments, and they received much support. In 1975, a series of demonstrations ended in the shooting of two police officers. Following this, the Front de Libération Nationale de la Corse (FLNC) was founded, a movement that committed many acts of terrorism in the following decades.

While the independence movement rapidly gained popularity, the island was again divided into two *départements*, Haute-Corse and Corse-du-Sud. In 1981, the University of Corte was reopened. The process of establishing a federal statute for Corsica began in 1991. The 1990s saw a boom in tourism, which created no environmental problems, partly because of the islanders' respect for their land. Today, Corsica has come to terms with the central government on the mainland and is working to build a peaceful future for its population.

1894 Inauguration of Ajaccio–Bastia railway line

1966 FRC founded

Logo of the University

1981 The University of Corte reopens

1942 Italian occupation

1900	1925	1950	1975	2000

1910–20 Great wave of emigration

1943 Liberation of Corsica

1976 FNLC founded

1991 Regional autonomy law is passed

CORSICA
AREA BY AREA

Corsica at a Glance

WITHIN A DISTANCE covered by a short drive, Corsica offers beaches that are not unlike those in tropical countries and wild mountains surrounded by woods. The island boasts extremely varied and fascinating landscapes, such as the coast carpeted with maquis vegetation, the hillside olive and chestnut groves, the valleys where rivers have created deep gorges, the mountains traversed by the GR20 long-distance path *(see pp20–25)*, and the beautiful surrounding waters and seabeds. In this natural setting, man-made splendour can also be found in prehistoric megaliths, Pisan Romanesque churches, Genoese citadels, and villages of old stone houses. The two cities that have played a major role in the history of the island, Ajaccio and Bastia, are joined by the "historical capital", Corte, along with Bonifacio, Calvi and Porto-Vecchio, famous for their beaches.

Calvi's Citadel
The strongholds of Genoese power, the citadels still dominate the main cities in Corsica, surrounded by massive bastions. Calvi's citadel was built in the 15th century.

AJACCIO AND
THE WEST COAST
see pp82–105

Pointe de la Parata
One of the most common sights along the coastline are the Genoese watchtowers, surrounded by the brilliant colours of the maquis. One such building features at Pointe de la Parata, the famous cape in the Golfe d'Ajaccio.

Megalithic Monuments
Relics of prehistoric Corsica can still be found in the interior of the island, which has many alignments of menhirs. The menhirs can be dolmens or the so-called castelli *(castles).*

0 kilometres   20

0 miles

◁ **The citadel of Corte dominating the Gorges du Tavignano and the Vallée de la Restonica**

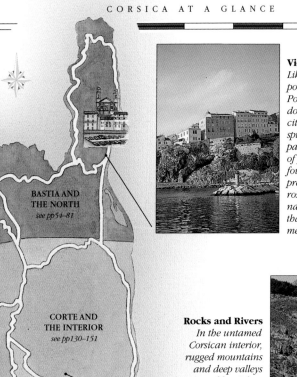

BASTIA AND
THE NORTH
see pp54–81

CORTE AND
THE INTERIOR
see pp130–151

BONIFACIO
AND THE SOUTH
see pp106–129

Vieux Port, Bastia
Like so many other ports, the Vieux Port of Bastia, dominated by the citadel, exudes the spirit of the island's past. Hundreds of years ago, the foundations of the present-day cities rose up around natural harbours that were used for merchant vessels.

Rocks and Rivers
In the untamed Corsican interior, rugged mountains and deep valleys crossed by violent torrents offer an exciting and challenging landscape for hikers.

The Cliffs of Bonifacio
The white limestone cliffs in the Bonifacio area are perhaps one of the most famous sights in Corsica. The cliffs are also geologically interesting, since limestone is an unusual presence in this mostly granitic island.

BASTIA AND THE NORTH

B ASTIA HAS A CHARM *of its own, which can be found in the citadel and the historic centre, with its narrow alleys reminiscent of Italian villages. Indeed, the town owes its development and commercial success to Genoa. To get a true sense of Bastia, the best thing to do is join the locals in their rituals: a coffee in Place St-Nicolas, a* pastis *at the Vieux Port and shopping at the Sunday market.*

Geographically closer to Italy than to France, Bastia aims to become a regular stopover port for Mediterranean cruises and a base for ecological tourism thanks to its proximity to the mountains inland. Cap Corse is nearby, with villages squeezed between the sea and mountains and small harbours protected by old watchtowers. This region is a world unto itself and has always been more similar to Pisa, Marseille, Genoa and Livorno than to the rest of the island.

With their sailing prowess, the inhabitants of this peninsula made it a port for the shipment of wine, firewood, oil, cork and other local products. Thanks to their farming traditions, they transformed the steep mountainsides into cultivable terraces. This can be seen in the Rogliano and Patrimonio vineyards, among the best on the island. The proximity to and close relations with Italy have left their mark on the language, with its Tuscan influence, and on the architecture, which resembles that of Italy's Ligurian coast. In fact, the islands in the Tuscan archipelago are visible from the east coast of Corsica.

The other "microregion" in the north is sunny Balagne, famous for its beaches and hamlets nestled in productive olive orchards. The history of this region is linked with that of Pisa, which developed Balagne's agriculture. Beautiful Pisan churches can be found in Aregno, Lumio and Calenzana. When the Genoese arrived, they built the citadels of Calvi and Algajola, exploited the cork oak groves, and planted the olive trees that still surround the old stone villages.

The small harbour at Meria, near Macinaggio, along the eastern coast of Cap Corse

◁ **Maquis vegetation covering the cliffs of Cap Corse; in the background, the Tour de l'Osse**

Exploring Bastia and the North

THE MAIN TOURIST LOCALITIES in the northern region
lie along the west coast, beyond the Col de
Teghime. St-Florent boasts a lovely yacht harbour
and boat service to the wild beaches in the Désert
des Agriates. Calvi is renowned for its nightlife and
its beach – a long stretch of white sand under the
shade of a pine grove. The relatively short distances
between interesting sights in this area make it
possible to organize one-day excursions inland
through Balagne or Nebbio. These villages have
preserved their centuries-old architecture, including
stunning Pisan Romanesque churches. The Cap
Corse peninsula is for those who love cliffs or
small pebble beaches. Visitors may also enjoy
hikes along the coast or among the maquis to
villages where time seems to have stood still.

**A slope in the Désert des Agriates
covered with maquis undergrowth**

Two villagers soaking up the sunshine and taking it
easy in the Balagne region

KEY

▨	Major road
▭	Minor road
▨	Scenic route
▬	River

L'ÎLE ROUSSE ⑰   N1197
N197
ALGAJOLA ⑱   ⑲ *PIGNA*
⑳   ㉑ *SANT'ANTONINO*
AREGNO   D71
LA REVELLATA ● *CALVI* ㉕   *SPELONCATO* ㉒
N197   *STRADA DI*   N197   D963
L'ARTIGIANI TOUR
㉔   *PIOGGIOLA* ●
D151   D151
㉓ *CALENZANA*
B A L A G N E
D147
Porto / D81B   D81 / *Porto*

SIGHTS AT A GLANCE

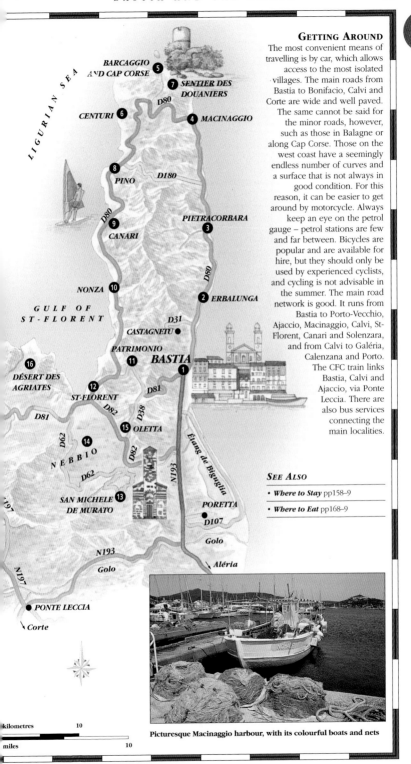

5 BARCAGGIO
AND CAP CORSE

7 SENTIER DES
DOUANIERS

D80

6 CENTURI

4 MACINAGGIO

8
PINO   D180

9
CANARI   PIETRACORBARA
3

10 NONZA

D80

2 ERBALUNGA

GULF OF
ST-FLORENT

D31
CASTAGNETU ●

PATRIMONIO   BASTIA
11   **1**

16
DÉSERT DES
AGRIATES

12
ST-FLORENT   D81

D81   D82   D38

15 OLETTA

N E B B I O   D82

D62   N193

D62

SAN MICHELE **13**
DE MURATO

14

Etang de Biguglia

PORETTA ●
D107

Golo

Aléria

N193

Golo

N197

● PONTE LECCIA

↘ Corte

GETTING AROUND

The most convenient means of
travelling is by car, which allows
access to the most isolated
villages. The main roads from
Bastia to Bonifacio, Calvi and
Corte are wide and well paved.
The same cannot be said for
the minor roads, however,
such as those in Balagne or
along Cap Corse. Those on the
west coast have a seemingly
endless number of curves and
a surface that is not always in
good condition. For this
reason, it can be easier to get
around by motorcycle. Always
keep an eye on the petrol
gauge – petrol stations are few
and far between. Bicycles are
popular and are available for
hire, but they should only be
used by experienced cyclists,
and cycling is not advisable in
the summer. The main road
network is good. It runs from
Bastia to Porto-Vecchio,
Ajaccio, Macinaggio, Calvi, St-
Florent, Canari and Solenzara,
and from Calvi to Galéria,
Calenzana and Porto.
The CFC train links
Bastia, Calvi and
Ajaccio, via Ponte
Leccia. There are
also bus services
connecting the
main localities.

SEE ALSO

• *Where to Stay* pp158–9

• *Where to Eat* pp168–9

kilometres   10

miles   10

Picturesque Macinaggio harbour, with its colourful boats and nets

Bastia ❶

WITH ITS COLOURFUL HOUSES overlooking the sea, Bastia is the second-largest city in Corsica and is considered its economic capital. This is because of the port and the industrial zone that extends south of the old centre. Although the ancient Romans founded the city of Mantinon, mentioned by the Greek geographer Ptolemy, on the hills, Bastia was for centuries only the small port of the village of Cardo in the neighbouring hinterland. Wine was loaded on to ships here in the Middle Ages and taken to Pisa. It was not until the 15th century that the Genoese began to construct a tower and enlarge the fortress that protected the port (*bastiglia* in Italian, hence the name of the city). Genoa was responsible for the prosperity of Bastia and left its mark there – including a certain coldness towards foreigners. With a little time and patience, however, this city can provide many surprises.

The simple, elegant façade of the Chapelle St-Roch

🏛 Place du Marché
Dominated by the old Mairie (town hall) and a lovely fountain shaded by plane trees, this square is the heart of Terra Vecchia (the ancient port area), with streets winding around the Vieux Port, or old harbour. The name "marché" (market) derives from the stalls, which, especially on Sunday mornings,

Detail of the fountain in Place du Marché

make for a colourful and noisy scene. As well as the stands with fruit, vegetables, cheese and charcuterie, there are those that make a sort of pancake with *brocciu*, the local sheep's-milk cheese, and an oyster and mussel vendor.

🔒 St-Jean-Baptiste
Place de l'Hôtel-de-Ville. ☎ 04 95 55 24 60. ⬜ *Mon–Sat, Sun am.*
The largest church in Corsica is flanked by two bell towers and has an imposing, austere façade that rises majestically among the roofs of the Terra Vecchia area. It was built in the mid-1600s and redecorated in the following century in Baroque style. The façade stands on a narrow alleyway and is one of the most recognizable images of the island. The two-aisle nave displays marble decoration, gilded stucco work and trompe-l'oeil decorations. The high altar, pulpit and font are made of polychrome marble.

🔒 Oratoire de l'Immaculée Conception
Rue Napoléon. ⬜ *daily.*
Constructed in 1611, this chapel reveals a rich Baroque interior. Wooden panels and red Genoese velvet cover the walls, and there is a fresco on the central vault representing the Immaculate Conception. On the small square outside, black and white pebblestones are laid out in the shape of a sun.

🔒 Chapelle St-Roch
Rue Napoléon.
⬜ *Mon–Sat, Sun am.*
This chapel was dedicated to the saint who protected the population from the plague. It was built in 1604 for the St Roch Confraternity, founded in 1588 (*see p61*). The work

of Ligurian architects and artists, the chapel has 18th-century, Genoese-style wooden panelling and features a statue of St Roch, which is borne in local processions. The organ was made in 1750 and is housed in an interesting tribune made of sculpted, gilded wood.

🔒 St-Charles
Rue du Général Carbuccia.
⬜ *Mon–Sat, Sun am.*
Preceded by a stairway, this church with its impressive façade was constructed in 1635 for the Jesuits' college and dedicated to St Ignatius Loyola, the founder of the order. When the Jesuits were driven out of Corsica in 1769, the church became the seat of the St Charles Borromeo Confraternity (*see p61*).
Inside is an altarpiece of the miraculous *Virgin of Lavasina* and a statue of the *Virgin Mary and Child* that is carried in a procession every year.

The view across the rooftops of the Terra Vecchia quarter

The jetty known as Môle Génois, on the north of the Vieux Port

Vieux Port

Nestled between Terra Nova, the citadel and the Terra Vecchia quarter, which frames it with its old buildings, the small cove of the medieval port has retained the atmosphere of an old maritime village. It was once the marina of Cardo, and fishermen still mend their nets here in the blue-and-white wooden boats that are flanked by luxury yachts. Lining the quays are cafés and restaurants that are frequented by the locals, who spend their evenings here. In the summer the road is closed to traffic and the old port is transformed into a large and lively pedestrian precinct, excellent for people-watching.

The tall façades lining the port have suffered erosion from the sea wind and salty air. Walks along the outer jetties are spectacular: the Môle Génois to the north, and the Jetée du Dragon to the south, ending at the 1861 lighthouse.

VISITORS' CHECKLIST

Road map D2. 👥 52,500.
✈ Poretta, 25 km (16 miles)
(04 95 54 54 54).
🚌 🚉 Place Maréchal Leclerc
(04 95 32 80 61).
⛴ from Genoa, Savona, Livorno,
La Spezia, Nice, Marseille, Toulon.
ℹ Place St-Nicolas (04 95 54
20 40). 🎬 Italian Film Festival
(Jan–Feb); Black Christ (Mar–Apr);
St John's Feast Day (24 Jun);
Relève des Gouverneurs (mid-Jul).
🌐 www.bastia-tourisme.com

Jardin Romieu

At the right-hand jetty of the Vieux Port are steps that go up to the citadel along a winding – but not particularly steep – path. It crosses over the Jardin Romieu, an oasis of greenery and tranquillity in the middle of Bastia. With palm, pine and laurel trees and succulent plants, it offers a splendid view of the city.

THE CENTRE OF BASTIA

Chapelle St-Roch ④
Jardin Romieu ⑦
Oratoire de l'Immaculée
  Conception ③
Place du Marché ①
Place St-Nicolas ⑨
Quai des Martyrs de la
  Libération ⑧
St-Charles ⑤
St-Jean-Baptiste ②
Vieux Port ⑥

0 metres   180
0 yards   180

KEY

ℹ Tourist information
🏛 Church
⚓ Port
🅿 Parking

Bastia: the Citadelle

THIS IMPRESSIVE STRUCTURE was built by the Genoese in the 15th–16th centuries. It is still surrounded by the original ramparts and lies in the Terra Nova quarter, which is quite different from Terra Vecchia. Unlike the ancient port area, which grew up almost at random, the Citadelle was laid out in keeping with rigorous town-planning principles, with houses of the same height and broad squares. After decades of neglect, a restoration campaign was initiated in the 1980s. The first houses to regain the original pastel colours typical of Ligurian tradition were those on Rue St-Michel, which has a splendid view of the Terra Vecchia quarter.

Cherub in the Oratoire Ste-Croix

The Citadelle seen from the sea, with the Jetée du Dragon in the foreground

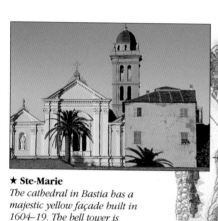

★ Ste-Marie
The cathedral in Bastia has a majestic yellow façade built in 1604–19. The bell tower is 71 m (233 ft) high. Ste-Marie was consecrated in 1570, when Bastia became a bishopric.

The rampart walls of the Citadelle were built between 1480 and 1521 by the Genoese governor Tomasino da Campofregoso. This section of the walls extends furthest into the sea.

★ Oratoire Ste-Croix
This gem of Rococo architecture boasts the Christ des Miracles, *the protector of fishermen, which is borne in procession every third year on 3 May. Other sculptures include this angel.*

STAR SIGHTS

★ Ste-Marie

★ Oratoire Ste-Croix

Louis XVI Gate
The monumental entrance to the citadel that directly connects Rue du Colle and Place du Donjon was built in the late 18th century.

The glacis of the Citadelle offers the best panoramic view of Terra Vecchia and the old port.

VISITORS' CHECKLIST

Palais des Gouverneurs
Place du Donjon.
04 95 31 09 12. for restoration until spring 2007.
Ste-Marie
Rue Notre-Dame-de-la-Citadelle.
daily.

Palais des Gouverneurs
From the 15th to the 18th centuries, this palace was the residence of the Genoese governors. It is now home to a museum, currently closed for renovation, of the history and art of Bastia.

Pavillon des Nobles Douze

Place Guasco
is a square among the old houses, protected by trees.

Luthiers in Bastia
In his workshop in Place Guasco, Christian Magdeleine makes stringed instruments, such as this cittern, decorated with wooden inlay.

RELIGIOUS BROTHERHOODS

Religious brotherhoods, or confraternities, are groups that carry out charitable works and organize religious celebrations, such as processions on Christian holidays and feast days. They grew up in the 17th century and many are still quite active throughout the island. At Bastia there are also brotherhoods of people with a common profession (artisans, fishermen) that meet in oratories decorated with stucco work, sculptures, fabrics and paintings of high artistic value. The chapels of the local confraternities are in the side aisles of the Bastia cathedral.

Singing during a religious procession

Exploring Bastia

Napoleon in Roman dress

THE CENTRE OF BASTIA, facing the commercial port, can easily be explored on foot. Those travelling by car can park in the garage under Place St-Nicolas, the heart of the city and the junction between Terra Vecchia and the modern area. Bastia is relatively small, but for those who would rather not walk there is a small electric train that starts off from the square, a short distance from the tourist-information office, and arrives at the citadel via the Quai des Martyrs and the tunnel under the Vieux Port. Guided tours of the Old Town are available, as is a tour of the outlying villages.

The Quai des Martyrs de la Libération

🜊 Quai des Martyrs de la Libération

This quay, enlivened by cafés and restaurants, provides a pleasant walk along the seaside from Place St-Nicolas to the Vieux Port. One of the buildings on the quay is the Palais Monti Rossi, a residence of one of Corsica's old families and one of the finest 19th-century constructions in the city. The building miraculously remained intact after the American bombings that destroyed 90 per cent of the Terra Vecchia quarter in the late summer of 1943. Its façade boasts a pediment, arches and pilasters.

This street is known for its lively nightlife during the tourist season.

🜊 Place St-Nicolas

Maison Mattei

🕻 04 95 32 44 38 for tastings.

Facing the new port and shaded by the old palm and plane trees, this 300-m (980-ft) long square occupies the site of an old hospital for the poor that was destroyed in the early 19th century. In the middle of the square is a music pavilion where concerts are held on summer evenings. On the south side of the square stands the white marble statue of Napoleon in the guise of a Roman emperor, while on the opposite side is a bronze sculpture group dedicated to widow Renno, a Corsican heroine who lost her sons in the wars of independence, and to all those Corsicans who lost their lives in war.

On the west side of the square are the bars and cafés where locals and visitors alike sit at alfresco tables. It is worth trying a glass of Cap Corse, the unique apéritif of the Maison Mattei, the historic establishment located on the square *(see opposite)*.

Every Sunday morning, Place St-Nicolas is enlivened by dozens of market stalls offering goods of every kind, and even some interesting

Bric-à-brac for sale on Sundays in Place St-Nicolas

antiques. Behind the charming cafés there are some elegant 19th-century buildings.

🏛 Cyrnarom

9 Avenue Monseigneur Rigo.
🕻 04 95 31 70 60. 🕐 Mon–Sat (Oct–Mar: pm only).

Old perfume bottles, alembics and stills, as well as vials and period labels make a fine display on the shelves belonging to pharmacist and chemist Guy Cecchini. This local establishment is a laboratory and museum specializing in Corsican scents, including myrtle, pine, rockrose, lavender, rosemary and broom. The buds, flowers or leaves are distilled, becoming aromatic oils used to cure or prevent illnesses. There are also essences that smell like the sea breeze or have the intense and oily aroma of the maquis.

🜊 Port de Toga

When the Vieux Port proved unable to take the number of pleasure boats arriving there

View of Port de Toga, also known as Port de Plaisance

in the high season, an area was created between Bastia and Pietranera to cope with all this heavy traffic.

The Port de Toga is a long quay that has become a lively, trendy place frequented by young people, especially on summer evenings. The restaurant and disco bar tables almost touch the sea, their multicoloured lights reflected in the water. Some of the best nightspots that are open until late are Le Bounty, Le Café Cézanne and Le Maracana.

Façade of the church of St-Étienne in Cardo

Cardo

Today a chic suburb in the hills above Bastia, Cardo used to be a fishing village. Its marina, Porto Cardo, was the original nucleus of the city of Bastia in the Middle Ages. It became a municipality in its own right in 1844, by order of Louis Philippe. Cardo offers a spectacular view of the coastline, and there are many paths popular with hikers and cyclists.

The main monument here is the Neo-Classical church of **St-Étienne**, which has painted wooden statues from the 17th century and a Neo-Gothic organ tribune.

From Cardo, the D231 and then D31, the **Route de la Corniche Supérieure**, is a panoramic road running at around 300 m (980 ft) above sea level. It goes through the village of Pietrabugno and proceeds to San Martino di Lota and Miomo. In clear weather, the islands of the Tuscan archipelago can be seen on the horizon.

THE MAISON MATTEI IN BASTIA

This renowned firm makes tobacconist's products, cork objects and, above all, liqueurs distilled from muscat grapes and flavoured with maquis herbs and quinine, including the famous Cap Corse *(see pp166 and 173)*. The Maison was established in Bastia in 1872 by Louis-Napoléon Mattei. Almost immediately the firm became a symbol of the spirit of enterprise, and its so-called "products of nostalgia" were exported throughout the world, especially where there

The stone sign on the façade of the Maison Mattei

were many Corsican emigrants. While the original cigarette factory at Toga closed in 1977, when the company was sold to a large group, the shop is still in Place St-Nicolas.

Étang de Biguglia
Lido de la Marana.
04 95 33 55 73.

On the southern outskirts of the city, between the airport, the industrial area and the strip of Marana coastline, is the Étang de Biguglia, a lagoon designated as a reserve to conserve the largest wet zone in Corsica. The lagoon consists of 18 sq km (7 sq miles) of pools and rivers that are part of the mouth of the Golo river and is connected to the sea in its northern part.

A flamingo in the wet Étang de Biguglia

The scourge of malaria, which was an endemic disease in Corsica for centuries, was finally eliminated after World War II. The land was reclaimed and partly used for farming. Now the canebrakes and grassland

are the ideal habitat for 100 species of birds, including the great cormorant, the purple heron and the flamingo. Other inhabitants of the lagoon are marsh tortoises. The reserve is also a habitual reserve, stop-over for birds migrating from Europe to Africa. The best seasons to observe the 60 or more species of migrators are spring and autumn.

The water, which until a few years ago was badly polluted, has been purified, and the mullets and eels have returned. They are caught using traditional methods by a local fishermen's cooperative.

Since 1994, the Étang has been a regional reserve, with nature walks, a cycling path, and guided tours. The town of Biguglia, which overlooks the lagoon, was the capital of the island under the Pisans and the residence of the Genoese governors until 1372. The sandy belt that separates the sea from the lagoon is one of the loveliest beaches in Bastia.

Étang de Biguglia from the sea

Sailing school in the peaceful Vieux Port of Bastia, with the church of St-Jean-Baptiste in the background ▷

White houses surrounding the small harbour of Erbalunga

Erbalunga ②

Road map D1. 🏛 *400.* ℹ *Port de Plaisance, Macinaggio (04 95 35 40 34).* 🎭 *Procession de la Cerca (Maundy Thu & Good Fri); Music Festival (1st week Aug).*

A GENOESE TOWER protects the small harbour lined with old stone houses and fish restaurants. Erbalunga, the marina of the district of Brando, was for centuries the port where Pisan ships landed to be loaded with local wine.

At the start of the village is the church of **St-Erasme**, home to the crosses of the Cerca procession: the men's crucifix weighs 60 kg (132 lb); the women's is 30 kg (66 lb). On the evening of Maundy Thursday, the procession winds through the streets to the Benedictine nuns' convent. On Good Friday it leaves early in the morning and proceeds for 7 km (4 miles), visiting the hamlets of Pozzo, Poretto and Silgaggia.

In Erbalunga, as in many other locations around Cap Corse, there are sumptuous country mansions known as *Maisons d'Américains*. These were built by Corsicans who had returned home wealthy after emigrating to Latin America. Rich families also had impressive mausoleums built, which can be seen from the D32 all over the cape *(see p27)*.

ENVIRONS: In **Castello**, 3 km (2 miles) inland, there is a 13th-century fortress. A 15th-century Italian nobleman murdered his wife here, and she is said to haunt Castello. The chapel of **Santa Maria di e Nevi** lies a short walk south towards Silgaggia. It houses the oldest frescoes in Corsica, dating from 1386. **Pozzo** is the starting point for the path to **Monte Stello** (1,307 m/ 4,288 ft), which takes 6 hours to walk.

North of Erbalunga, along the D80, is the **Sisco Valley**. In Sisco is the Chapelle de St-Martin, housing a precious 13th-century silver mask of St John Chrysotom. From the main road a path leads to the Romanesque Chapelle de San Michele, built by the Pisans. Closer to the coast is the former Couvent de Santa Catalina, famous for once having housed relics of a fantastic nature, such as a lump of clay from which Adam was made and almonds from Paradise.

🏛 Santa Maria di e Nevi
Castello. ☎ *04 95 33 20 84.* 📷 *Visits by guided tour only. Book one day in advance (06 86 78 02 38).*

Pietracorbara ③

Road map D1. 🏛 *350.* ℹ *Port de Plaisance, Macinaggio (04 95 35 40 34).*

A BROAD, GREEN cultivated valley behind a long, sandy beach enclosed by a canebrake protects the village of Pietracorbara. A skeleton found here in 1990 and dating from 6000 BC is proof of the prehistoric origins of the site, which was later used by the Greeks and Romans as a base.

ENVIRONS: Northwards, along the coast, is the 16th-century **Tour de l'Osse** (Bone Tower), one of best preserved in the area, and **Porticciolo**, a tiny marina with houses grouped around the pier.

Fishing boat in Macinaggio's busy harbour

Macinaggio ④

Road map D1. 🏛 *480.* 🚢 ℹ *Port de Plaisance (04 95 35 40 34).* 🎭 *Nautival, Sea Festival (end of May).*

F ISHING BOATS ARE anchored next to the yachts that stop at Macinaggio after sailing across from Italy. The most popular tourist harbour in Cap Corse, it has always been a military and commercial port. Controlled by the Genoese for a long time, it was liberated by Pascal Paoli, after years of struggle, in 1761 *(see pp46–7)*. Plaques on the quay announce that Napoleon landed here, as did the empress Eugénie on her return trip from the Suez Canal inauguration in 1869, and that Paoli also stopped here. The port is divided into three basins that can take in over 500 boats and is surrounded by visitors' facilities.

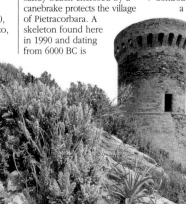

The Genoese Tour de l'Osse near Pietracorbara

ENVIRONS: Around the village are vineyards, extending as far as **Rogliano**, which cling to the slopes of Monte Poggio. Inhabited in Roman times, from the 12th to the 16th centuries it was ruled by the da Mare family, which had trade relations with Genoa.

At **Bettolacce**, the area's main village, a round tower bears witness to its former splendour. The church of Sant'Agnellu boasts a beautiful altar of white Carrara marble.

Île de la Giraglia opposite the tip of Cap Corse

Barcaggio and Cap Corse ❺

Road map D1. 🗠 480. 🛈 *Port de Plaisance, Macinaggio (04 95 35 40 34).*

ON THE NORTHERN TIP of the peninsula are some villages that have retained the spirit of the past. One of these is Barcaggio, which has a beautiful beach where cows go to graze and a small harbour where time seems to have come to a halt.

The road leading here, the D80 followed by the D253, is simply spectacular. It descends among the maquis, holm oak groves and pastures covered in white asphodel, offering a fine view of the **Île de la Giraglia**. The northernmost part of Corsica, this green serpentine rock island is separated from the coast by 2 km (1 mile) of treacherous,

fast-flowing sea. This island has a square 16th-century Genoese tower and a lighthouse built in the 1940s that, until 1994, was inhabited by a keeper; now it is wholly automatic. Giraglia is famous because the sailing regatta that goes from Sanremo, in Liguria, to Le Lavandou, Provence, and back passes by here.

About 2 km (1 mile) west of Barcaggio is **Tollare**, another small harbour with a tuna fishery. From here, a small road winds back to the D80 and **Ersa**, whose church of **Ste-Marie** has a 17th-century wooden tabernacle. West of here, on Col de Serra is **Moulin Mattei**, an old, round mill offering a fabulous panoramic view. In a poor state of preservation, it was restored in the past by the Maison Mattei, the renowned apéritif makers (*see p63*).

Centuri ❻

Road map D1. 🗠 200. 🛈 *Port de Plaisance, Macinaggio (04 95 35 40 34).*

A NARROW INLET lined by ochre, grey and white houses with green serpentine roofs is an apt description of the small port of Centuri, which for centuries was a loading point for wine,

A fisherman from Centuri making a lobster pot

wood, oil and citrus fruits that were then shipped to Italy and France. Today, Centuri, the ancient Roman Centurium mentioned by Ptolemy, is in fact the leading fishing centre in Cap Corse. The docks are covered with fishing nets and lobster pots that are still handmade. The port is full of the typical double-ended fishing boats that return laden with lobsters (3,000 kg/6,600 lb a year) that can be enjoyed in the local restaurants.

The sea floor here is a paradise for scuba divers, especially around the islet of Centuri, at the mouth of the bay, which was fortified in the 13th century.

From the port, an hour's walk up a path leads through luxuriant vegetation to the village of **Cannelle** (also accessible by car from the D80 road). Its simple stone houses hugging the mountainside are rich in bougainvillea, and its narrow streets and covered passageways offer views of the sea. On the D80 road, 3 km (2 miles) from Centuri, is the 16th-century **Couvent de l'Annonciation** dedicated to Our Lady of the Seven Sorrows. The church is considered the largest in Cap Corse. The monastery is not open to the public.

Fishing boats anchored in the Centuri harbour

Tour of the Sentier des Douaniers **❼**

O NCE USED BY CUSTOMS OFFICERS to
control smuggling activities (hence
the name, "path of customs officers"), this
coastal footpath runs along the tip of Cap
Corse, in places offering stunning views.
Similar paths run along the entire perimeter of Corsica, but the Sentier des
Douaniers, going from Macinaggio to
Centuri – among the junipers, mastics and
asphodels, and over beaches and craggy
cliffs – is simply breathtaking. This tour
can be divided into three stages:
Macinaggio–Barcaggio, Barcaggio–Tollare
and Tollare–Centuri. It is not particularly
difficult, but watch out for brush fires,
especially in the summer. Drivers can
reach the separate sights via inland
paved roads.

Barcaggio ③
Past the Punta d'Agnello tower and
promontory – one of the most panoramic
spots in Cap Corse – is Barcaggio *(see p67)*.
This is the first stage of the tour that is
directly accessible by car, from the D253.
The water in the bay is crystal clear.

Tollare ④
Tollare, a tiny port with a
Genoese tower, is another stage
in the tour that can be accessed
by car, from the D153 road.

*Île de la
Giraglia*

*Punta
d'Agnello*

L'Acqua Tignese

④

③

⑤

D153

D253

Poggio

Granaggiolo

*Moulin
Mattei*   *Botticella*

Capo Grosso ⑤
There is a great
viewpoint at Capo
Grosso. From here
a road leads to the
Moulin Mattei
(see p67).

⑥

D80

D53

D80

D35

Rogliano

D8

NONZA

0 kilometres   2

0 miles   1

Centuri ⑥
Those who decide
to hike this far
along the Sentier
des Douaniers will
have a challenging
but interesting
day. At Centuri
(see p67), delicious
seafood makes for
an excellent reward.

KEY

▬   Tour footpath

═   Motorable road

☀   Viewpoint

TIPS FOR HIKERS

Port de Plaisance, Macinaggio (04 95 35 40 34).
Length of tour: 20 km (12 miles). **Duration:** Macinaggio–Barcaggio 3 hours; Barcaggio–Tollare 45 minutes; Tollare–Centuri 4 hours.
Footpath: of average difficulty; can be taken all year long.
Stopping-off points: Macinaggio, Barcaggio, Tollare and Centuri.

Chapelle de Santa Maria ②
Further along the path is the chapel of Santa Maria, built in the 12th century over an early Christian church. The ruins of a Genoese tower can be found on the coast along Santa Maria bay.

Macinaggio ①
The tour begins at Macinaggio *(see p66)* and leads to the beautiful beach of Tamarone, the entrance to a reserve opposite the Îles Finocchiarola. These craggy rocks with a watchtower inhabited by colonies of marine birds are also a nature reserve. The path then skirts the high coastline, with continuous fine views of the sea and the coves below, where it is possible to take a swim.

BASTIA

CAP CORSE AND PATRIMONIO WINES

Appreciated since ancient times, the white wines of Cap Corse come from terraces carved out of the mountainside. The two AOC *(appellation d'origine controllée)* labels here are Coteaux du Cap Corse and Muscat du Cap Corse *(see p167)*. They produce Malvasia, Muscat and Sciaccarellu wines, and Rappu, a sweet white wine that can be purchased only at the wineries. Among the most famous wineries is

A wine label of Patrimonio, a famous AOC region

the Clos Nicrosi, which produces one of the best Corsican whites. Another AOC area is Patrimonio *(see p70)*; Domaine de Pietri at Morsiglia has been in business since 1786 and at St-Florent there is the Domaine Gentile. Both make reds and whites, as well as Rappu and Muscat.

Pino ❽

Road map D1. 🏛 *145.* 🛈 *Port de Plaisance, Macinaggio (04 95 35 40 34).*

THIS SMALL VILLAGE at the foot of Col de Ste-Lucie lies in the midst of luxuriant vegetation. Umbrella pines protect the Maisons d'Américains *(see p66)*, including the Maison Savelli and the family mausoleum with its tile roof. Other monumental tombs surrounded by cypress trees lie at the junction of the D80 and D180 roads. The church of **Ste-Marie** has a Baroque façade and, inside, two fonts: one decorated with fish and salamanders, the other with lions. The **Couvent St-François**, built in 1486 in Marina di Scalu, is flanked by a Genoese tower.

ENVIRONS: About 5 km (3 miles) from Pino, on the D180 road going up to Col de Ste-Lucie, is the footpath for the **Tour de Sénèque**. The tower is at the top of **Monte Ventiggiola**, 564 m (1,850 ft) above sea level, where the great Roman playwright Seneca is said to have been exiled. In reality, the tower is medieval. It can be reached after a steep climb through the maquis that can take over an hour. The view is well worth the climb.

🏛 **Ste-Marie**
🕽 *04 95 35 12 32.* ⭘ *by appt.*
🏛 **Couvent St-François**
🕽 *04 95 35 12 70.* ⬤ *to the public.*

Canari ❾

Road map D1. 🏛 *290.* 🛈 *Port de Plaisance, Macinaggio (04 95 35 40 34).* 🎌 *St Thomas's and St Erasmus's feast days (Jul).*

RATHER ISOLATED from the D80 highway and divided into various hamlets, the medieval fiefdom of Canari boasts two interesting churches. The 12th-century Pisan Romanesque **Santa Maria Assunta** has a cornice decorated with animal heads and human figures. This church is open to the public only on 15 August. **St-François** was built in 1506 and then rebuilt in Baroque style.

From 1932 to 1966, Canari grew significantly due to a local asbestos mine. Although the mine was closed when this mineral was found to be toxic, it has left an ugly scar on the landscape. The **Marine d'Albo**, protected by a watchtower, is where, in 1588, Hassan Pasha's fleet landed and his men sacked the area.

🏛 **St-François**
🕽 *04 95 37 80 17.*
⭘ *ask for the keys at the Town Hall.*

The old watchtower at Marine d'Albo

Panoramic view of Nonza, dominated by the cliff overlooking the sea

Nonza ⑩

Road map D1. 🏘 *85.*
ℹ️ *Port de Plaisance, Macinaggio
(04 95 35 40 34).* 🎭 *Culture in
the Limelight (2nd week of Aug).*

ONE OF THE MOST fascinating
villages in Corsica, Nonza
clings to a black rock falling
steeply down to the sea. Its
old, pastel-coloured stone
houses are surrounded by
terraces and small gardens,
and many are reached by
steps rather than streets.
    Steps also lead up to the
church of **Ste-Julie**, built in the
16th century but enlarged in
the 19th. Inside is a Baroque
altar, a chapel dedicated to St
Erasmus, patron saint of sailors,
and a painting of St Julia, one
of Corsica's patron saints.
According to legend, this girl
was crucified by a Roman
prefect after refusing to take
part in some pagan revelry.
Nearby, 54 steps lead down
to the **Fontaine de Ste-Julie**,
which is said to have sprung
up as she was martyred and
to have miraculous water.
    More steps lead down to the
beach, 160 m (525 ft) below
the village. Until the early
19th century, the inhabitants
left from here in boats every
morning to reach the then-
fertile Désert des Agriates (see
p72). Today, the beach offers
an awe-inspiring view up to
the village and its 18th-century
green schist tower built by
Paoli. The dark colour of the
sand is the result of pollution
from an asbestos mine up the
coast that was closed in 1966.
It is safe to walk here, but
bathing is not allowed. On
the D80 road to Albo there are
many mortuary chapels and
mausoleums *(see p27)*. These
belonged to Corsican families
that emigrated to find their
fortunes and returned rich
enough to have elaborate
tombs built for themselves.

Patrimonio ⑪

Road map D2. 🏘 *650.* ℹ️ *Route du
Cap Corse, St-Florent (04 95 37 06 04).*
🎭 *Guitar Nights (3rd week of Jul).*

AT THE FOOT of the Col de
Teghime and the Serra di
Pigno, this village in the heart
of the Nebbio region is one
of the main wine-producing
centres on the island *(see p69)*.
The vineyards, which all
belong to small, family-owned
wineries, dot the limestone
hills that dominate Patrimonio.
    While driving along the
highway, it is worth stopping
at one of the many wineries to
taste and purchase the white
Vermentino, or a fine red wine
made from the Niellucciu
grape. The latter is the
ideal accompaniment for
charcuterie and game.
    Overlooking the
village is the church of
St-Martin, built in 1570
and reached by a stair-
way. At sunset, its
façade takes on golden
hues. Just down the
lane, next to the church,
is a megalithic menhir
with a carved face.

🏛 **St-Martin**
📞 *04 95 37 08 49.*
⭕ *daily; make enquiries
at the Mairie (Town Hall).*

St-Florent ⑫

Road map D2. 🏘 *1,350.*
🚌 ℹ️ *Route du Cap Corse (04 95
37 06 04).* 🎭 *Porto Latino: Latin-
American music (mid-Aug).*

AT THE END OF a long gulf,
the village of St-Florent
sits with its brightly coloured
houses along the harbour and
a lively promenade with
boutiques, restaurants and
cafés. In summer these are
open till late at night.
    Although it was inhabited
in the Neolithic era and was
an ancient Roman base, the
village only really developed
in the 15th century around
the Genoese fort. The area
was marshy and unhealthy,
however, and was abandoned
between the 17th and 19th
centuries because of malaria.
    The homes in the old town
surround the parish church,
which houses a statue of
St Florent the Martyr.
    At the edge of the village is
Santa Maria Assunta, the
old cathedral of the Nebbio
region. This splendid Romanesque church dates back to
1140. Made of pale limestone,
its façade has two super-
imposed tiers of blind arches
and a niche with a *Virgin
Mary and Child* statue. The
basilica-style interior has pillars
and pilasters whose capitals
are decorated with shells and
animal figures. In a glass case
are the remains of St Flor, a
Roman soldier mummified
in the 3rd century AD.

🏛 **Santa Maria Assunta**
⭕ *ask for the keys at the
tourist office.*

The quay at the port of St-Florent

San Michele de Murato ⑬

VISITORS' CHECKLIST

Road map D2. 📞 04 95 37 60 10. ○ to view the frescoed interior ask for the keys at the Mairie (Town Hall) in Murato

THIS 13TH-CENTURY CHURCH is one of Corsica's best examples of Pisan Romanesque architecture. It lies just north of Murato village, 475 m (1,560 ft) above sea level, dominating the valley of the Bevincu river and the Nebbio region. San Michele de Murato has a simple structure, with a rectangular nave ending in a small semi-circular apse. The porticoed bell tower is set against the middle of the façade. The materials used were white limestone and green serpentine. All around the church are tiny blind arches. The consoles and cornices of the small windows have bas-reliefs with animal and plant motifs, as well as allegorical scenes, such as Eve taking the forbidden fruit or the Lamb attacked by other animals.

The central window of the apse with green serpentine decoration

The square bell tower in the middle of the façade was rebuilt and enlarged in the 19th century. It is the truly original element in this church, forming a colonnaded portico around the entry door.

Consoles
The blind arches lie on consoles with various sculpted nature motifs.

The sculpture decoration in the church includes geometric patterns and scenes with birds and human figures.

Façade
Dominated by the bell tower, the façade has one entrance and three blind arches on the consoles of which are bas-relief sculptures of animals.

A feature of the Pisan Romanesque style is the irregular checkerboard arrangement of different-coloured stone blocks.

On the two columns
framing the portal, the limestone and serpentine alternate in irregular bands.

Capitals
A garland surrounds the columns at the base of the capitals, which are carved in the shape of two simple volutes.

Symbols
The two figures flanking the three blind arches may be symbols of the political and religious power in Murato during that time.

The village of Oletta, perched on the slopes of the Nebbio hills

Nebbio ⑭

Road map D2. ﹗ *Route du Cap Corse, St-Florent (04 95 37 06 04).*

CALLED THE GOLDEN shell (Conca d'Oro) for its fertile land, the Alisu basin is an area with vineyards and olive and fruit orchards. Via the D38, D82 and D62 roads, there is a semi-circular route that departs from and returns to St-Florent, passing through the Nebbio region's main towns, from Oletta up to Rapale. The roads lead to the passes of Col de Teghime (a small road goes up to Serra di Pigno, for an even better view) and Col de San Stefano. From here the stretch of D62 known as Défilé de Lancone descends to the coast in dangerously steep curves. A 30-minute walk from Rapale is the 13th-century **Chapelle de San Cesario**, with its green shale and white limestone façade. The parish church of **Murato** has a painting attributed to Titian, but the village is famous for the Romanesque church of San Michele *(see p71)*.

Oletta ⑮

Road map D2. 🏠 880. ﹗ *Route du Cap Corse, St-Florent (04 95 37 06 04).*

IMMERSED IN THE GREENERY of the hills of Nebbio is the small village of Oletta. It seems to be clinging to the hillside and is characterized by simple houses of white, ochre and pink. Oletta offers spectacular views of the Golfe de St-Florent and the Nebbio region, including the bell tower of the old **Couvent St-François**, the only remaining architectural element from the original complex. Dominating the view towards the hilltop is the **Mausoleum of Count Rivarola**, governor of Malta, one of the many monumental family tombs in this region. The 18th-century parish church of **St-André** has a bas-relief of the Creation on its façade and a wooden triptych inside dating from 1534.

Detail of a monumental tomb in the Nebbio area

The area around Oletta is renowned for its sheep's-milk cheese, which was once used to make Roquefort.

Désert des Agriates ⑯

Road map C–D2. ﹗ *Route du Cap Corse, St-Florent (04 95 37 06 04).*

SITUATED BETWEEN St-Florent and the mouth of the Ostriconi river, this 160 sq km (60 sq miles) of green desert is virtually uninhabited. Only some shepherds and a few people in the hamlet of Casta live here. Until the mid-19th century, however, this area was the "bread basket" of Bastia and Cap Corse, and it produced wheat, olives and olive oil, wine and fruit. The farmers arrived by boat from Nonza, Canari and St-Florent to work the land. Today, the only remains of this area's fertile past are the barns and stone granaries. The fields are abandoned and the maquis has invaded the terrain.

The panoramic D81 highway crosses this sweet-smelling desert, which is extraordinary in spring. There are also two detours, negotiable only by four-wheel drives, that lead to the beaches of **Saleccia** *(see p19)* and **Guignu**. It is worth spending a few days on the 35-km (22-mile) coastal path, taking lodgings in the renovated barns. Boats also sail from the St-Florent port to the **Loto** beach, which is a 30-minute walk from Saleccia. The lovely, white-sand beach of **Ostriconi**, bounded by sand dunes and a pool, is more convenient and accessible.

Spring blossoms on the slopes of the Désert des Agriates

Mediterranean Maquis

KNOWN IN the Corsican language as *macchia*, maquis is one of the most luxuriant types of vegetation in southern Europe. The low, thick undergrowth and bushes occupy vast areas along the coast and in the interior, covering a surface area of about 2,000 sq km (770 sq miles). The maquis is spectacular in spring, when it blossoms covering entire hills with white and pink rockrose flowers and yellow broom. The flowers are used to produce

White Montpellier cistus

essences, as well as honey with a particular aroma. Despite the frequent fires, the maquis manages to grow back in a relatively short time compared to trees and tall shrubs. Besides rockrose, other herbaceous plants are asphodel thistle, cyclamen, lavender, heather and sarsaparilla. Typical shrubs include rosemary, juniper, myrtle, mastic shrub, phillyrea and strawberry trees. Among the trees are two kinds of oak – the cork oak and evergreen holm oak.

Wild fennel has umbrella-shaped flowers that look like small white or yellowish clouds. It also has a strong, almost oleaginous scent that is quite characteristic of the maquis. It can be used for pot-pourri after being dried.

Cistus, or rockrose, *is a typical maquis plant that can also grow in the mountains, up to an altitude of 1,200 m (3,950 ft). This is a low-growing shrub with slightly fleshy leaves. Its five-petalled flowers frame a centre of golden-yellow stamens.*

Wild rosemary *exudes an intense scent that infuses the entire maquis. Its aromatic leaves are used to flavour food and as a perfume and a medicine.*

Myrtle is considered a sacred plant, the symbol of fertility. It has aromatic leaves, white flowers and dark berries from which a liqueur is distilled.

Broom *inflames the sides of hills and mountains from April to late summer with its dazzling yellow flowers, which cover the green, arched and spiny stems.*

The red granite rocks around the bay of L'Île Rousse

L'Île Rousse ⑰

Road map C2. ⛪ 2,800. 🚂
🚉 Route du Port. ⛴ from Genoa,
Savona, Marseille, Nice, Toulon.
🛈 Place Paoli (04 95 60 04 35).
🎭 Festimare (early May).

A BUSY BEACH with fine sand,
a pleasant, Riviera-style
promenade, shops and a lively
port sum up L'Île Rousse. It
was founded in 1758 by Pascal
Paoli, who had the port built
to counter the presence of the
Genoese at Calvi and Algajola.
L'Île Rousse revolves around
Place Paoli, with its mix of
cafés, shops and *pétanque*
players in the shade of palm
and plane trees. In the middle
of the square is a fountain
with the statue of Paoli.

The square is the starting
point for the little train that
skirts the bay and goes to Isola
di La Pietra. This islet is linked
to the mainland by a pier with
a tower and a lighthouse built
by Paoli in 1857.

At one end of Place Paoli
is the covered market, a 19th-
century structure similar to
a Greek temple, which sells
charcuterie, vegetables,
cheese, maquis-flower honey,
fish and home-made bread.
For shops and restaurants, try
the old quarter north of the
square, with its well-kept
houses and paved streets
that descend to the seaside.

Outside the town is the
popular but less urban
Rindara beach, which can
be reached by a dirt track.
L'Île Rousse is also the
starting point for excursions
in the Balagne region (see

pp76–7). This area of Corsica
boasts the island's best
artisans, whose products are
exported all over the world.

The area is also renowned
for its idyllic villages surrounded by olive groves, such as
Monticello, overlooked by
the 13th-century Castel
d'Ortica. Further inland, the
road climbs up to **Santa
Reparata di Balagna**. Here
the church of Santa Reparata,
with its origins in the 11th
century, offers a great view
from its terrace.

Algajola ⑱

Road map C2. ⛪ 200. 🚉
🛈 Tourist office (04 95 62 78 78).

F RINGED by a beach of
golden sand some 2 km
(1 mile) long, Algajola makes
an excellent base for water
sports, especially windsurfing.

Founded by the Phoenicians,
Algajola was used
by the Romans
as a base for
their legions,
and then chosen
by the Genoese
because of its
central position
in the region.
Sacked repeatedly
by the Saracens, the village
enjoyed a period of splendour
in the 1600s, when the
bastions were built.

The church of **St-Georges**
was also fortified after a Barbary pirate raid. Its interior
houses a 17th-century painting
of the Deposition attributed
to the Italian artist Guercino.

🔒 **St-Georges**
📞 04 95 62 78 32. ⬜ summer: ask
for the keys at the tourist office.

**Music box by Scat'a
Musica in Pigna**

Pigna ⑲

Road map C2. ⛪ 90. 🛈 Place
Paoli, L'Île Rousse (04 95 60 04 35).
🎭 Estivoce (Jul).

T HIS THRIVING HAMLET in the
Balagne is perched on a
slope alongside olive orchards.
It has retained its medieval
character, with stepped paths,
narrow alleys and vaulted
passageways. By the tree-lined
central square stands the local
church with two bell towers.

Pigna has become famous
as a centre for traditional
Corsican music and for its
many handicraft workshops.
The **Casa Musicale** (Music
House), which also has hotel
facilities (see p159) and a
restaurant, is the centre for
the safeguarding of Corsican
music and the island's major
traditions. In the workshops,
ancient instruments are built
in traditional style, including
various types of cittern. Another workshop,
Scat'a Musica,
sells musical
boxes. In
summer, the
Estivoce festival
celebrates tradi-
tional singing.
The Corsican-
produce boutique A
Merendella is also worth a visit.

🎵 **Casa Musicale**
📞 04 95 61 77 31.
🌐 www.casa-musicale.org

ENVIRONS: About 2 km (1 mile)
from Pigna is the Franciscan
Couvent de Corbara, founded
in 1456, destroyed during the
French Revolution and rebuilt
by the Dominicans in the
1800s. Pascal Paoli and Guy de
Maupassant were guests here.

The sea wall at Algajola protecting the port at the foot of the citadel

Aregno ⑳

Road map C2. 👥 *600.* ℹ️ *Place Paoli, L'Île Rousse (04 95 60 04 35).* 🎭 *Almond Festival (early Aug).*

THE VILLAGE of Aregno, surrounded by olive and citrus-fruit trees, should be visited for its two churches: the Baroque parish church of **St-Antoine** and the Pisan Romanesque church of the **Trinité et San Giovanni**. Built in 1177 of green, white and pink granite, the latter has a façade with four blind arches over the portal. It also has a pediment decorated with small arches, in the centre of which is a statue of a man holding his foot while pulling a thorn from it. The chapel interior has two 15th-century frescoes: *St Michael and the Dragon* and *The Four Doctors of the Church.*

🏛 **Trinité et San Giovanni**
📞 *04 95 61 70 34.* ⏰ *Jul–Aug; during other months, ask for the keys at the Mairie (Town Hall).*

Sant'Antonino ㉑

Road map C2. 👥 *60.* ℹ️ *Place Paoli, L'Île Rousse (04 95 60 04 35).*

AN EAGLE'S NEST 447 m (1,467 ft) above sea level, this hamlet overlooks the Regino and Tighiella river valleys. Its unique position affords a magnificent view, from the snow-capped mountains to the sea. Sant'Antonino is laid out in a circle and was one of the

Steps going up to the village of Sant'Antonino

The Baroque church and campanile at Feliceto, near Sant'Antonino

fiefdoms of the Savelli family. It was an impregnable fortress that took in the entire valley population when Saracen pirate ships appeared on the horizon. Along the alleys of this hamlet, which are for pedestrians only, there are steps and passageways. The dark-granite houses have been restored and shops featuring local handicrafts have been opened.

ENVIRONS: About 10 km (6 miles) along the D663 road is **Feliceto**, which has a Baroque church and a mill producing olive oil.

In the opposite direction is the Giussani region, with the villages of **Pioggiola** and **Olmi-Cappella**, linked by a number of footpaths. The latter is known for its olive oil.

Speloncato ㉒

Road map C2. 👥 *194.* ℹ️ *Place Paoli, L'Île Rousse (04 95 60 04 35).*

PERCHED ON a spur of Monte Tolo, this village offers a fine view of the surrounding Balagne region. It is named after the *spelunche,* the caves in the vicinity, which include the 8-m (25-ft) long **Pietra Tafonata**. Supposedly, twice a year, on 8 April and 8 September, the setting sun is visible through the tunnel, briefly illuminating the village square with the Baroque church of **San Michele**.

Calenzana ㉓

Road map C2. 👥 *1,535.* ℹ️ *Place Paoli, L'Île Rousse (04 95 60 04 35).* 🎭 *Ste-Restitute's Feast Day (end of May).*

OLIVE OIL, WINE and honey are still the mainstays of the economy of this town, one of the liveliest in the Balagne region. It is also the starting point of the GR20 long-distance path *(see p20).*

The Baroque collegiate church of **St-Blaise**, designed by the Milanese architect Domenico Baina, was built in the late 17th century. The ceiling over the nave has an 18th-century fresco, *St Biagio Healing a Child.* At the foot of the campanile, a plaque commemorates the battle of Calenzana, fought on 14 January 1732 between Corsican nationalists and the Genoese Republic, in which 700 German mercenaries lost their lives.

About 1 km (half a mile) away is **Ste-Restitute**, a 12th-century church built over a Roman necropolis. It is dedicated to a martyr killed in Calvi in the 3rd century and venerated in the entire region. Her story is told in two 14th-century frescoes, and her sarcophagus is in the crypt.

ENVIRONS: A short way along the D151 is **Montemaggiore**. This village, built on a promontory, has a lovely Baroque church and a superb view of the Golfe de Calvi.

Tour of the Strada di l'Artigiani ㉔

A typical music box made in Pigna

T HE "ARTISANS' ROAD" is a route that covers the most characteristic craftsmen's workshops in Balagne, the fertile region behind Calvi and L'Île Rousse. These shops are located in villages perched on hilltops and are a popular tourist attraction thanks to their handicraft production. The main centre is Pigna *(see p74)*, with its Casa Musicale, an organization committed to safeguarding the island's rich cultural heritage. The road signs indicate different ways to reach Calenzana, Corbara, Santa Reparata, Feliceto, Pigna, Lumio, Monticello, Occiglioni, Lozari, Palasca, Olmi-Capella, Cateri and Occhiatana, all of which are fascinating villages thanks to their architecture and panoramic views.

Pigna ④
Musical instruments, music boxes and pottery, along with many natural products such as wine, honey, olive oil and cheese, can be found in Pigna. This village is the leading handicraft centre in the region, with all kinds of workshops – as if the best artisans in Corsica had decided to settle here.

Corbara ③
For those interested in artistic pottery, original tableware and crockery in general, Corbara is a must. Here, the craftsmen work mainly with sandstone, a versatile and robust material.

Lumio ②
There is a small, family-run production of essential oils just south of Lumio, with a shop selling massage and aromatherapy oils distilled from the fragrant plants and shrubs in the surrounding countryside. The area also boasts wineries producing fine *appellation d'origine controllée* red, white, rosé and muscat wines, as well as some cutlery makers.

Punta di Valli

Algajola

Golfe de Calvi

Fiume seccu

Bartasca

PORTO

KEY

▬	Tour route
═	Other roads
⊥⊥⊥	Railway line

Calenzana ①
This prosperous little village in the Balagne interior is renowned for its delicious asphodel-and-lavender honey, as well as for its sandstone ceramics known as *raku*.

OLIVE OIL IN BALAGNE

Among the many local gastronomic specialities in the Balagne region, the extra-virgin olive oil is outstanding.

Olive trees and their products are an integral part of Corsican tradition. It has been proven that the trees are endemic to the island, as are myrtle and the Corsican pine, and many of them are over 500 years old. The olives are gathered by setting large nets under the trees and shaking the branches. The olives are then pressed in hydraulic presses. Olive oil is a true "fruit juice", wholly natural, with many nutritious qualities.

Olive harvesting

VISITORS' CHECKLIST

i *Calvi tourist information, 97 Port de Plaisance (04 95 65 16 67), or any other in the Balagne region have leaflets about the tour.*
Length of tour: *50 km (30 miles).*
Duration: *one day for the route suggested here, while more time will be needed for an extended tour to take in other localities in the area or to make an additional gastronomic tour.*
Stopping-off points: *there are many in all the localities.*

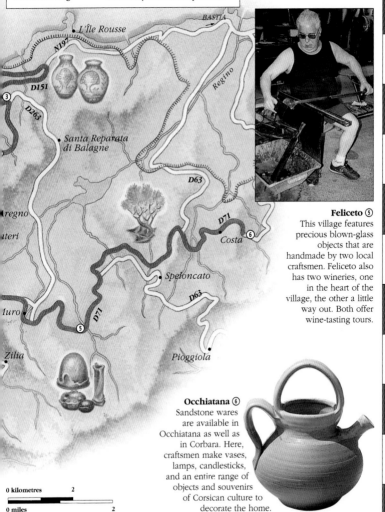

Feliceto ⑤
This village features precious blown-glass objects that are handmade by two local craftsmen. Feliceto also has two wineries, one in the heart of the village, the other a little way out. Both offer wine-tasting tours.

Occhiatana ⑥
Sandstone wares are available in Occhiatana as well as in Corbara. Here, craftsmen make vases, lamps, candlesticks, and an entire range of objects and souvenirs of Corsican culture to decorate the home.

0 kilometres 2

0 miles 2

Calvi ㉕

CIVITAS · CALVI ·
SEMPER · FIDELIS ·

**Plaque over the
citadel entrance**

Sɪᴛᴜᴀᴛᴇᴅ ᴏɴ ᴀ ʀᴏᴄᴋʏ promontory, the 15th-century Genoese citadel dominates the yacht harbour and the promenade of Calvi. Massive bastions protect it on all four sides, three of which overlook the sea. In 1794, the citadel was bombarded by 30,000 cannon shots fired by the British fleet. Inside, there is a quiet atmosphere, which contrasts with the liveliness of the rest of the town. A series of alleys leads to the Palais des Gouverneurs Génois and the cathedral of St-Jean-Baptiste. The latter was almost destroyed in 1567, when an arsenal of gunpowder exploded. A walk along the ramparts, including the Tour de St-Antoine and the Teghiale and Malfetano bastions, offers magnificent views.

**Sentries'
lookout
walkway
along the
ramparts
of the citadel**

**Citadel
Entrance**
*A sign made of
glass with the
symbols of the
Genoese maritime
republic greets
visitors before they
enter the citadel.*

Porte
Entrée de la Citadelle
1

**Palais des
Gouverneurs Génois**
*The former Castel Nuovo
was built in 1492. It was
the residence of the Genoese
governors from 1545–47
and after 1652. It is now
the barracks of a division
of the Foreign Legion.*

**Oratoire
St-Antoine**
*Built in 1510, this
structure was used for
meetings of the St Anthony
and Annunciation
confraternities (see p61).
Inside are some 15th- and
16th-century frescoes
and an ivory statue of
Christ attributed to the
Italian artist Sansovino.*

Sᴛᴀʀ Sɪɢʜᴛs

★ St-Jean-Baptiste

According to legend, Christopher Columbus, though Genoese, was born here

Teghiale Bastion

VISITORS' CHECKLIST

Road map B2. 🏚 *5,600.*
🛬 *Ste-Catherine, 4 km (2 miles)*
(04 95 65 88 88). 🚌 🚃 *Avenue
de la République (04 95 65 00 61).*
⛴ *from Marseille, Nice, Toulon
and Savona.* 🛈 *97 Port de Plaisance (04 95 65 16 67).* 🎭 *La
Granitula (Holy Week); Jazz Festival
(late Jun); Polyphonic Music (mid-
Sep); Festiventu (mid- to late
Oct).* Ⓦ *www.tourisme.fr/calvi*

★ St-Jean-Baptiste
*Calvi's cathedral houses
a 15th-century ebony
crucifix known as* Christ
des Miracles, *and the*
Virgin of the Rosary.
*Carried in processions,
she is dressed
differently for each
religious festival.*

HOLY WEEK

The Holy Week Procession

The Holy Week celebrations are among the
most fascinating and beautiful in Corsica.
They begin on Maundy Thursday in the
church of Ste-Marie-Majeure *(see p80)*, with
the benediction of the *canistrelli* (biscuits
made from chestnut flour). Another
benediction of *canistrelli* takes place in the
Oratoire St-Antoine after a procession of
penitence by Calvi's two confraternities,
St Erasmus and St Anthony. On Good
Friday evening, the Granitula procession
starts off from St-Jean-Baptiste and winds
through the streets of the lower city and
the citadel. Members of the confraternities
carry the statues of the *Christ des Miracles*
and the *Virgin of the Rosary*, who is
dressed in black. Some penitents follow
the procession barefoot, wearing a white
habit and carrying wooden crosses.

View from the Bastions
*The impressive citadel walls and
Tour de St-Antoine overlook the
yacht harbour and the lower city.*

Exploring Calvi

Frieze, Notre-Dame-de-la-Serra

THE CAPITAL OF BALAGNE is one of the most beautiful seaside resorts in Corsica, partly because of its long beach. Calvi was founded by the Romans in the 1st century AD. From 1278 onwards it was the main Genoese stronghold – the wealthy capital of the island governed by this maritime republic. It comprises the upper sector, the citadel with its centuries-old Genoese ramparts, and the lower town, with houses overlooking the harbour and the animated atmosphere typical of seaside resorts. Calvi claims to be the real birthplace of Christopher Columbus.

Sunbathers enjoying the white-sand beach paradise at Calvi

⚑ Place Christophe Colomb

At the foot of the citadel is a square linking the old and new towns, the ideal starting point for a walking tour of the city (partly thanks to the large car park). In the middle of the square is a bronze statue commemorating those who died in World War I, while a stone pays homage to the first battalion of the French Liberation Army, which liberated Corsica in 1943. A stairway descends to the Rue Clemenceau, a pedestrian precinct with restaurants and shops selling beach accessories.

The Calvi War Memorial

♠ Ste-Marie-Majeure

Rue Clemenceau. ◯ *daily.*
This rose-coloured church can be found on a small square next to Rue Clemenceau, in the heart of the lower city. Begun in 1765, with the bell tower added in 1838, it is Baroque in style, with a softly rounded dome. It houses some statues, including one of St Erasmus, the fishermen's patron saint who is popular here, and an *Assumption* that is carried through the city in a procession. The chapel in the choir has a 15th-century oil painting on leather from Cordoba.

⚑ Marina

The Marina in Calvi is one of the loveliest in all Corsica, with luxury yachts berthed next to simple fishing craft and other small boats. The marina is the starting point for boat tours of the west coast that go to the Scandola Nature Reserve *(see pp104–5)*, between Galéria and Porto, or even as far as Ajaccio. The harbour also hosts the boats that belong to the diving centres. These take scuba divers to the best spots, such as those around Punta della Revellata *(see p183)*.

⚑ Quai Landry

This promenade, with its hotels, cafés and restaurants shaded by palm trees and colourful awnings, is the liveliest spot in Calvi. Many relaxing hours can be spent at one of the tables, enjoying a refreshing drink, watching the boats anchoring or setting off or observing the passers-by along the quay.

Under the citadel at the end of the quay is the Tour du Sel, a medieval lookout post once used as a salt storehouse. Further along is the lighthouse, which dominates the entrance to the harbour.

⚑ The Beach

Calvi's beach is 4.5 km (3 miles) long, from the marina to the mouth of the Figarella river. It is bordered by a pine grove that was laid out in the 19th century, when the marshland was reclaimed. It has fine white sand and low dunes protected by fencing.

Camp sites and establishments offering deckchairs and other beach items can be found among the pines.

ENVIRONS: About 4 km (2 miles) along the road leading south out of Calvi there is a steep road on the left that goes up into the maquis among rocks sculpted by wind erosion. From here there is a view of the **La Revellata** promontory, a scuba divers' paradise. The road ends at **Notre-Dame-de-la-Serra**, a 19th-century chapel built over the ruins of a 15th-century complex destroyed during the 1794 siege, when British and Corsican troops surrounded Calvi. The terrace with the statue of Notre-Dame-de-la-Serra affords a fabulous view of the bay and the city.

The lively Quai Landry, with Ste-Marie-Majeure in the background

The French Foreign Legion

Founded in 1831 by King Louis Philippe during the conquest of Algeria, the French Foreign Legion is a professional army of volunteers from different countries. It is part of the French Armed Forces and is trained for military interventions throughout the world. In the past, it has often fought in the French-speaking African countries, but also in the Crimean War and in the Battle of Marengo. Algeria became independent in 1962, and a year later the Foreign Legion headquarters were transferred from Sidi-bel-Abbès to

Monument to the Foreign Legion, Bonifacio

Camp Raffalli, near Calvi. A military police division is located in the citadel. The Foreign Legion is thought to be a corps of coarse and ruthless men that attracts misfits and renegades. In fact, such personalities as the Danish Prince Aage, Luigi II of Grimaldi, the Prince of Monaco, and the German author Ernst Junger have served in its ranks. The Foreign Legion has inspired many film writers and producers, and its men have been portrayed by such famous actors as Gary Cooper and Ronald Colman.

A parade is a key moment in the Foreign Legion. On these occasions, the soldiers wear their ceremonial uniforms with red epaulettes and green ties, the colours of the Legion.

All the soldiers, except for a few officers, are foreigners, and even the French enlist as foreigners, hence the name of this special corps.

HONNEUR ET FIDELITÉ

In an army whose soldiers hail from more than 100 countries – with nothing in common except the fact that they have burned all their bridges – honour and fidelity to the Legion become absolute values. Nothing of the soldiers' past remains, not even their names, if they so choose, and they have to embrace fully the motto *Legio Patria Nostra* ("The Legion is our home").

Captain Jean Danjou is a hero of the Foreign Legion. Decorated many times, he died on 30 April 1863 at Camerone, Mexico, where 63 legionnaires fought an army of almost 3,000 men.

White kepi

Green tie, the symbol of celibacy

Red epaulettes are typical of the infantry regiment and have been worn by legionnaires since 1868.

The blue belt is 4.2 m (14 ft) long and 40 cm (16 inches) wide. The soldiers need help to put it on.

Black boots

The trousers, like the shirt, have a certain number of folds that is stipulated in the Legion regulations.

Parade flash

The Code of Honour

1 Every legionnaire is a volunteer serving France with honour and fidelity.
2 Every legionnaire is a brother-in-arms.
3 Discipline and comradeship are a legionnaire's strength, courage and loyalty his virtues.
4 Each legionnaire is an elite soldier, who will train with

rigour, treat his weapons as his most precious possessions and always stay in peak condition.
5 Any mission is sacred and will be carried out immediately and at any cost whatsoever.
6 In combat, a legionnaire will always act without passion, will respect the defeated enemy and will never abandon the dead and wounded nor his weapons.

AJACCIO AND THE WEST COAST

RUGGED, CRAGGY COASTLINE *beaten by the wind, white sandy beaches and red granite cliffs: Corsica's west coast offers no end of grand, natural scenery. This stretch of land has three gulfs – Porto, Sagone and Ajaccio – that highlight the jagged nature of the western coastline, which is so different from the rather straight profile of eastern Corsica.*

The Golfe de Porto has retained its wild beauty thanks to the regional nature reserve that protects the Scandola peninsula and the smaller Golfe de Girolata, which can be reached only on foot or by sea.

The sandy beaches of the gulfs of Ajaccio and Sagone have led to the creation of tourist facilities, which fortunately have not altered the beauty of the area. Most of this coastline can also be explored on foot by following the shrub-lined mule tracks that go to Girolata or traverse the rock formations of the Calanques, between Piana and Porto.

Just outside Ajaccio there are other panoramic footpaths, ending opposite the Îles Sanguinaires and the beaches of Capo di Feno. The capital of Corse-du-Sud *(see p49)*, Ajaccio owes its foundation and prosperity to the Genoa Maritime Republic *(see pp41–5)*, but it is linked mostly to Napoleon Bonaparte, who was born here. Ajaccio jealously preserves Napoleon's memory: his name and effigy are everywhere to be seen in the city, on plaques, statues and souvenirs.

As well as a stunning coastline and some of the most interesting sea beds in the Mediterranean, Corsica offers valleys full of olive, pine and chestnut trees. Some mountain villages have maintained their old pastoral traditions, linked to wild-pig breeding and the exploitation of the woods. The rivers have created deep and spectacular canyons, such as the Gorges de Spelunca at Evisa and the Gorges du Prunelli near Bastelica. On the old stone bridges the sounds of sheep and mules have been replaced by those of hikers on the panoramic *Mare a Mare* (Sea to Sea) and *Mare e Monti* (Sea and Mountains) paths.

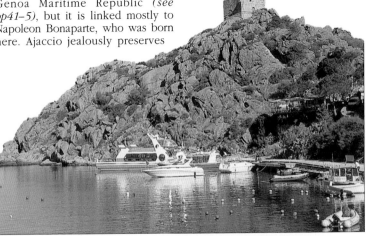

The Genoese tower, dominating the Golfe de Porto, still seeming to be defending the city

◁ Dramatic granite cliffs along the Château Fort path, a classic route in the Calanques de Piana

Exploring Ajaccio and the West Coast

THE WEST COAST OF CORSICA, with the gulfs of Porto, Sagone and Ajaccio, offers spectacular marine landscapes, from the porphyry cliffs in the Scandola Nature Reserve *(see pp104–5)* to the white beaches of Porticcio. Apart from Ajaccio, with its museums and stylish streets, the most interesting sights in western Corsica are nature-based. Some of them are part of the Parc Naturel Régional de la Corse *(see p99)*: Evisa and the Forêt d'Aïtone, the Vallée du Fango, the Gorges de Spelunca, the Calanques de Piana, the Gorges du Prunelli and the Golfe de Girolata. This area is ideal for hiking, especially the region around Porto, which offers numerous waymarked routes of varying degrees of difficulty.

PUNTA CIUTTONE ●

GALÉRIA ⑱

GIROLATA ⑰

⑲ RÉSERVE NATURELLE DE SCANDOLA

CALANQUES DE PIANA ⑬   PORTO ⑭

PIANA ⑫

⑪ CARGÈSE

⑩ SAGO

Plage de Verghia, a cove with a sandy beach and transparent sea in the Golfe d'Ajaccio

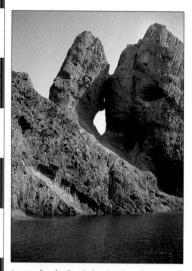

A natural arch of typical red rock in the Scandola Nature Reserve

GOLFE DE SAGONE   TIU

KEY

〰 Minor road

〰 Scenic route

〰 River

CAPO DI FENO ●

POINTE DE LA PARATA ③

ÎLES ④ SANGUINAIRES

D111   AJA

②

ROUTE DE LA PARATA

L'Île Rousse/Calvi

0 kilometres 10

0 miles 5

ezza

ARC NATUREL
ÉGIONAL DE
LA CORSE

FORÊT D'AÏTONE **16**

GORGES DE
SPELUNCA

D84

D70

D23

Young Laricio pines in the intriguing Forêt d'Aïtone

SIGHTS AT A GLANCE

SEE ALSO

Guagno

Liamone

Cruzini

CINARCA   N193 / *Corte*

Tavera

● *CARBUCCIA*

N193

● *PERI*

8 *VALLÉE DE LA GRAVONA*

**View of a village in one of the
interior valleys on the west coast**

GORGES DU PRUNELLI
7

Prunelli   D27

Bastelica

D83

PORTICCIO

Frasseto

Sartène

6 *FORÊT DE*
CHIAVARI   *Pila-Canale*

-to-Pollo

GETTING AROUND

Around Ajaccio, the roads to Corte and Sartène are wide
and quite fast. However, minor mountain roads and those
on the stretch of coast between Galéria and Porto are
very narrow and overhang the sea, so careful driving is
required. A car is the best way to get around Corsica, but
you can also use the Ajaccio–Bastia railway line, which
stops at Bocognano, the starting point for many paths
going through the Vallée de la Gravona. Boat excursions
along the west coast are quite interesting: those from
Ajaccio and Sagone go to the Îles Sanguinaires and the
Golfe de Porto. Porto is the starting point for trips to
Girolata and the Scandola Nature Reserve.

Ajaccio ❶

Notre-Dame-de-la-Miséricorde

T HE LARGEST CITY IN CORSICA, as well as the island's political centre, Ajaccio has a typically Mediterranean look. It is divided into three sectors: the old Genoese town, with its narrow streets and houses with pastel-coloured façades; the modern city, with tree-lined avenues and outdoor cafés; and the outskirts, which extend up to the hills and offer a marvellous view of the gulf, dominated by the Citadelle.

A Roman settlement during the Imperial Age, Ajaccio began to develop in 1492 thanks to the Genoese. In 1553 the city was conquered by Sampiero Corso *(see p45)* for the French, but in 1559 it was returned to the Genoese as part of the treaty of Cateau-Cambresis. Under Genoa Ajaccio prospered, thanks to commerce, agriculture and coral fishing, but not until 1592 were the locals granted the right to live here. In 1723 the city became the capital of West Corsica. Ajaccio is famous because Napoleon Bonaparte was born here on 15 August 1769.

The Tino Rossi harbour, bordered by the Jetée de la Citadelle

🏰 Citadelle

🚫 *to the public.*

The construction of the Citadelle, on a rocky spur jutting over the sea, began in 1554, by order of the French Marshal de Thermes, and was completed by the Genoese in 1559. The building faces the innermost part of the gulf and overlooks the Jetée de la Citadelle, a jetty that encloses the Tino Rossi harbour. With its sentry walkways, walls and ramparts, the Citadelle towers over the old Genoese quarter.

As a military zone, the Citadelle is not open to the public, but its majestic profile can be admired from the beach, from the breakwater or from Boulevard Danielle Casanova, named after the Ajaccio-born French-Resistance heroine who died in Auschwitz in 1943.

🏛 Musée du Capitellu

18 Boulevard Danielle Casanova.
📞 *04 95 21 50 57.* 🕐 *Apr–Oct: Mon–Sat, Sun am.* 📷 ♿

This tiny but interesting private museum illustrates the history of Ajaccio by means of the collections of an old Corsican family, the Bacciochi. On display are religious artifacts, paintings and porcelain and silver objects, including a precious gilded silver dinner service that Napoleon used during his military campaigns.

🏠 St-Erasme

Rue Forcioli-Conti.

Founded in 1617 as the chapel of the Jesuit College, St-Erasme later became the chapel of the Royal College. During the French Revolution the church was closed to the public and turned into a city office. In 1815 it was reconsecrated and dedicated to the sailors' patron saint, Erasmus. Inside are model ships, three processional crosses and a statue of St Erasmus with angels. On 2 June the statue is carried in a procession down to the seaside.

🏠 Notre-Dame-de-la-Miséricorde

Rue Forcioli-Conti.
📞 *04 95 21 07 67.* 🕐 *daily.*

Dedicated to the Virgin Mary, the cathedral of Ajaccio was built in 1582–93 by Giacomo della Porta in Venetian Renaissance style, but has Baroque elements. The simple façade contrasts with the lavish interior, which features polychrome marble and gilded decoration. In July 1771, when he was almost two, Napoleon was baptized at the font.

The first chapel on the left has a painting by Eugène Delacroix, the *Madonna of the Sacred Heart*. The next chapel, dedicated to Our Lady of Mercy, the patron saint of Ajaccio, contains an impressive 18th-century marble statue of the Virgin Mary. The high altar, made of white marble with black tortile columns, was donated to the cathedral in 1811 by Elisa Bacciochi, Napoleon's sister and princess of Lucca and Piombino.

The simple façade of Notre-Dame-de-la-Miséricorde

The study of Napoleon's father, furnished in the style of a bedroom of the late 1700s

🚇 Rue Bonaparte

This street was the old *carrugio dritto* (straight alley) of the Genoese city, inhabited by merchants and leading citizens. During Genoese rule Rue Bonaparte divided Ajaccio into two quarters: to the north was the Macello, where the poor lived, and to the south was the area of the upper middle classes. Today this is a pleasant, lively street with antique shops and boutiques catering to all tastes.

🏛 Maison Bonaparte

Rue St-Charles.
📞 *04 95 21 43 89.*
○ *Mon pm–Sun.* 🅖

The house that belonged to the Bonaparte family from 1682, and where Napoleon was born, has an austere façade overlooking the small, tree-lined Place Letizia, where there is a bust of the emperor's son.

In 1793 Napoleon and his family were forced to flee the house (through a trap door) by supporters of Pascal Paoli *(see pp46–7)*. The Paolist mob was seeking revenge because Napoleon (then an officer in the French army) had ordered his troops to fire at a local rally. The house was then impounded by the British (1794–6)

Marble bust of Napoleon

VISITORS' CHECKLIST

Road map B4. 🏚 *58,500.*
✈ *Campo dell'Oro, 7 km (4 miles) E (04 95 23 56 56).*
🚌 🚉 *Place de la Gare (04 95 23 11 03).* ⛴ *from Porto Torres, Marseille, Nice, Toulon.*
ℹ *3 Boulevard du Roi Jérôme (04 95 51 53 03).* 🎎 *Our Lady of Mercy Feast (18 Mar); Blues Festival (Jul); Celebrations in Honour of Napoleon (mid-Aug).*
🌐 *www.ajaccio-tourisme.com*

and partly used as an arsenal.

In 1797 Letizia Bonaparte, Napoleon's mother, returned to Ajaccio and obtained compensation to refurbish the house. Since 1923 Maison Bonaparte has been a state-managed, three-storey museum illustrating the history of the Bonaparte family.

AJACCIO CITY CENTRE

Boulevard du Roi Jérôme ⑨
Chapelle Impériale ⑪
Citadelle ①
Cours Napoléon ⑩
Maison Bonaparte ⑤
Musée du Capitellu ②
Musée Fesch pp90–91 ⑫
Musée Napoléonien ⑦
Notre-Dame-de-la-
    Miséricorde ④
Place Foch ⑥
St-Erasme ③
Yacht Harbour ⑧

Musée d'Histoire Corse A Bandera

Place d'Austerlitz POINTE DE LA PARATA

KEY

ℹ Tourist information

✝ Church

⚓ Port

🚌 Bus station

P Parking

0 metres   170

0 yards   170

Exploring Ajaccio

The
Petit Train **logo**

AJACCIO IS A RELATIVELY SMALL TOWN and can easily be explored on foot. One of its main thoroughfares, Rue Cardinal Fesch, is a pedestrianized area with craft shops and boutiques. In Cours Napoléon and along the seafront, on the Quai Napoléon and Quai l'Herminier, it is quite enjoyable to sit at one of the outdoor cafés and watch the world pass by. Ajaccio can also be discovered by *Petit Train (see p176)*. It leaves from Place Foch for a tour of the city (45 mins) or goes to the Pointe de la Parata (90 mins).

The *Petit Train* leaving Place Foch for a tour of the city

🚇 Place Foch

The true heart of Ajaccio, this square is lined with cafés with tables outside in the shade of the palm and plane trees. Formerly called Piazza Porta, it used to be the only gate to the Citadelle. Place Foch is dominated by the white marble statue of Napoleon as First Consul, in the middle of the Four Lions Fountain, sculpted by Jérôme Maglioli.

At the end of the square, in Rue Serafini, is the statue of *Our Lady of Mercy*, the patron saint of Ajaccio, placed in a niche that is lit in the evening.

First Consul Bonaparte, detail

🏛 Musée Napoléonien

Avenue Antoine Serafini.
📞 04 95 51 52 62. ⏰ Mon–Fri.
⦿ public hols. 🎫

Housed on the first floor of the town hall (Hôtel de Ville), the rooms of the Napoleonic Museum are accessed via a grand staircase. The museum displays documents and paintings relating to the life of Napoleon and his family. In the Grand Salon, under the large Bohemian crystal chandelier donated for the 200th anniversary of the birth of Napoleon, there are large portraits of the family and several busts, including one of Napoleon's mother, Letizia. A painting by Domenico Frassati celebrates the *Glory of the Emperor* (1840). Other interesting items are Napoleon's baptism certificate and a replica of his bronze death mask. The Hall of Medals features a fine collection of coins and gold, silver and bronze medals.

🚢 Marina

At the foot of the Citadelle, a long breakwater protects this harbour from the west wind. Next to the passenger terminal of the port, where the large ferries land, are the yacht harbour and the fishermen's port, with many brightly coloured boats filled with fishing nets. Every morning from 7am, in the open space in front of Place Foch, there is an animated market offering fresh fish.

This quay is also the departure point for the boats taking visitors on excursions to the Îles Sanguinaires, the Golfe de Porto and Porticcio.

🚇 Boulevard du Roi Jérôme

Lined with hotels and restaurants, this boulevard is a favourite with locals, who gather here to have a *pastis* or play a game of *pétanque*. Every morning, the area behind the town hall facing the sea becomes a colourful open market offering typical Corsican products: *brocciu* cheese, *lonzu* (smoked fillet of pork), *coppa* (pork neck), *prizuttu* (cured ham), pâtés, honey, fig jam and myrtle liqueur. Vegetables and flowers also fill the market with their scents and colours.

The hubbub and gaiety invade the adjacent streets and the pedestrianized Rue Cardinal Fesch, once the main thoroughfare in the Genoese quarter, which from the 16th century onwards grew outside the city walls. Halfway down this street is the Palais Fesch, built by Cardinal Fesch, one of Napoleon's uncles, in 1827–37 and now a museum containing part of his huge fine art collection (see *pp90–91*).

Typical Corsican products for sale on Boulevard du Roi Jérôme

Detail of the statue of Napoleon on horseback in Roman dress

🚩 Cours Napoléon

The main street in Ajaccio crosses the city from northeast to southwest. It is intersected by smaller streets that go down to the sea or up to the hills. Cours Napoléon is lined with cinemas, shops, banks and cafés, including the famous Café Napoléon, built in 1821 by the architect Carrayol. Towards the railway station the street becomes wider, forming Place Abbatucci, which was once the border between the old town and the countryside.

About halfway down Cours Napoléon is the Chapelle de St-Roch, built in the late 1800s, while towards the southern end of the street is the Palais Lantivy, now home to the prefecture and the General Council. The street ends at Place de Gaulle, a large square dominated by a statue of Napoleon in the guise of a Roman emperor on horseback, surrounded by his four brothers.

⚓ Chapelle Impériale

Rue Fesch. 📞 04 95 21 48 17.
🕐 same as Musée Fesch
(see pp90–91). 📷

When Emperor Napoleon III had Cardinal Fesch's palace restored in 1857 by the architects Corona, Casanova and Paccard, he decided to use the right-hand wing as a chapel to house the remains of the nine members of the Bonaparte family, including Napoleon I's parents – Carlo Bonaparte and Letizia Ramolino (Napoleon's tomb is in Les Invalides, Paris), and Cardinal Fesch himself. The sober Renaissance exterior is made of light St-Florent limestone. Inside, the trompe-l'oeil dome was painted by the Ajaccio-born architect Jérôme Maglioli, and is decorated with the cardinal's insignias, which are also on the stained-glass windows. On the high altar is a gold crucifix that Napoleon gave to his mother when he returned from his campaign in Egypt. The remains of the nine family members are all in the round crypt under the dome.

🏛 Musée Fesch

See pp90–91.

🏛 Musée d'Histoire Corse A Bandera

1 Rue du Général Levie.
📞 04 95 51 07 34. 🕐 daily.
🌙 Sun (winter). 📷

Just behind the prefecture is a picturesque building, the façade of which is decorated with portraits of the leading figures in Corsican history. This is the home of a museum that illustrates the history of the island through its main political and military events, from prehistory to World War II. This is done over five halls with documents, objects, photographs and large maps.

The museum is a good starting point for an understanding of Corsican culture.

Mural in the Musée A Bandera

Of particular interest are the maps showing the location of the megaliths on the island, the models of Genoese ships, the paintings of the battles for independence, and the accounts of the Resistance against the Italian and German occupation and the liberation of Corsica in September 1943.

🚩 Place d'Austerlitz

At the western end of Place Foch begins Cours Gandval, a street running parallel to the sea in the direction of the Pointe de la Parata (see p92). Cours Gandval ultimately leads to Place d'Austerlitz, a square dominated by an imposing structure, known as U Casone, which features a statue of Napoleon. Preceded by two eagles and a stone that commemorates his victories and exploits, this monument represents the emperor in a riding coat and wearing his famous two-cornered hat as he looks towards Ajaccio, his native town.

To the left of U Casone is the cave where, according to legend, Napoleon pretended he was an emperor when he was a child. Every year, around 15 August, his birthday, Ajaccio commemorates Napoleon's imperial period with impressive parades in period costumes (see pp33–4) during the lively *Journées Napoléoniennes*.

The monument to Napoleon in Place d'Austerlitz

Ajaccio: Musée Fesch

Cardinal Joseph Fesch's insignia

Jesus and the Samaritan
This work is by Étienne Parrocel, an 18th-century Corsican artist. Above is a detail of the Samaritan.

CARDINAL FESCH, Napoleon's uncle, had this palace built in 1827. He dedicated three wings to housing works of art, which were donated to the city when he died, in 1839. The main building has the most important collection of Italian paintings in France after the Louvre, as well as works by Spanish, Flemish and Dutch artists. The first floor contains 13th–17th-century Italian art, including many canvases of the Virgin Mary and Child. On the second floor are works dating from the 17th and 18th centuries, with a fine collection of still lifes. The basement is given over to Napoleon, with statues and paintings of the emperor, as well as various objects bearing his image. The left wing houses the City Library, founded by Lucien Bonaparte, Napoleon's brother. It boasts books and manuscripts that for the most part were confiscated from religious orders.

Holy Family
This detail of a painting by 17th-century Italian artist Benedetto Gennari shows the attention he paid to minutiae.

The Grande Galerie contains large-scale Italian paintings.

The collection of early Italian Renaissance paintings is the core of the museum.

Auditorium

CARDINAL FESCH

Joseph Fesch (1763–1839) was Napoleon's uncle, but he was only six years older than the emperor. He was the archdeacon of Ajaccio and archbishop of Lyon. In 1803

Cardinal Fesch he became a cardinal and moved to Rome, where he collected 16,000 works of art, some of which are on display in the museum, while others were donated to many churches in Corsica. It was thanks to his diplomatic intervention that Pope Pius VII agreed to go to Paris in 1804 to crown Napoleon emperor. In 1811 Fesch fell into disgrace for siding with the Church in the conflict between the Pope and Napoleon.

★ Virgin Mary and Child with Angel
This early masterpiece by the Italian artist Sandro Botticelli (1445–1510) is one of the loveliest works in the museum. It is innovative from an iconographic point of view because the Virgin is standing, and also because of her open display of affection.

Landscape
Paul Brill, a late 16th-century Flemish painter, makes surprising and refreshing use of cool colours highlighted by brilliant ochre hues. His works helped to revolutionize landscape painting.

VISITORS' CHECKLIST

50 Rue du Cardinal Fesch.
04 95 21 48 17.
Oct–Mar: Tue–Sat; Apr–Jun, Sep: Mon pm–Sun; Jul–Aug: Mon pm–Sun without lunchtime break (open evenings on Fri).
W www.musée-fesch.com

★ **Portrait of a Man with a Glove**
This work by Titian (1485–1576), depicting an unknown Venetian aristocrat, is the twin of a portrait kept in the Louvre, Paris.

Second floor

First floor

The Chapelle Impériale *(see p89)* occupies the right wing of the palace.

KEY

- 15th-century Italy
- 16th-century Italy
- 17th-century Italy
- 17th-century Rome
- 17th–18th-century Naples
- 16th–17th-century Flanders
- 18th-century Italy and France
- 18th–19th-century Corsica
- Grande Galerie
- Temporary exhibitions

Visitors' Entrance

Entrance to the Chapelle Impériale

The statue of Cardinal Fesch in the museum's court of honour is by Vital-Dubray.

Entrance from Rue Fesch

The Library is on the ground floor and first floor in the right wing of the complex.

Entrance to the Library

STAR FEATURES

★ **Virgin Mary and Child with Angel**

★ **Portrait of a Man with a Glove**

One of the many beaches on the Route de la Parata

Route de la Parata ➋

Road map B4. ℹ️ *3 Boulevard du Roi Jérôme, Ajaccio (04 95 51 53 03).*

THIS PANORAMIC ROAD, the D111, runs along the northern shore of the Golfe d'Ajaccio, passing by the locals' favourite sandy beaches. There are also many cafés and restaurants with terraces from where it is possible to admire the cormorants in flight and, with a bit of luck, see dolphins playing.

As well as by car or bicycle, this coastline can be explored by bus or by the *Petit Train* (departure from Place Foch in Ajaccio, *see p88*).

The coastal route begins at Boulevard Lantivy and continues along Plage St-François, the most central beach in Ajaccio, at the foot of the walls of the Citadelle. It then proceeds along Boulevard Pascal Rossini, where every Sunday from 8am to noon there is a colourful flea market in front of the Fesch Lyceum, with second-hand objects and antiques.

The road continues through residential quarters, which offer a view of the gulf and are surrounded by lush Mediterranean gardens.

At the edge of the city, at Place Emmanuel-Arène, is the **Chapelle des Grecs**, a small Greek Orthodox church built in 1632 and used by the Greek community that had fled from the Peloponnese seeking political asylum. Not far from the main road is the cemetery, with Baroque and Neo-Classical chapels.

Some 5 km (3 miles) from the heart of town, the road skirts the beaches of Scudo, with bathing facilities and restaurants, the beautiful Marinella cove, and Vignola beach. The latter also marks the end of the **Chemin des Crêtes**, a popular, easy-to-follow ridge path with a superb view of the gulf. Waymarked with spots of paint, it starts in the centre of Ajaccio, at Bois des Anglais, behind Place d'Austerlitz *(see p89)*, and takes about three hours. The number 5 bus travels back into town.

Pointe de la Parata ➌

Road map B4. 🚌 *from Place de Gaulle, Ajaccio.* ℹ️ *3 Boulevard du Roi Jérôme, Ajaccio (04 95 51 53 03).*

A BLACK GRANITE headland, the Pointe de la Parata makes for a dramatic end to the D111 road. The cape is dominated by the **Tour de la Parata**, a tower built by the Genoese in 1608 to defend the island from pirate raids. A path leads to the end of the cape (about 30 minutes there and back). From here the view of the red Îles Sanguinaires is grandiose, especially at sunset.

Another, longer route starts about 500 m (1,600 ft) before the restaurant at the Pointe de la Parata. Once on the far side of the headland, a path winds through tall maquis to a lovely beach at Anse de Minaccia (90 mins), also accessible via the D111-B road from Ajaccio. From here it is possible to continue to windswept Capo di Feno, with its Genoese watchtower (60 mins).

Îles Sanguinaires ➍

Road map B4. 🚢 *from Ajaccio.* ℹ️ *3 Boulevard du Roi Jérôme, Ajaccio (04 95 51 53 03).*

THE RED ROCK SEEMS to have been the reason behind the name ("sanguinary") of the maquis-covered cliffs that emerge from the sea a short distance from the Pointe de la Parata. However, because the islands mark the southern border of the Golfe de Sagone, some people claim that the name derives from the Latin *Sagonares Insulae*, or Islands of the Gulf of Sagone.

The largest of the islands is the Grande Sanguinaire, also called Mezzumare. There is a lighthouse, built in 1840, as well as the ruins of the Genoese tower and a leprosy hospital. In spring this island is clad in white thanks to Montpellier rockrose in bloom. The Grande Sanguinaire is home to cormorants, herring gulls and other birds.

In 1863 the French author Alphonse Daudet lived in the lighthouse. He described the Sanguinaires as wild islands populated by wild goats, Corsican ponies and an osprey.

The other three islands are very small, little more than cliffs emerging from the sea.

View of the Îles Sanguinaires with their reddish rocks

The long beach at Porticcio, with its fine white sand

Porticcio ❺

Road map B4. 🏛 *320.*
🚌 🛈 *Porticcio (04 95 25 10 09).*

JUST OPPOSITE Ajaccio, on the southern coastline of the gulf, is Porticcio. This seaside resort has developed in recent years and is now filled with hotels, residential complexes and lovely beaches with fine sand and facilities for watersports, from sailing to diving.

The beach with the best facilities is **La Viva**, while the most spectacular are **Agosta** and **Ruppione**, separated by the Isolella peninsula, which has coves with turquoise water.

On the headland is an old Genoese tower called Tour de l'Isolella. Another tower, Tour de Castagna, is further south, at Punta di a Castagna. Built in 1584, it is now off limits, since it stands in a military zone. The headland can be reached by taking the D55 road, past the Port de Chiavari and the little Portigliolo cove. From here are fine views of the Golfe d'Ajaccio and of Île Piana, a maquis-covered island.

Forêt de Chiavari ❻

Road map B5. 🛈 *Parc Naturel Régional de la Corse, 2 Rue Sergent Casalonga, Ajaccio (04 95 51 79 00).*

THE LARGE Forêt de Chiavari extends for 18 sq km (7 sq miles), from the coast to an altitude of about 600 m (1,970 ft) on top of the hills separating the Golfe d'Ajaccio from the Golfe de Valinco.

The forest consists mainly of holm oaks, eucalyptus (imported from Australia in the 19th century to reclaim the land and help eliminate malaria), maritime pine and shrubs such as strawberry trees, mastic trees, ruscus and thyme. It also has many footpaths and mountain-bike paths of all levels of difficulty and for all tastes. One of the most pleasant is the Sentier de Myrte ("Myrtle Path"), which starts and ends at Plage de Verghia, a beach with a café.

At 485 m (1,600 ft), perched on a hill at the edge of the forest, is the hamlet of **Côti-Chiavari**, with a tree-lined terrace offering a splendid panoramic view of the gulf. Destroyed in the 16th century by Barbary pirates, this village was repopulated in 1713, when the Genoese government decided to transfer here the inhabitants of Chiavari, a locality in the Gulf of Tigullio, in Liguria, hence the name.

Not far from Côti-Chiavari there are interesting viewpoints that take in both sides of the surrounding hills and the two large gulfs on the west coast, Golfe d'Ajaccio and Golfe de Valinco.

On the narrow D55 road that leads up to Côti-Chiavari from Verghia is the old agricultural penal colony that was constructed in 1855. The mortality rate of the prisoners who worked the land here was very high because of malaria and the unhealthy climate. The prison was therefore abandoned in 1906 and the inmates were transferred to Cayenne.

A village at the edge of the Forêt de Chiavari

THE COASTLINE TOWERS

As well as the fortified cities that defended their ports, the Genoese rulers left another symbol in Corsica: the series of 67 coastline towers that were constructed in the early 16th century along the entire perimeter of the island. Built to spot pirates and, in some cases, to afford refuge for the populations of the small seaside villages, these towers are either square or round and their size differs to quite an extent. Some, such as the towers of Girolata (*see p103*) or Campomoro (*see p128*), were the centres of true fortresses, while in other cases the towers were merely outposts built on sites that could easily be seen from the villages or from the neighbouring towers. Normally, a tower contained storehouses and a cistern to collect rainwater, since sources of drinkable water were very scarce so close to the sea.

Round watchtower

A characteristic sight on the west coast: craggy granite rocks and a Genoese watchtower at Porto ▷

Gorges du Prunelli ❼

Road map C4. ℹ️ *Parc Naturel Régional de la Corse, Rue Sergent Casalonga, Ajaccio (04 95 51 79 00).*

THE PRUNELLI TORRENT flows from Monte Renoso, which stands 2,352 m (7,716 ft) high, to the Golfe d'Ajaccio. The torrent has carved a deep canyon, or gorge, partly irrigated by the water from an artificial lake created by a dam.

From Ajaccio, the D3 twists along the north bank of the torrent. At the village of **Eccica-Suarella** a stone commemorates the site where Sampiero Corso, the enemy of Genoa in the 16th century *(see p45)*, was killed.

A little further along the D3, at the pass of **Col de Mercuju**, 716 m (2,349 ft) above sea level, a path begins. It leads to a belvedere with great views of the surrounding area.

Overlooking the lake is **Tolla**, a small village surrounded by orchards. From here the road joins the D27 leading up to **Bastelica**. This hamlet on the slopes of Monte Renoso is known for its wild-pig charcuterie and for being the birthplace of Sampiero Corso. The national hero is portrayed in a bronze statue in front of the parish church. The house he was born in is in Dominacci, a nearby hamlet.

If driving back towards Ajaccio, it is possible to follow the D27 along the south side of the gorge. Here, between Col de Cricheto and Col de Marcuggio, is the **Forêt de Pineta**, with pine, beech and chestnut trees. A footpath descends from the road towards the Èse torrent and the Genoese bridge of Zipitoli.

ENVIRONS: Continuing north from Bastelica, the D27 first ascends to Col de Scalella, then descends to Tavera, a village in the Vallée de la Gravona. Another panoramic road from Bastelica is the D27-A, leading southeast to the Val d'Èse ski resort, 1,700 m (5,577 ft) above sea level.

Convolvolus berries

Vallée de la Gravona ❽

Road map C4. ℹ️ *Parc Naturel Régional de la Corse, Rue Sergent Casalonga, Ajaccio (04 95 51 79 00).*

THIS WIDE VALLEY is traversed by the N193 highway, one of Corsica's main roads, which leads to Corte and Bastia. Parallel to the N193, but further up on the slopes, are the winding and panoramic roads leading to the villages of **Peri**, **Carbuccia**, **Ucciani** and **Tavera**, on the south side of the Vallée de la Gravona.

At the hamlet of Carbuccia is **A Cupulatta**, a reserve for 166 species of tortoise and the largest of its kind in Europe. **Bocognano**, the main village in the valley, lies at the foot of Monte d'Oro and is surrounded by chestnut trees. The village marks the start of many paths. The most popular of these begins 4 km (2 miles) southwest of the village centre, down the D27, and leads to the Cascade du Voile de la Mariée ("Bride's Veil Falls").

The dam at Gorges du Prunelli

View of coves and beaches on the road to Tiuccia

Tiuccia ❾

Road map B4. 👥 *150.* ℹ️ *Sagone (04 95 28 05 36).*

ON THE GOLFE de Liscia, between the Genoese towers of Ancone and Capigliolo, is Tiuccia. This small seaside resort is dominated by the ruins of the Capraja Castle, which once belonged to the Counts de la Cinarca. In the 13th–16th centuries, this family resisted Genoese rule and established its hold over the south of the island.

The mouths of the Liscia river and, further north along the coast, of the Liamone river have created long, sandy beaches surrounded by hills covered in maquis. These secluded beaches and coves can be reached via the Ancone footpath along the coast.

Tiuccia is also the starting point for boat excursions towards Girolata *(see p103)*, the Calanques de Piana *(see pp100–1)* and Capo Rosso.

ENVIRONS: The valley of the river Liscia forms **La Cinarca**, a fertile area covered with woods, olive and orange trees and vineyards. Livestock raising is still the main activity here. At an altitude of 400–600 m (1,300–2,000 ft) are villages with splendid views of the coast, such as Sari d'Orcino and Calcatoggio.

This area was once the home of some famous bandits, including Spada, also known as "the Tiger of Cinarca".

Corsican Charcuterie and Cheeses

Nuts to be eaten
with cheese

THE GASTRONOMIC products *prisuttu* (cured ham), *lonzu* (smoked pork fillet), *coppa* (smoked pork shoulder) and *figatellu* (smoked liver sausage) are typical of Corsica. They are prepared by hand and smoked on the *fucone*, an open fireplace that burns chestnut wood and grapevine stumps. The wild pigs used for these products are allowed to roam freely, a factor reflected in the meats' unique flavour. Other typical products are cheeses made of goat's and sheep's milk. They are named after their areas of production, such as Niolo, Balaninu, Orezzincu, Bastelicaccia and Venaco. Niolo is one of the best-known strong, aged cheeses. Usually, cheese is eaten with fig preserves and nuts.

Sheep can be found almost anywhere, especially in upper Corsica. Their milk is used to make a variety of cheeses, including brocciu and toma. Goats are common above all in the Balagne and Castagniccia regions.

There are about 45,000 wild pigs in Corsica. They live in woods along the roads, feeding on chestnuts, acorns and aromatic herbs that give their meats a special flavour.

Lonzu is raw pork fillet rolled with salt and pepper, tied into thick sausages and smoked.

Partly aged cheeses

Salsiccia

Goat's milk cheese

Lonzu

Cheese with herbs

Fresh herbs

CORSICAN FLAVOURS
In tourist resorts there is no shortage of delicatessens selling gift baskets filled with tempting food items. But produce can also be purchased directly from the farmers.

Prisuttu is a very savoury cured ham. It is best when it is cut by hand in thick, compact slices, so that its taste can be enjoyed to the full.

FROMAGE DE LACTOSERUM DE CHÈVRE
ET DE LAIT FRAIS DE BREBIS
BROCCIU
PASSU
Appellation d'Origine Contrôlée

Fromagerie Xavier SALVINI

Brocciu is a ewe's-milk cheese similar to ricotta, prepared with whey and heated milk. It can be fresh or salted to last longer. Since 1983 its trademark has been registered.

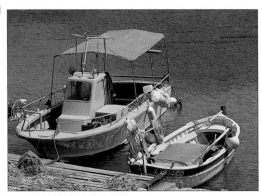

Boats moored in the Golfe de Sagone

Sagone ❿

Road map B4. 🏘 250.
🛈 04 95 28 03 46.

THE WIDE GOLFE de Sagone, between Punta di Cargèse to the north and Capo di Feno to the south, has long, sandy beaches formed by the silt carried by the Liamone, Sagone and Liscia rivers.

The small village of Sagone was once a major Roman city and owed its prosperity to timber from the Forêt d'Aïtone. In the 6th century AD it became a bishopric, and in the 11th century the cathedral of **Sant'Appiano** was built near the port. Its ruins can still be seen there. In the Middle Ages, however, the town declined because of malaria from the stagnant river water.

Thanks to land reclamation, Sagone is now a pleasant seaside resort. Among the activities on offer are sailing, scuba diving and boat trips to Scandola and Girolata.

ENVIRONS: A beautiful 15-km (9-mile) road goes up the Liamone river valley to **Vico**, a large, hilly village with narrow houses packed around two squares. Until the 18th century, Vico was the residence of the bishops of Sagone.

The church of the Couvent St-François has a lovely wooden crucifix that was sculpted in the 15th century and that is traditionally considered one of the oldest in Corsica.

The road continues through lush vegetation to **Guagno Les Bains**, a tiny spa with two springs: the Occhiu (37° C/ 98.6° F), which is used to cure eye and throat ailments, and the Venturini spring (52° C/125.6° F), used by those afflicted by sciatica, rheumatism and obesity. Among the illustrious guests at this spa were Pascal Paoli and Napoleon's mother, Letizia. Further along the road is the village of Soccia, the starting point for a footpath to the **Lac de Creno**, a lake surrounded by Laricio pines (2 hours return trip).

Sign for the spa of Guagno Les Bains

Cargèse ⓫

Road map B3. 🏘 1,000. 🛈 Rue Dr Dragacci (04 95 26 41 31). 🎭 Greek-Orthodox procession (Easter Monday).

IN THE MID-17TH CENTURY a group of Greek families that had fled from the Peloponnese following the Turkish invasion asked the Genoese for political asylum. First they settled at Paomia, 50 km (31 miles) from Ajaccio, and then at Cargèse, where they were allowed to retain their traditions and religion. To this day this village, which is about 100 m (330 ft) above sea level, reflects its Greek history. Two churches, both from the 19th century, stand opposite each other: a Greek-Orthodox church, with Byzantine-style icons and a 13th-century double-sided panel of the *Deposition of Christ*; and a Latin church, with a Neo-Classical interior. The terraces of both offer fine views of the Golfe de Sagone.

Piana ⓬

Road map B3. 🏘 500. 🛈 Place de la Mairie (04 95 27 84 42). 🎭 Brocciu Day (date depends on cheese production).

WITH ITS WHITE houses, large Baroque church and the granite formations of the Calanques in the background, Piana occupies a panoramic position overlooking the Golfe de Porto. The village is the ideal base for excursions along this stretch of coastline, which has many beautiful beaches and is one of the most fascinating in Corsica.

Among the beaches is the **Anse di Ficajola**, situated among red rocks at the end of a winding road descending to the sea. The panoramic D824 road leads to **Plage d'Arone**, a pretty, undeveloped beach surrounded by maquis.

A difficult hike (4 hours return trip) from the roadside 2 km (1 mile) above the beach leads to **Capo Rosso** and the Tour de Turghiu, which, from its position 300 m (1,000 ft) above sea level, offers a spectacular view of the area.

Panoramic view of Piana, surrounded by forest

Parc Naturel Régional de la Corse

WITH A SURFACE AREA of 3,300 sq km (1,274 sq miles) and 143 towns, this park occupies nearly two thirds of Corsica, including the peaks of Monte Cinto, Rotondo, d'Oro, Renoso and Incudine, up to the Aiguilles de Bavella and the Massif de l'Ospédale. The park was founded in 1972 to support the mountain

The park logo

economy and protect the island's natural wonders: its forests (Aïtone, Valdu-Niellu, Vizzavona, Bavella and Ospédale), its rugged gorges (Spelunca, Restonica, l'Asco), the Calanques, and lakes such as Creno and Nino. The park is traversed by all the main hiking paths, including the GR20 long-distance path (*see pp20–25*).

Cork oak is one of the most widespread species of trees in Corsica and is protected in the park.

LOCATOR MAP

☐ *The park area*

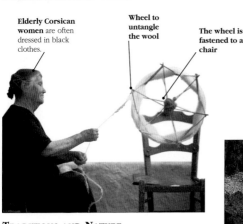

Elderly Corsican women are often dressed in black clothes.

Wheel to untangle the wool

The wheel is fastened to a chair

TRADITIONS AND NATURE

The Parc Naturel Régional was established not only to protect the Corsican flora and fauna, but also to safeguard the traditional activities of the hill and mountain environments. Most of the inhabitants in the park area are people whose families have lived and worked here for centuries and have forged the region's history and traditions.

The Gorges de l'Asco are a stunning example of the many deep canyons created by the rivers that flow from inland Corsica to the sea.

The donkey is one of the many domesticated or semi-domesticated animals linked to the economic activities of mountain life.

*This **bergerie** at Cagna exemplifies mountain architecture. Bergeries are used in the summer for transhumance (the movement of livestock). In 1973–8 Father Doazan wrote about 20 notebooks describing this activity and the life of Corsican shepherds.*

Tour of the Calanques de Piana ⑬

THE GRANITIC ROCK FORMATIONS known as the Calanques de Piana feature sensational colour changes from gold to pink to bright red depending on the time of day. The wind and water have sculpted the granitic rock, creating awesome cavities, known as *tafoni*, and intriguing formations. Although it is possible to cover this whole route in half a day, or a full day with a lunch break, it might be more relaxing to explore the Calanques in the course of two separate walks, especially during the hottest period of the year. For those who are driving, this stretch of the D81 road is at its most beautiful and impressive at sunset.

Typical rock in the Calanques

Tête du Chien ①
The "dog's head" rock, eroded by the sea and wind, is one of the many intriguing shapes in the Calanques. It is near the parking area on the D81 road and is the starting point for many excursions.

Château Fort ②
This massive block of granite that looks like a fortress forms a panoramic terrace overlooking the gulfs of Porto and Girolata and Capo Rosso. It can be reached on foot in 30 minutes from the Tête du Chien through a maze of sculpted rocks, cavities and pinnacles that in spring are covered by flowering shrubs.

Dardo

Café les Roches Bleues ④
In one of the most spectacular spots along the D81 highway is the Roches Bleues café. Drinks are served on the terrace over-hanging fantastically shaped rocks: to the left is the Tortue ("turtle", seen here), and to the right the Aigle ("eagle").

PIANA ← **D81**

Mezzanu

The D81 Road ⑥
Once back on the D81, walk about 500 m (500 yards) towards Piana. Along this stretch of road the Calanques can be appreciated at their most beautiful. Turn back and follow the D81 all the way back to the parking area.

KEY

▦	Tour route
═	Other roads
☀	Viewpoint
🅿	Parking

THE *TAFONI*

In Corsican *tafone* means a large hole, and this term is used to indicate a natural cavity in the rock of areas where the dry season is very long and the terrain is steep. Erosion begins when even just one crystal of granite is corroded

by the humidity and swings in temperature that occur in this area. The shapes the rock then takes on are truly astonishing. The *tafoni* became part of the Corsican way of life in ancient times, when these holes were used as burial sites or as primitive dwellings.

A *tafone* formation in the Calanques de Piana

TIPS FOR HIKERS

🛈 *Place de la Mairie, Piana (04 95 27 84 42).*
Length of tour: *3 km (2 miles).*
Duration: *about four hours, without stops, to do the paths, plus 45–60 minutes to get back to the parking area.*
Difficulty: *average. Wear comfortable shoes and carry a hat and sunglasses, a supply of water and a detailed map of the area (free from local tourist offices).*
Stopping-off point: *Café les Roches Bleues.*
W www.sipiana.com

Corniche ③

Once back at the Tête du Chien, a path east of the D81 road zigzags through the Laricio pine forest for about an hour before returning to the road a short distance from the Café les Roches Bleues. Marked with blue dots, the strenuous path offers splendid views of the rocks and the Golfe de Porto.

Chemin des Muletiers ⑤

Just after the café, near a small shrine to the Virgin Mary, begins the Chemin des Muletiers. This was the old mule track that connected Porto and Piana. A short but tough climb leads to the path, which runs through rocks and scented woods. One hour of easy walking leads back on the D81.

Forêt Domaniale de Piana

0 metres   400

0 yards   400

The Genoese watchtower at Porto

Porto ⓮

Road map B3. 👥 *460.*
🚌 **ℹ** *La Marine (04 95 26 10 55).*

A MODERN SEASIDE resort with facilities for watersports of every kind, Porto is also an ideal base for visitors who want to make inland excursions. Its favourable geographic position was providential for Porto, which, during the Genoese period, was the only outlet to the sea in the agricultural zone of Ota.

On either side of the village are tall cliffs that conceal enchanting beaches. Overlooking the village's harbour is the impressive Genoese tower that defended the small port, the river and the valley. This quadrangular construction was built in 1549 on levelled red-granite cliffs and offers magnificent views of the gulf, where the red rock contrasts with the blue sea.

Next to the village, with its many hotels, cafés and boutiques, is the **Marina**, which has a wide beach of grey pebbles backed by a large grove of centuries-old eucalyptus trees. The Marina can be reached via a charming wooden footbridge leading over the estuary of the little river where fishing boats and yachts are anchored. This tiny port is the departure point for many excursions by boat along the entire coastline. The Golfe de Porto, part of the Parc Naturel Régional *(see p99),* can be seen in all

A strawberry tree laden with fruit

its splendour from the sea – the tourist boats go as far as the Scandola Nature Reserve *(see pp104–5)* and the Calanques de Piana *(see pp100–1).*

ENVIRONS: South of Porto loom the magnificent Calanques, which reach an altitude of 1,294 m (4,245 ft) at Capo d'Orto. North of Porto, among the coast's granite cliffs, are some beautiful beaches that can be reached either by car (by taking turn-offs from the D81 road) or by boat. Among the most scenic are the pebble beaches of **Bussaglia** and **Gradelle**, the latter on the way to Osani; and the **Caspio** beach, with its dark rocks. Caspio can be reached by taking the detour after the hamlet of Partinello.

The stretch of the D81 road to Galéria is arguably the most difficult and spectacular in all Corsica. This high, narrow road with numerous bends offers wide-ranging views of the Golfe de Porto and coast. Small lay-bys along the road make for good viewpoints, as does the **Col de la Croix**, from which a path leads to the beaches of Tuara (75 minutes return) and Girolata (3 hours return; also accessible by boat).

Gorges de Spelunca ⓯

Road map B3. **ℹ** *La Marine, Porto (04 95 26 10 55).*

B EHIND PORTO is a splendid valley from where it is possible to admire this gorge, formed by the Aïtone and Tavulella torrents. Fine views of the Gorges de Spelunca can be had from the D84 road that goes up to Evisa on the south side of the valley.

On the north side of the valley, at an altitude of 310 m (1,017 ft), is **Ota**, a mountain village with simple stone houses that was once famous for its citrons, which were exported to Europe. Today the orchards are partly overrun by scrub. Ota is one of the stops on the *Mare e Monti* path *(see p25)* in the Parc Naturel Régional *(see p99).*

Interesting sights in this area are the Genoese bridges, about 2 km (1 mile) along the road to Evisa. The first of these, at **Pianella**, is a perfect arch. The nearby bridge of **Ota** lies where the Aïtone and Tavulella torrents meet and passes over both of them. This point also marks the start of the old mule track that once linked Ota and Evisa through the spectacular gorges, passing over the **Vecchju** and **Zaglia** bridges (90 minutes return). The latter, built in 1745, is one of the gems of Genoese architecture.

The entire area is reminiscent of American canyons, and there is a ravine that can be followed along the path hewn out of the rock.

The Genoese bridge of Ota, with its characteristic arch

Laricio pines in the Forêt d'Aïtone

Forêt d'Aïtone ⓰

Road map C3. **ℹ** *Jun–Sep: Paesolu d'Aïtone (04 95 26 23 62). Other times: Parc Naturel Régional de la Corse, Ajaccio (04 95 51 79 00).*

WITH THE ATMOSPHERE of an enchanted forest, the Forêt d'Aïtone can be explored through its easy, enjoyable and well-marked footpaths.

An ancient forest, its name seems to have derived from the Latin word *abies*, meaning fir tree. The forest covers an area of 24 sq km (9 sq miles) at an altitude of 800–2,000 m (2,600–6,500 ft). The Genoese used the wood to make their ships and, in the 16th century, built a road to transport the trunks to Sagone (*see p98*). The forest is made up mostly of Laricio pines, a sweet-scented variety of *Pinus nigrus* that can grow to more than 45 m (150 ft) high and live for 200 years. There are also maritime pines, firs, beeches and larches that protect the rich undergrowth and its wild fruit and mushrooms. The forest is inhabited by foxes, wild boars and moufflons.

Just west of the forest, at 830 m (2,723 ft) above sea level, is **Evisa**. Surrounded by chestnut groves that yield high-quality fruit, this village plays host to a famous chestnut festival in November. Evisa is situated at the junction of the *Mare a Mare* and *Mare*

e Monti footpaths (*see p25*) and is therefore a great starting point for excursions.

About 4 km (2 miles) from Evisa, on the road to Col de Verghio (*see p151*), is the starting point of the path that leads to the **Cascades d'Aïtone** (30 minutes return), a series of waterfalls formed by the Aïtone torrent, at the foot of which are limpid pools perfect for a swim.

The **Sentier de la Sittelle** (the French word for the nuthatch, a local bird) is a path beginning by the park information centre of **Paesolu d'Aïtone** and going through the forest along the **Sentier des Condamnés** (2 hours 30 minutes), a circular path named after the convicts who, in the 19th century, felled the trees for firewood.

The ramparts and keep of the Genoese fort at Girolata

Girolata ⓱

Road map B3. **👥** *100.* **ℹ** *La Marine, Porto (04 95 26 10 55).*

A FISHERMEN'S hamlet facing a splendid cove sheltered from the wind, Girolata can be reached only on foot (90 minutes from Col de la Croix, *see p102*) or by one of the boats that offer excursions from Porto in the summer. On the headland is the majestic square Genoese fort, which is protected by a defensive wall.

It was in the sea in front of Girolata, that, in 1540, the Genoese led by Andrea Doria captured the infamous Turkish pirate Dragut Rais.

In the summer the bay area becomes crowded with yachts and loses much of its charm, even though the sea beds and red cliffs are still beautiful.

Galéria ⓲

Road map B3. **👥** *300.* **🚌** **ℹ** *Carrefour des Cinq Arcades (04 95 62 02 27).*

THE ONLY RESIDENTIAL area of any importance between Calvi (*see pp78–80*) and Porto, this isolated village is a great base for visits to the Scandola Nature Reserve (*see pp104–5*), dives and watersports in general. Galéria is also the departure point for excursions along the coast, where a panoramic path that also penetrates the maquis skirts the Golfe de Galéria from Punta Ciuttone to the north to Punta Stollu to the south.

Just behind Galéria is the **Vallée du Fango**, created by the river Fango, the mouth of which forms a vast pebbled beach. The valley was a trans-humance route along which flocks of sheep from the mountains above the Vallée de Niolo were moved to the sea for winter. They stayed there until spring, when they made the return trip.

The D351 road penetrates the valley for about 10 km (6 miles), traversing the Forêt du Fango. Here the Fango river flows between low rock faces, creating transparent water-holes ideal for a swim. Shortly before the village of Barghiana is the spectacular meeting point of the Fango and the Taita torrent.

The Taita torrent in the Vallée du Fango

Réserve Naturelle de Scandola ⑲

R ED GRANITE CLIFFS plunge into the transparent sea at the
Scandola Nature Reserve, while cormorants and shear-
waters perch on the rocks and ospreys circle in the sky.
Under the water's surface is a blaze of colours created by
sponges, yellow anemones and corals. The reserve, which
is on the UNESCO World Heritage list, protects 9.2 sq km
(3½ sq miles) of land and 10 sq km (4 sq miles) of sea
between Punta Mucchilina to the south and Punta Palazzo
to the north. The park boasts an unparalleled wealth of
flora, rare bird species and an abundance of underwater
fauna: 450 species of algae and 125 species of fish are
protected by bans on fishing, on mooring for more than
24 hours, and on gathering marine fauna and flora.

**Cliffs of beautiful red
volcanic rock**

Volcanic Rock
*The entire Scandola peninsula
is part of a volcanic complex, the
rocks of which date back to the
Upper Permian era (248 million
years ago). Among these are
porphyry flows at Cala Ficaccia,
the lava and rhyolite domes
at Punta Palazzo, and the
prismatic organ-pipe shapes
at Elbo, shown above.*

Algae platform

**Clinging to the
volcanic rocks**, at the
water's surface, are sea
urchins and anemones,
as well as numerous
crustaceans.

THE ALGAE PLATFORM

Lythophyllum is a calcareous alga
forming encrustations that hang
over the surface of the water and
are often as thick as 30 cm (12 in).
At Punta Palazzo is the largest algae
platform in the Mediterranean, about
100 m (330 ft) long and 2 m (6½ ft)
wide. Though they seem robust,
algae platforms are extremely fragile.

Underwater layers

Algae platform above the water

Euphorbia Dendroides

Growing as much as 1 m (3 ft) high, this shrub is one of the most common in the reserve. It blossoms in May, when it tinges the cliffs yellow; at the end of spring, as it becomes dry, it takes on a bright-brown hue. Only in late summer, with the first autumn rain, does it become green again.

VISITORS' CHECKLIST

Road map B3. 🛈 *La Marine, Porto (04 95 26 10 55).*

🚤 *excursions (by boat) from Ajaccio, Calvi, Cargèse, Galéria, Porto, Propriano, Sagone. (Snorkelling excursions are also available.)*

🕐 *Jul–Aug: six excursions a day; Apr–Jun & Sep–Oct: four excursions a day.*

The nest of the osprey, a large white bird of prey with brown wings, is one of the features of these cliffs. After being close to extinction, there are now about 20 pairs of ospreys in the Scandola Nature Reserve.

Fauna in the Reserve

The Scandola Nature Reserve is above all the domain of marine birds and fish. Here the birds find shelter and abundant food in the crevices of the rocks, where they nest. Cormorants, peregrine falcons and ospreys can all be observed here, as can a species of bat. The pure water also favours underwater life: flora lives as deep as 45 m (150 ft) down and the range of sea creatures is truly exceptional.

The cormorant, *one of the largest sea birds, makes acrobatic manoeuvres on the water.*

The osprey *builds its nest on the steep cliffs of the Scandola Nature Reserve.*

The grouper *is a large fish that can be as much as 1.5 m (5 ft) long. It is recognizable by the light spots on its brownish dorsal portion.*

The sea bream *is highly prized and much in demand for its tasty meat, but in this park it is protected by the ban on fishing.*

Over 450 species of algae live here as a result of the exceptional clarity of the water.

Panorama

The coast along the Scandola Nature Reserve is one of the most evocative in Corsica. Here steep red rock formations plunge into the crystalline sea.

BONIFACIO AND THE SOUTH

THE FORTIFIED CITY *of Bonifacio, with its narrow streets from which Sardinia can be seen on the horizon, is one of the most ancient on the island. But long before the Pisans, Genoese and Spanish fought for control here, southern Corsica was the centre of a prehistoric indigenous population that left amazing traces of its presence in the alignments of menhirs and* casteddi.

The inlet of Bonifacio, on the cliffs of which are the defensive walls of the old Genoese city, is an ideal starting point for boat excursions along the precipitous white coastline. The menhirs at Filitosa are among the best-known aspects of Corsican history, but this is only one of the many sites where it is possible to admire Neolithic architecture. North of the Golfe de Porto-Vecchio are the impressive walls of the *casteddu* (castle) of Arraggio, while south of Sartène the alignments of menhirs at Palaggiu, Stantari and Renaggiu are eloquent reminders of Corsica's early history.

The natural scenery in this area is quite varied and splendid: from the forests around the Aiguilles de Bavella to the white rocks on the islands of Lavezzi and Cavallo – protected by an international marine park that extends over the Straits of Bonifacio – the landscape offers incomparable views.

There are many walking tours, and indeed the interior of southern Corsica should be explored, at least to some degree, on foot. A series of small villages occupies the most protected part of the mountain valleys, where olives and chestnuts grow and where traces of Corsica's medieval past can be found.

Amid small churches and old houses there is still an atmosphere of peace and quiet – the region is far removed from the world most of the year, becoming animated with tourists only in the summer. A low-season visit is highly recommended.

Three of the best-known anthropomorphic megaliths at the prehistoric site of Filitosa

◁ **The famous cliffs of Bonifacio, resembling the hull of a huge ship**

Exploring Bonifacio and the South

SOUTHERN CORSICA IS DIVIDED into two adjacent areas that are quite different to one another. Starting off from Bonifacio, two main routes are worth exploring. Along the south coast there are many small coves, peaceful beaches and sheer rocks overlooking the sea. This is the area with the most popular tourist resorts, such as Bonifacio, Propriano, Solenzara and Porto-Vecchio, which in summer all become crowded. The inland route, after crossing the Alta Rocca region, leads to the Col de Bavella zone, which offers wonderful spots for nature hikes and many small secluded villages. The best-preserved prehistoric sites in Corsica – Filitosa, Palaggiu, Renaggiu, Fontanaccia and Stantari – are only a short driving distance from the town of Sartène, while near Levie, the sites of Cucuruzzu and Capula are also worth a visit.

View of the citadel of Bonifacio

Alignment of menhirs at Palaggiu, one of the prehistoric sites in the area of the Cauria plateau

GETTING AROUND

The main communication routes on the south coast of Corsica are the N196 and N198 roads, connecting Bonifacio to Propriano and Sartène, and Porto-Vecchio respectively. The N198 then proceeds northwards towards Bastia. The D368 road, with its many hairpin bends, goes from Porto-Vecchio into the mountains; in the village of Zonza it merges with the D268 road and leads to Col de Bavella. To explore the prehistoric sites it is necessary either to take minor roads, some of which are unpaved, or to go on foot. The main coastal towns are connected to Ajaccio and Bastia by bus service, while Bonifacio is a stopover for the ferries from Sardinia.

SEE ALSO

- **Where to Stay** pp160–61
- **Where to Eat** pp170–71

Sights at a Glance

Arraggio **5**
Bonifacio pp110–17 **1**
Campomoro **18**
Cascade Piscia di Gallo **10**
Col de Bavella
pp122–3 **8**
Cucuruzzu & Capula **13**
Filitosa **21**

Levie **12**
Massif de l'Ospédale **4**
Porto-Pollo **20**
Porto-Vecchio **3**
Propriano **19**
Punta Fautea **6**
Quenza **11**
Roccapina **16**

Ste-Lucie de Tallano **14**
Sartène **15**
Solenzara **7**
Tappa **2**
Zonza **9**

Tour
Megaliths of Cauria **17**

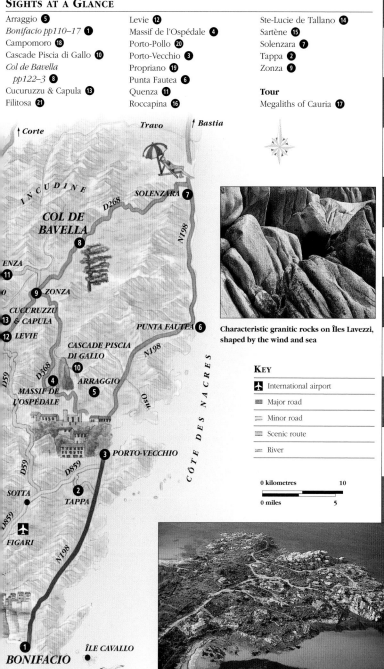

Characteristic granitic rocks on Îles Lavezzi, shaped by the wind and sea

↑ Corte

Travo   ↑ Bastia

I N C U D I N E

SOLENZARA **7**

D268

COL DE BAVELLA
8

ENZA
11

9 ZONZA

O

CUCURUZZU
13 **& CAPULA**

12 LEVIE

N198

PUNTA FAUTEA **6**

CASCADE PISCIA
DI GALLO
10

N198

D368

D59

4

ARRAGGIO
5

MASSIF DE
L'OSPÉDALE

Osu

C Ô T E   D E S   N A C R E S

D59

3 PORTO-VECCHIO

D859

SOTTA

2
TAPPA

D859

FIGARI

N198

1
BONIFACIO

ÎLE CAVALLO

ÎLES LAVEZZI

AITS OF BONIFACIO

Key

✈	International airport
	Major road
	Minor road
	Scenic route
	River

0 kilometres   10

0 miles   5

Transparent water and wild beauty on
the exclusive Île Cavallo

Bonifacio ❶

Rose window, Ste-Marie-Majeure

THIS STUNNING MEDIEVAL TOWN on a striking limestone promontory was developed by Bonifacio, Marquis of Tuscany, who passed by upon his return from an expedition in Africa in 828. For three centuries the fortified harbour lived on fishing and piracy and was partly under the rule of Pisa. In 1195, Bonifacio became a Genoese colony and took in a number of immigrants from Liguria. At about the same time, it became a republic, was granted the right to mint its own money and began construction of the massive walls. Bonifacio was conquered in 1553 by the French before being recaptured by the Genoese, and in the 17th century it was fortified with modern military structures. Although the town fell definitively under French rule in the 18th century, it has kept an Italian flavour and a certain sense of isolation from the rest of Corsica.

Outdoor cafés along the Marina

🏛 Marina
The quays of the old port of Bonifacio are now a popular promenade filled with cafés and restaurants. This is the departure point for cruises to the Grotte du Sdragonatu *(see p114)* and the Îles Lavezzi *(see p117)*. In the summer, this area remains quite lively until late at night.

Further along, towards the mouth of the inlet, is the commercial port with the Gare Maritime (passenger terminal). In the Middle Ages the port was entrusted to the benevolence of St Erasmus, the patron saint of sailors and fishermen who is celebrated on 2 June *(see p33)* and honoured by a church named after him in the Marina.

To the Haute Ville
The old town can be reached by walking up the stairs known as Montée Rastello, next to St-Érasme, and then up Montée St-Roch, which leads to the old Porte de Gênes. It is also possible to drive along the road that goes past the Porte de France. This road skirts the foot of the Bastion de l'Étendard and a war memorial that consists of an ancient Roman column found on a nearby islet, and leads to the car park in the upper town *(haute ville)*, next to the monument to the Foreign Legion soldiers

🏰 Bastion de l'Étendard
⭕ *Jul–Aug: daily; Apr–Jun & Sep–Oct: Mon–Sat.* 📷
The silhouette of this massive bastion towering over the quays of the Marina and the port is one of the most famous features of the city. The bastion was built in the 16th century by modifying the existing fortifications, and its function was to house the powerful heavy artillery that at that time was bringing about a drastic change in military architecture. Along with the Porte de Gênes, it was the strong point of the walls of Bonifacio, which proved impregnable on several occasions.

The upper platforms of the bastion afford a magnificent panoramic view of the narrow inlet of Bonifacio and the Marina below.

Four halls in the interior are now a small museum featuring reconstructions of significant moments in Bonifacio's history.

🏰 Porte de Gênes
During Genoese rule, the Porte de Gênes was the only entrance to Bonifacio's upper town. Surrounded by tall ramparts, the gate gave access to the Place d'Armes, beyond the walls. These walls were so thick that, to get to the square, one had to pass through eight successive barriers made of wood reinforced with iron.

In 1588, a drawbridge was added at the end of these barriers. The drawbridge was raised and lowered by a complex system of counterweights that can still be seen inside the structure.

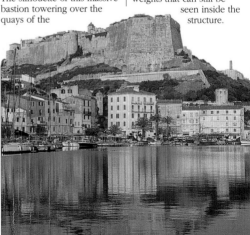

The massive Bastion de l'Étendard towering over the Marina

Open and blind double lancet windows, Ste-Marie-Majeure

🏠 Ste-Marie-Majeure

Rue de la Loggia. ◯ *daily.*

Bonifacio's cathedral was the heart of the city's religious and cultural life for centuries. At the front of the building is a vast loggia with porticoes, which, in the past, was the meeting point for the town notables and the seat for administering justice. The structure was built over a large cistern that is now used as a conference room.

Construction of Ste-Marie-Majeure was begun in the 12th century, before the Genoese conquered the city, by Pisan artisans, and was completed a century later. This extremely long delay has led to a mixture of styles that does not, however, diminish the beauty of the whole. The first floor of the bell tower, for example, is Romanesque, while the upper three are Gothic with some Aragonese relief decoration. The three-aisle interior is partly Baroque.

Inside, to the left of the entrance, is a 3rd- or 4th-century Roman sarcophagus surmounted by a magnificently wrought tabernacle executed by Genoese masters in the mid-1400s. The high altar dates from 1624 and is clearly Baroque in style. In the sacristy is a relic of the True Cross.

VISITORS' CHECKLIST

Road map C6. 🏘 *3,400.*
✈ *Figari-Sud-Corse, 21 km (13 miles) NW (04 95 71 10 10).*
🚌 🚢 *from Sardinia.* 🛈 *2 Rue Fred Scamaroni (04 95 73 11 88).*
🎉 *St Erasmus's Feast Day (2 Jun); St Bartholomew Procession (24 Aug).* Ⓦ *www.bonifacio.fr*

In the past, during particularly dangerous times and when there were heavy storms, the curate and mayor carried the Cross in a procession through the streets of Bonifacio.

The loggia of Ste-Marie-Majeure

BONIFACIO OLD TOWN

Bastion de l'Étendard ②	Porte de France ⑤
Escalier du Roi d'Aragon ⑦	Porte de Gênes ③
	Ste-Marie-Majeure ④
Marina ①	St-Dominique ⑥

KEY

🛈 Tourist information

⛪ Church

⚓ Port

🅿 Parking

Exploring Bonifacio

THE HEART OF BONIFACIO is the *haute ville* (upper town), which perches on the promontory high above the fjord-like inlet that forms Bonifacio's harbour. Bordered by Avenue Charles-de-Gaulle and the massive ramparts, this is the oldest section of the city. Around the cathedral, tall, narrow houses line the streets, the outer rows balancing dangerously on the cliff's edge. Further out on the promontory, west of the city walls, the wind-battered Bosco area stretches out towards the sea, offering panoramic views from the Esplanade St-François.

🏛 Porte de France

In addition to the Porte de Gênes, a second entrance to the *haute ville* was created in 1854, when the French Army Engineers' Corps built a road to the St-Nicolas fort. This new gate also featured a drawbridge. Within the city walls around the Porte de France, traces of the oldest quarters of Genoese Bonifacio can still be seen. These include the Fondaco, or staple (commercial warehouse), that once stood in the Place Montepagano area.

The bell tower of St-Dominique

⛪ St-Dominique

Haute Ville, near Place Birhakeim. 🕐 *Jul–Aug.*

Outside the city walls, but inside the fortifications that once protected the Pisan quarter, is this church dating from 1343. It stands on the site of an earlier Romanesque church, which was begun by the Pisans and finished by the Knights Templars. The present church was built by the Dominicans and, until the French Revolution, was part of a monastery complex.

The Gothic bell tower is unusual: its square base is surmounted by an octagonal section topped with battlements, and the white limestone façade is decorated with an ogival portal. Inside are groups of statues depicting Mary and the other holy women at the foot of the Cross and an image of St Bartholomew.

Opposite the church doorway are the Montlaur barracks, which were built by the Genoese. Later this building became the home of the Foreign Legion troops.

Next to the church is the Mairie (Town Hall), which is linked to St-Dominique by an arch that was once part of the old Dominican monastery.

🏕 Bosco

At the tip of Bonifacio's promontory is the Bosco area. Here there is a cemetery, with many small, light-coloured mortuary chapels. Near the edge, the structure of the St-Antoine battery was constructed in the period between the two World Wars. The position of the battery allowed complete control of the maritime traffic in the Straits of Bonifacio.

🏛 Escalier du Roi d'Aragon

Rue des Pachas. 🕐 *Apr–Oct.*

On the west side of the headland, where the craggy cliff is at its most precipitous, this steep rock-cut stairway descends to sea level. According to legend, its 187 steps were hewn in only one night, during the Aragonese siege of 1420. It is, in fact, more likely that the stairway was built in a much earlier period and served as access to a well with good drinking water.

The Escalier could be clearly monitored from above, and was never used by any of the foreign troops that tried to storm Bonifacio.

The impressive Escalier du Roi d'Aragon

THE TRINITÉ PROCESSIONS

When heading out of Bonifacio on the D196 road towards Sartène, after about 3 km (2 miles) there is a junction, the left branch of which leads to the Ermitage de la Trinité. A narrow road winds between two walls of maquis to the open space in front of this little church, which affords a magnificent view towards Bonifacio and the Anse de Paragnano. On 13 May (feast day of Our Lady of Fatima) and on 8 September *(see p34)*, the inhabitants of Bonifacio come here in procession, creating such a traffic jam that it is advisable to go to the Ermitage on foot. The small church dedicated to the Trinity contains offerings and vows left by people who survived dangerous trips in the Straits of Bonifacio during heavy storms.

View from the hermitage

Parc Marin de Bonifacio

To preserve the coastal habitats of southern Corsica, the first marine reserves were established in the early 1980s. They now include the islands of Lavezzi, Bruzzi, Monaci and Cerbicale. Underwater fishing was prohibited and rigorous regulations were applied even to professional fisher-

A yacht in the straits

men. In 1986, the idea for an international marine park in the Straits of Bonifacio – the stretch of sea between Corsica and Sardinia – started to take shape. In 1992 the Italian and French ministers of ecology decided to

work together for the park. Although they could not block shipping of loads that could cause damage in case of an accident, the authorities did restrict the limits of the navigable channel and set up an emergency plan that goes into effect whenever the wind, which is quite strong in this part of the sea, blows at more than 4 or 5 knots. Because the wind is never lacking here, the straits are a paradise for yachtsmen, whose boats can always be seen slicing through the frothy waves, often during a regatta.

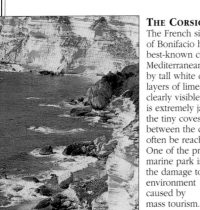

THE CORSICAN COAST
The French side of the Straits of Bonifacio has one of the best-known coasts in the Mediterranean, characterized by tall white cliffs in which layers of limestone are clearly visible. The profile is extremely jagged and the tiny coves squeezed between the craggy rocks can often be reached only by boat. One of the problems of the marine park is how to limit the damage to the environment caused by mass tourism.

Red coral, according to popular legend, originated from the blood of Medusa after Perseus cut off her head and tossed it into the sea.

The sea anemone is an inhabitant of the coast of the straits. Although it seems to be an immobile plant, the sea anemone is an exceptional predator.

Lobsters, crustaceans with highly prized meat, find refuge in this area, where fishing is strictly regulated.

THE SARDINIAN COAST
On the other side of the Straits of Bonifacio, the Sardinian coastline is as jagged as Corsica's, but generally much lower, with beautiful sandy coves and colourful sea beds. Not far away to the east is the Maddalena archipelago, made up of seven main islands, including La Maddalena and Caprera, and several smaller islets, such as Isola Budelli, famous for its pink-sand beach.

Bonifacio: the Coast and the Cliffs

Perched on its promontory, keeping guard over the deep inlet below, the fortified city of Bonifacio owes its charm and importance to the sea, fishing and commerce. Only an exploration from beneath the cliffs, at sea level, reveals all of Bonifacio's particular beauty and the reason why it has been likened to a ship carved out of rock. On the jetties of the Marina many companies offer boat tours of the coastline as far as the sea caves, the Grain de Sable and to the open sea, skirting the headlands and coves that lead to the Îles Lavezzi.

The houses of Bonifacio on the steep cliffs overlooking the sea

Grotte de St-Antoine

Esplanade de St-François

Escalier du Roi d'Aragon

The marine cemetery, with its aligned mortuary chapels surrounded by greenery, is a fine panoramic viewpoint.

The *haute ville* of Bonifacio dominates the port situated in the inlet.

Grotte du Sdragonatu
Created by water erosion, this sea cave is illuminated by the sun, which penetrates through a crack in the vault. The local tourist guides claim that this long, narrow opening resembles the shape of Corsica.

A GEOLOGICAL ANOMALY

The coast around Bonifacio is made up of a chalk outcrop that created the famous cliffs. Extending as far as south as Capo Pertusato and towards Pointe de Sperone, these cliffs are friable sedimentary rocks that over time have been sculpted by the wind and sea to create this much-admired craggy coastline. The presence of lime-stone here is a geological anomaly on an island mostly made up of magmatic rocks, in particular granite (Col de Bavella and the Calanques de Piana) and volcanic rhyolite (Scandola Nature Reserve).

Typical layers of limestone in the cliffs

Grain de Sable

This solitary stack, which now has the curious nickname of "grain of sand", broke off from the cliff 800 years ago. It is one of the most recognizable cliffs around Bonifacio.

VISITORS' CHECKLIST

Road map C6. 2 Rue Fred Scamaroni, Bonifacio (04 95 73 11 88). Apr–Oct: excursions leave from the Marina of Bonifacio every 15 minutes for the sea caves and the Grain de Sable (duration: 1 hour). W www.bonifacio.fr

Capo Pertusato Lighthouse

Clearly visible at night from the coast of Sardinia, this lighthouse was built on the southernmost point of Corsica.

Craggy Cliffs

The cliffs near Bonifacio have many fine belvederes from which the beauty of this splendid coastline can be fully enjoyed. Among the birds that nest in this wild stretch are shags, herring gulls and the rare Andouin's gull.

Capo Pertusato

Viewed from the sea, the southernmost point of Corsica appears quite rugged and shaped by the waves. A view from the land highlights a colossal cave carved out of the limestone. Capo Pertusato was named after this natural opening – in Genoese dialect, the language of the former rulers of Bonifacio, the word pertusato means "perforated".

Bonifacio: the Îles Lavezzi

Continuing along the coast after Capo Pertusato, the cliffs remain quite high, and the few beaches here can only be reached via steep paths. Past the Pointe de Sperone, the view opens on to the group of the Îles Lavezzi and Île Cavallo. This fascinating archipelago is made up of granitic-rock islands fringed by small sandy beaches. Inland, although the scenery appears to be extremely barren, there are plenty of endemic plant species. The Îles Lavezzi lie in the middle of a large marine reserve and mooring is strictly regulated. Today, there are about 20 people working here, including park wardens and marine biologists.

Aerial view of Île Cavallo, with its runway in the middle

Capo Pertusato

An exclusive golf club, the Sperone (see p185), is situated on the promontory.

Granite and Limestone
Shortly after Pointe de Sperone is the "border" between granite and limestone formations. Here the layers of white rock are lined with pink granitic crevices. The vegetation also changes, with limestone shrubs giving way to maquis.

The *Sémillante* Shipwreck

The Straits of Bonifacio have been the dramatic scene of many shipwrecks. One of the most famous was that of the *Sémillante*, a French frigate that set sail from Toulon in February 1855 with a crew of 301 to take 392 French soldiers to Crimea. On the night of 15 February a terrifying storm caused the ship to crash against the rocks of Île Lavezzi. The *Sémillante* sank quickly and there were no survivors. The bodies found were buried in the two small cemeteries of Lavezzi. A year after the tragedy, a monument commemorating the victims of this shipwreck was built on one of the island's promontories.

The monument to the victims of the *Sémillante* shipwreck, on a promontory of Lavezzi

VISITORS' CHECKLIST

Road map C6.
2 Rue Fred Scamaroni, Bonifacio (04 95 73 11 88).
excursions from the Marina of Bonifacio, with frequent departures for Îles Lavezzi (duration: 3 hours).

Pointe de Sperone
This wind-beaten, maquis-covered promontory is a perfect example of the untamed nature of this stretch of coast. Many sea birds nest and live here.

Île Cavallo
This beautiful island is private property. Hidden among the rocks and low vegetation are luxury villas, and there is even a small airport. Mooring is forbidden along the entire coastline.

The islet of San Bainsu was used by the ancient Romans as a granite quarry.

Cormorants and Corsican gulls find ideal nesting places among the rocks of Lavezzi.

The flora on Lavezzi includes endemic species, the presence of which is somewhat of a mystery. Some of these exist only here, in Australia and in South Africa.

Île Lavezzi
Like the rest of the archipelago, this island is a nature reserve. Little more than a rock, it is full of fascinating stone formations but also has a range of flora and fauna that is interesting from a scientific point of view.

The Marina of Bonifacio, dominated by the massive Bastion de l'Étendard ▷

Tappa ❷

Road map C6. ℹ️ *Rue Camille de Rocca Serra, Porto-Vecchio (04 95 70 09 58).* 🔘 *daily.*

T HE IMPRESSIVE *casteddu (see p39)* of Tappa stands about 7 km (4 miles) from Bonifacio, in the village of Ceccia. This Neolithic settlement, which consists of fortified dwellings built around two gigantic structures, went through some difficult times in recent years, when it was treated as an open-air quarry. Tappa was saved from a worse fate by a private citizen who bought the land to protect it.

From above, the plan of the site reveals stretches of walls that were added to fortify the natural defence of the small settlement. On the basis of their finds, archaeologists have established that Tappa was already inhabited by the Torréens *(see p37)*, so called because of their tower structures, in the second millennium BC, which makes this one of the most ancient settlements in Corsica.

On the southwestern side of the settlement is a round, non-fortified monument dating from 1350 BC. Access was gained via a steep rock-cut stairway. A round cell in the interior was used to preserve foodstuffs and other valuable materials. Besides serving as a store-house, this monument was probably also used as a place of worship and as a watchtower.

Boats moored in the sheltered port of Porto-Vecchio

Porto-Vecchio ❸

Road map C6. 🏠 *8,400.* 🚌 🚢 *from Genoa, Livorno, Marseille, 04 95 70 06 03.* ℹ️ *Rue Camille de Rocca Serra (04 95 70 09 58).*

I T WAS THE GENOESE governors of the Bank of St George *(see pp44–5)* who decided, in the early 16th century, to found Porto-Vecchio. Its function was to fill a long gap in the series of strongholds on the coastline between Bastia and Bonifacio. Porto-Vecchio was also known as the "City of Salt" after its most precious natural resource. However, due to its proximity to the marshes created by the Stabiacciu and Osu rivers, Porto-Vecchio was plagued by malaria for centuries.

Around 1553, the period of the revolt headed by Sampiero Corso *(see p45)*, Porto-Vecchio became a refuge for pirates; then, until the mid-1900s, the town lived off the cork industry and the local salt works.

At the end of World War II thorough land reclamation stemmed the danger of malaria, paving the way for future development, such as tourism, small industries and commerce. Porto-Vecchio is now an important town, famous above all for the lovely beaches in its vicinity. In the upper part of town there are still traces of the Genoese fortifications and in the historic centre, in the summer, tourists flock to the many outdoor cafés and restaurants.

ENVIRONS: Along the southern coast of the Golfe de Porto-Vecchio there is a series of very popular tourist resorts. Past the watershed that ends at **Punta di a Chiappa** are the famous white sand beaches of **Palombaggia** and **Santa Giulia** *(see p19)*, which face the Îles Cerbicale reserve.

The beach at Palombaggia, south of Porto-Vecchio

Massif de l'Ospédale ❹

Road map C5.
ℹ️ *Rue Camille de Rocca Serra, Porto-Vecchio (04 95 70 09 58).*

B EHIND THE TOWN of Porto-Vecchio is a large wooded and rocky region that offers panoramic views of the sea and many fine footpaths.

The village of **Ospédale** lies 800 m (2,600 ft) above sea level, halfway up the mountain of the same name. It may owe its name (hospital) to the fact that, in the past, affluent Porto-Vecchio families used to come here to spend the hot season away from the unhealthy marshes.

The panorama from here includes a broad section of the coastline below.

The ruins of the *casteddu* at Tappa, a prehistoric settlement

The artificial lake below the peaks of the Massif de l'Ospédale

One of the recommended hikes starts from the hamlet of **Cartalavonu**, 4 km (2 miles) further up the hill, and leads to the 1,315-m (4,300-ft) high **A Vacca Morta** peak, which offers marvellous views.

Beyond Ospédale, a maritime pine forest spreads out, covering the entire massif and surrounding the artificial lake of Ospédale. The whole area is part of the Parc Naturel Régional *(see p99)*.

Arraggio (Araghju) ❺

Road map C5.
🛈 *Rue Camille de Rocca Serra, Porto-Vecchio (04 95 70 09 58).*

NORTH OF PORTO-VECCHIO, towards the interior and the hills, the small hamlet of Arraggio is the departure point for a steep walkway leading to the nearby *casteddu (see p39)*. This mule track is quite narrow and hard to climb, ascending without a break along a stony ridge. Then, suddenly, the loose stones

and sheepfolds are interrupted by the light-coloured walls of a massive fortress standing on a rocky spur. The walls of the *casteddu* of Arraggio are about 4 m (13 ft) high and 2 m (6 ft) thick. The megalithic complex inside the fortifications consists of a series of rooms that in prehistoric times (16th–12th centuries BC) served as living quarters, kitchen and storehouse for foodstuffs. Close-up these structures are reminiscent of the great prehistoric nuraghi complexes in Sardinia. From here there is a splendid view of the gulf and the countryside around Porto-Vecchio.

Punta Fautea ❻

Road map D5. 🛈 *Solenzara (04 95 57 43 75).*

NORTH OF THE low coastline of the gulf of Porto-Vecchio is the Cala Rossa promontory, which marks the beginning of a rocky stretch interspersed by a few beaches, including the beautiful **Plage de Pinarellu**. About 20 km

(12 miles) from Porto-Vecchio, towards Solenzara, is the turn-off for Punta Fautea. Here, not far from the main road, is a restored **Genoese watchtower** built in the late 16th century and partly destroyed by fire in 1650.

From here to Solenzara is the **Côte des Nacres**, a rocky coast with many coves, crystal-clear waters and fascinating sea floors. The name of this coast derives from the large triangular shells that can be found locally. They are as much as 50 cm (20 in) long and the inside is covered by a thin layer similar to mother-of-pearl (*nacre* in French).

Mermaid mural at the port of Solenzara

Solenzara ❼

Road map D5. 🚶 *1,200.*
🛈 *04 95 57 43 75.*

WHAT WAS ONCE only a tiny hamlet at the mouth of the Solenzara torrent has become one the most lively and well-appointed tourist resorts in southeast Corsica. Solenzara has a port that can take in about 450 boats and a sandy beach bounded by eucalyptus trees. **Sari**, a tiny hamlet above Solenzara, overlooks the plain and is worth visiting for the splendid views of the Bavella.

The restored ruins of the 16th-century Genoese watchtower at Punta Fautea

Col de Bavella

A moufflon

THE JAGGED PINNACLES of the Aiguilles de Bavella make for one of the most thrilling landscapes in Corsica. This group of needle-shaped peaks lies at the foot of the Monte Incudine massif, which, at 2,134 m (7,001 ft), is the highest mountain range in south Corsica. The road going over the Col de Bavella passes through rocks that glow red at sunset, pine groves and meadows covered with thyme flowers in spring, and offers one of the most breathtaking views in Corsica. The area boasts many footpaths, including the southernmost stretch of the GR20 *(see pp20–25)* and the more demanding alpine route through the Aiguilles themselves.

One of the marvellous views from the Trou de la Bombe

Laricio pines are very tall. They often live for a considerable time; many are three or four centuries old and some have even reached the venerable age of 800 years. In the past the pine trunks were used to build ships.

Calamint in Bloom
When spring arrives, the meadows lining the road and the footpaths take on the pink colour of calamint flowers, which bumblebees love for their abundant nectar.

THE TROU DE LA BOMBE

There are several holes *(tafoni, see p101)* created by wind erosion in the hard rocks of Corsica. Expertise in hiking or climbing is not necessary to get to the Trou de la Bombe, a hole about 9 m (30 ft) high at the Punta Tafonata di Paliri. The walk, which takes a couple of hours there and back, starts off from the U Canone fountain, a short distance beyond the Col de Bavella in the direction of Solenzara. From here a forest road, then a footpath with red markings lead to a rocky amphitheatre and then to the base of the huge *tafone*. From here the view of Monte Incudine and of the pines among the rock crevices is remarkable.

Approaching the Trou de la Bombe

VISITORS' CHECKLIST

Road map C5.
🛈 *Office du Tourisme de l'Alta Rocca, Zonza.*
📞 *04 95 78 56 33.*
GR20 long-distance path
🛈 *Parc Naturel Régional de la Corse, 2 Sergent Casalonga, Ajaccio (04 95 51 79 00).*
🖳 www.parc-naturel-corse.com

Aiguilles de Bavella

The rugged needles of these peaks are a real favourite with hikers and rock climbers. Those with no head for heights can enjoy the spectacular beauty of the Aiguilles while travelling along the D268 road.

The Aiguilles massif is the habitat of many species of birds of prey. Moufflons (called *muvrini* in the Corsican language) can also be spotted.

Paths and Signs

The many hiking itineraries in this area are all well marked. Easy-to-read wooden signs show the altitudes and distances of the hikes, while other markings painted on rocks or trees indicate the direction to take.

The shrubs are a sign that the wooded area is ending to give way to alpine meadowlands.

Inspiring Landscape

The Bavella area has always been popular, even at the time when tourism was only for the privileged few. Edward Lear, the English artist and traveller, depicted the region in this 1870 watercolour called Forest of Bavella, Corsica.

The village of Zonza; in the background, the famous profile of the Aiguilles de Bavella

Zonza ❾

Road map C5. 🏚 1,800. 🚌
ℹ️ Office du Tourisme de l'Alta
Rocca, Zonza (04 95 78 56 33).

IN THE MIDDLE of the Alta
Rocca region, among pine
and oak forests and high along
the course of the Asinao river,
is Zonza. During the summer
this small town, with the bulk
of the Aiguilles de Bavella in
the background, is a magnet
for those who love outdoor
activities. Along the main
street are shops selling guides
with descriptions of climbing,
rafting, trout fishing and hiking
itineraries. There are also many
associations of tourist guides.

In 1953, the sultan
Mohammed V of Morocco
lived in Zonza in exile, but
the climate proved too harsh
for him, and he asked to be
transferred to L'Île Rousse
(see p74), on the north coast.

Cascade Piscia di Gallo ❿

Road map C5. ℹ️ Office du Tourisme
de l'Alta Rocca, Zonza (04 95 78 56 33).

ALTHOUGH THE Cascade
Piscia di Gallo can only
be reached on foot, it is
possible to park in the
vicinity, near the top of the
D368 road leading to the pass
of the Massif de l'Ospédale.

After some streams is a
larger watercourse, where,
over time, the current has
sculpted large round pools,
commonly known as

Marmitte dei Giganti.
Further along the path, the
river suddenly rushes through
a narrow rock crevice, creating
a waterfall that is about 46 m
(150 ft) high. The best viewpoint for the Cascade Piscia
di Gallo can be reached by
following the path that goes
around the rocks and then
descends to the right. The
whole walk will take about 90
minutes to the viewpoint and
back and for a long stretch
consists of rocky terrain,
so suitable hiking boots or
robust shoes should be worn.

Quenza ⓫

Road map C5. 🏚 750. ℹ️ Office
du Tourisme de l'Alta Rocca, Zonza
(04 95 78 56 33).

THIS VILLAGE AT THE FOOT of
the ascent leading to the
Col de Bavella is surrounded
by a thick oak and chestnut

The façade of the Chapelle de
Ste-Marie, just outside Quenza

forest. Quenza has two
churches, **St-Georges**, in the
village, has a pulpit carved in
the form of a Moor's Head
supported by sea monsters.
The second church, the
Romanesque **Chapelle de
Ste-Marie**, was founded
around the year 1000 and
stands on the road to Aullène.

Levie ⓬

Road map C5. 🏚 2,200. 🚌
ℹ️ Office du Tourisme de l'Alta
Rocca, Zonza (04 95 78 56 33).

THE AREA AROUND Levie, a
short distance from the
Aiguilles de Bavella, is one
of the most interesting
prehistoric zones in Corsica,
with many important sites
unearthed by digs.

Levie also houses one of the
main archaeological museums
in Corsica. Recently moved to
a new and more modern
home, the **Musée Départemental de Levie** boasts the
famous *Dame de Bonifacio*,
the skeleton of an old woman
who was buried in 6570 BC.
It is the most ancient relic of
the island's past. The museum
also features a fascinating
display of cardial ware
(named after the decorative
patterns carved with the use
of the sharp edges of the
Cardium cockle shell; see
p38), skeletons of small
mammals and an ancestor
of the cow. The explanations
and descriptions given by
the museum staff are very
enlightening and offer a

The ancestor of the cow at the Musée Départemental de Levie

better understanding of the evolution of prehistoric civilization on the island.

🏛 Musée Départemental de Levie
📞 04 95 78 47 98. ⬜ Tue–Sat (Jul–Sep: daily). ⬛ public hols. 🖼

ENVIRONS: About 8 km (5 miles) from Levie, across the deep Fiumicicoli river valley, is **Carbini**. It was in this small village that, around the end of the Middle Ages, the religious sect of the Giovannali was founded (1352) and thrived. Inspired by St John the Baptist and founded by Giovanni Martini, a Franciscan monk from Marseille, this cult found fertile ground in Carbini and then spread throughout the island. The meeting place of the followers was the Pisan Romanesque church of St-Jean-Baptiste, which was built in the 14th century. The church is flanked by a structure – still visible – thought to correspond to the foundations of an earlier church dedicated to San Quilico and destroyed during the tragic repression of the Giovannali. As a result of the 1362 crusade ordered by Pope Urban V against the "satanic heretics", the members of this sect were burned at the stake at the foot of the Monte Kyrie Eleison, the name of which (Greek for "Lord, have mercy") has a particularly poignant ring in this context.

Cucuruzzu and Capula ⑬

Road map C5. 🛈 *Maison d'Accueil des Sites Archéologiques, Office du Tourisme de l'Alta Rocca, Zonza (04 95 78 56 33).* ⬜ *Apr–Oct: daily. By request during the other months.* 🖼⬛🔲

THE VISIT to the archaeological site of Cucuruzzu and the medieval castle of Capula is organized as a pleasant walk in the oak and chestnut forest on the plateau.

Right by the ticket office, where audio-guides are handed out, is the start of a mule track. The ruins of Cucuruzzu appear after a 15-minute walk. This *casteddu (see p39)*, with its wall, fireplaces, and inner stairway leading to the upper levels, dates from the second millennium BC. Digs carried out in the 1960s brought to light an entire citadel covering a surface area of 1,200 sq m (12,900 sq ft). Some of the enormous blocks that make up the citadel's walls weigh more than one tonne.

Once back on the trail, a short walk leads to the Chapelle San Lorenzo, which was built using stone blocks from an earlier church, the ruins of which can also be seen here.

A short distance above these are the ruins of the medieval castle of Capula, a Roman fortification that was destroyed in 1259 by Giudice della Rocca, who had been made count of Corsica

The bell tower at Carbini

by the Pisans. This site of Capula had already been inhabited in prehistoric times, as confirmed by the nearby menhir-statue of an armed prehistoric warrior (Capula I), which was unearthed during the course of archaeological digs.

Ste-Lucie de Tallano ⑭

Road map C5. 🏠 *520.* 🛈 *Office du Tourisme de l'Alta Rocca, Zonza (04 95 78 56 33).*

ON THE ROAD descending west from the Alta Rocca plateau towards the Golfe de Valinco, is the village of Ste-Lucie de Tallano, famous for its **Couvent St-François**, a monastery founded in 1492 by the local lord, Rinuccio della Rocca. St-François is now being restored.

On the village square is the church of **Ste-Lucie**, which contains a beautiful Catalan-style altarpiece with Christ, St Peter and St Paul in the middle, and three small figures of saints below them. The altarpiece is attributed to the Master of Castelsardo, an artist from the late 15th to the early 16th centuries who probably came from the large Franciscan monastery of Castelsardo, in Sardinia. The church of Ste-Lucie also boasts a *Crucifixion*, which some art historians have attributed to the same artist.

🔐 Ste-Lucie
⬜ *ask for the keys at the only café in the square.*

View of the hamlet of Ste-Lucie de Tallano

The austere grey houses of Sartène perched on the rocks

Sartène ⑮

Road map C5. 🏚 *3,600.* 🚌
ℹ️ *Cours Soeur Amélie (04 95 77 15 40).* 🎭 *Catenacciu Procession (Good Friday).*

PROSPER MERIMÉE, who in the mid-1800s was the Inspector of Antiquities in Corsica, described Sartène as "the most Corsican of Corsican towns". Located in the middle of an area rich in prehistoric ruins, this town with a history of vendettas lies halfway up the hill in the valley of the Rizzanese river.

The old town has a maze of narrow streets lined with dark-coloured houses as well as many aristocratic mansions. The alleyways are often surmounted by arches and vaults.

On Good Friday evening, the Baroque church of **Ste-Marie**, in Place de la Libération, is the starting point for the Catenacciu Procession *(see p32).* One of the most ancient religious ceremonies in Corsica, it re-enacts the crucifixion walk to the Golgotha. The *Catenacciu* ("chained one") represents the Great Penitent. After spending two fasting days in isolation, he dons the traditional long red tunic and a hood covering his face while bearing the Cross and heavy chains through the streets. The White Penitent, who represents Simon of Cyrene, helps him carry the large oak cross, while behind them eight black-clad figures bear the

statue of the Dead Christ. A traditional chant, "*Perdonu miu Diu*" (Forgive me, Lord), accompanies the slowly moving procession, which comes to a halt back in front of the church where it started. After the blessing, the ceremony ends.

Sartène is also worth a visit for the **Musée de Préhistoire Corse et d'Archéologie**, which is similar to the one in Levie *(see pp124–5)* and features the long, ancient history of the island. The museum will soon be transferred to a larger, more modern building. Among the items on display, the cardial ware *(see p38)* is worth a look, as are the obsidian

arrowheads from Sardinia and the collection of funerary vases dating from the second and first millennia BC.

🏛️ **Musée de Préhistoire Corse et d'Archéologie**
1 Rue Croce. 📞 *04 95 77 01 09.*
⛔ *Closed until further notice. Call for updated information.* 📷

Roccapina ⑯

Road map B6.

ABOUT 25 KM (16 miles) south of Sartène, on the N196 road towards Bonifacio, a terrace on a hilltop affords a fine panoramic view of the Golfe di Roccapina and the Pointe de Roccapina promontory, with its characteristic pink granite rocks, which were inhabited in prehistoric times. One of these rocks, which is flanked by a massive Genoese tower, looks very much like a colossal crouching lion, hence the name **Le Lion de Roccapina**, or Lion's Rock.

View of the Golfe di Roccapina

HANDMADE KNIVES

With their curved blades and handles that fit perfectly in the hand, knives have always been one of the shepherds' most indispensable work tools. Traditionally, the top of the blade also had a sawtoothed section and the handle was made of wood or goat's horn. Called *cursina* in the local language, this type of knife is now protected by a registered trademark and is still handmade by a dozen craftsmen. Their size and the ratio between the blade and handle have always been the same, but the artisans' creativity has led to the use of new materials. Thus, the blades are now made of damask steel and the handles range from white cedar to manta-ray skin. Corsican tradition has also produced the *runchetta*, a jackknife, and the *temperinu*, a small, pointed knife. Most famous of all is the *stiletto*, which, along with pistols, was part of the bandits' arsenal in the 19th

Two *cursine*, typical knives

century and is now sold as a souvenir, with the word "Vendetta" carved on it.

Tour of the Megaliths of Cauria ⑰

IN THE REGION OF SARTÈNE ALONE, after almost two centuries of archaeological research, no fewer than 500 prehistoric sites have been explored. According to the experts, the southern part of Corsica was much more densely populated than the north in prehistoric times. A tour of the barren plateau of Cauria, south of Sartène, allows the chance to visit some of the island's most important sites with megalithic monuments (see p39), which here are in the form of alignments. Although it is not easy to reach Palaggiu, it is worth the effort, because this is one of the most important menhir alignments in the world.

TIPS FOR DRIVERS

ℹ Cours Soeur Amélie, Sartène (04 95 77 15 40).
Length of tour: from Sartène to Palaggiu, ca 15 km (9 miles); from D48-A turn-off to Stantari, ca 5 km (3 miles). **Duration**: 1 day. **Stopping-off points**: Sartène and Tizzano.

Palaggiu ①
With its 258 menhirs, discovered in the late 1800s, Palaggiu is an amazing sight. About 5 km (3 miles) after the Cauria turn-off on the D48 road, on the right is a mule track marked by a metal gate. A 20-minute walk leads to the "stone forest".

SARTÈNE

0 kilometres | 1
0 miles | 0.5

TIZZANO
Avena

Stantari ②
Tall, pink at sunset and made smooth by animals rubbing against them, the Stantari menhirs have traces of faces and weapons.

Chiusu di a casa

KEY

▬ Tour footpath
═ Other roads

Fontanaccia ④
Discovered in 1840 by Prosper Merimée, then Inspector of Antiquities in Corsica, this is the island's best-preserved dolmen. It stands about 100 m (320 ft) from the parking area.

Renaghju ③
Here is the most ancient Neolithic settlement in Corsica, with two alignments of menhirs. The most ancient ones date from 4000 BC; around their bases are remains of round fireplaces.

The tranquil bay of Campomoro, with its crystal-clear sea

Campomoro ⓲

Road map B5. 🏠 *260.* 🛈 *Port de Plaisance, Propriano (04 95 76 01 49).*
Tour de Campomoro
⭕ *summer: daily.*

Sᴵᴛᴜᴀᴛᴇᴅ ᴏɴ the south coast of the Golfe de Valinco, the small village of Campomoro is a peaceful place to relax, even during the tourist season.

A ten-minute walk along a well-marked path dotted with informative signs leads to the door of the **Tour de Campomoro**, built in the 16th century by the Genoese. This fortress, the largest in Corsica, allows visitors to explore the interior of a typical defensive tower and offers magnificent views of the gulf.

Another splendid coastal path running south from Campomoro has recently been inaugurated.

The round Genoese tower at Campomoro

Propriano ⓳

Road map B5. 🏠 *3,500.* 🚌
🛈 *Port de Plaisance (04 95 76 01 49).* Ⓦ *www.propriano.net*

Tʜᴇ ᴛᴏᴡɴ of Propriano lies at the innermost point of the Golfe de Valinco, tucked in between the green hills behind it and the transparent blue sea. It is a popular yacht harbour and seaside resort thanks to the beautiful beaches and coves dotting the gulf.

Because of its strategic position, Propriano was much sought after throughout its history. In ancient times it developed as a famous port, and as a landing place and trade centre for Etruscans, Greeks, Carthaginians and Romans, especially in the 2nd century BC. In the 1980s, while restructuring work was being carried out on the port, numerous remains from this period were found.

During the Middle Ages Propriano was governed first by the Pisans and, then, from 1230 onwards, by the Genoese. In 1563 Sampiero Corso (*see p45*) landed here and initiated a period of anti-Genoa revolts. His actions, however, proved to be disastrous for Propriano, because the village was then left at the mercy of pirate raids and virtually destroyed. The same period also saw the demise of the beautiful Santa Giulia di Tavaria abbey, mentioned in chronicles but now in ruins.

In the 19th century Propriano came to life again, becoming a commercial port for the entire region, a role consolidated in the early 20th century.

Now the village is a lively tourist locality.

The beautiful beaches and well-developed facilities make it one of the leading resorts on the island.

Eɴᴠɪʀᴏɴs: About 9 km (6 miles) from Propriano, going northwest on the N196 road, is **Olmeto**, a large hamlet 870 m (2,850 ft) above sea level that dominates the gulf. Just above the village are the ruins of the **Castello della Rocca**, the fortress that Arrigo della Rocca used as a base when he began his rebellion against the Genoese rulers. In 1376–90, he governed the entire island, leaving only Bonifacio and Calvi to the foreign invaders.

The white lighthouse at Propriano looming over the sea

Porto-Pollo ⓴

Road map B5. 🏠 *340.*
🚌 🛈 *Office du Tourisme de Sollacaro (04 95 74 07 64).*

Aᴛ ᴛʜᴇ ᴍᴏᴜᴛʜ of the Taravo river, Porto-Pollo is a small seaside resort. During the summer it is popular with people who are attracted by the tranquillity of the place and its delightful beach along the Golfe de Valinco.

Not far from the village, on top of the Pointe de Porto-Pollo, is the Genoese **Tour de Capriona**.

The sea and sea bed along the promontory are very popular with scuba divers, who love to dive down to the so-called *cathédrales*, rocky pinnacles at a depth of about 10 m (32 ft).

Filitosa ㉑

Road map B5. ℹ️ *Office du Tourisme de Sollacaro (04 95 74 07 64).* ◯ *Apr–Oct: daily; Nov–Mar: by appointment (04 95 74 00 91).* 🗓️

THE MOST FAMOUS prehistoric site in Corsica is managed with great care by the heirs of Charles-Antoine Cesari, who made the first discoveries here in 1946.

Filitosa offers almost 5,000 years of history. Populated in very ancient times because it was both fertile and easy to defend, the area was filled with large constructions and menhirs from 1800 BC to 1100 BC. The fortified town dominated the valley of the small Taravo river. It was here, among the stones of one of the structure's walls, that one of the most significant alignments of

The front of Filitosa V

anthropomorphic menhirs *(see below)* was found. Details of the faces, weapons and helmets of ancient warriors are still clearly visible on the surface of these rocks.

Most of the ruins of Filitosa date from between the late second millennium BC and 700 BC. With the rise of Christianity, the menhirs were considered pagan and therefore destroyed. Their remains were heaped together in piles, like mere stones, and had to wait many centuries to be rediscovered.

The tour of Filitosa begins with a splendid statue (Filitosa V) standing on the track that leads to the fortified settlement, also known as *oppidum.* Here are the ruins of a village and three monuments, the middle one

Detail of the central monument

of which is well preserved. Below, in a small valley, is the quarry where the stone for the sculpture was extracted. Some statues found in the surroundings have been placed around the quarry.

Next to the entrance to the site is a small museum that illustrates the history of the site. It displays fragments of three menhir statues, the most famous of which is the Scalsa Murta menhir (1400 BC). Armour and weapons can be seen on these menhirs, as well as holes on the upper part of the head, probably where ornamental ox horns were placed.

THE EVOLUTION OF THE ANTHROPOMORPHIC MENHIRS

Megalithic monuments, used to worship the dead in the Neolithic era (6000–2000 BC), were found on five Mediterranean islands: Corsica, Sardinia, Malta, Majorca and Minorca.

The Corsican megalithic culture (3500–1000 BC) is divided into three periods – Megalithic I, II and III – which show an evolution in burial practices. The early subterranean tombs on mounds of earth sealed with long stone slabs were replaced by outdoor monuments known as dolmens, consisting of horizontal monoliths representing the souls of the deceased.

In the Megalithic III period, which, in turn, is divided into six stages, the horizontal

monolith becomes a vertical anthropomorphic statue, that is, one resembling a human.

These statues have different features, depending on the populations that sculpted them. In the period of invasions, for example, they were armed, but later they became plain again. Near the end of

The front of Filitosa IV

Megalithic III the so-called Torréens *(see p37)* settled in Corsica, introducing tower-like structures. Over time these towers replaced the anthropomorphic statues.

Statues of Stages 5 and 6 of the Megalithic III period. The statues seen below are among the most famous in Corsica. They were named after the localities in which they were discovered; their numbers indicate that more than one statue was found on the same site.

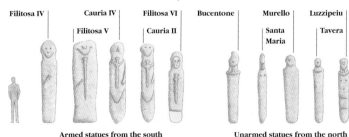

Filitosa IV | Cauria IV | Filitosa VI | Bucentone | Murello | Luzzipeiu
Filitosa V | Cauria II | | Santa Maria | Tavera

Armed statues from the south | **Unarmed statues from the north**

CORTE AND THE INTERIOR

THE ANCIENT ROMANS *who conquered Corsica in 259 BC were aware of the strategic importance of Corte as the geographical heart of the island. Originally a fortress, the city soon became the symbol of all Corsica and its struggle for independence, the home of the island's parliament, university and national heroes. Corte is also the starting point for excursions into the valleys in the interior.*

The colours of the sea, the jagged coastline and the iridescent sea beds are perhaps the best-known features of Corsica. But also deserving of a visit are the mountains inland, which, with Monte Cinto, reach a height of 2,706 m (8,877 ft). Traversed by valleys and paths leading to refuges, in the summer the mountains are ideal for a wide range of hiking excursions.

In the middle of this natural setting made up of rocks, spring waters and forests, lies Corte. The town's fortunate geographic location meant that on several occasions potential conquerors, including the Romans, had to stop short of this region. In the 18th century, Corsica's first National Constitution was drafted here and ever since then Corte has been the symbol of the island, of its culture and yearning for independence. From its Citadelle, which is the home of the Musée de la Corse, there are commanding views of the surrounding territory. To the west are the wildest valleys and tallest peaks; to the east are hills covered with woods, small villages and remains of the past. These hills descend towards the sea of Aléria, the first Roman colony in Corsica. The regions of Bozio, Fiumorbo and Castagniccia (named after its rich chestnut groves) have a series of chapels and churches that bear witness to various artistic styles and that reach in the Romanesque church of La Canonica and the Baroque church of La Porta the apogee of Corsican religious tradition.

Fresco decoration in the small church of San Pantaleo, Castagniccia

◁ **Punta Larghia, one of the peaks in the Haut-Asco area**

Exploring Corte and the Interior

CORTE IS THE GEOGRAPHIC HEART of Corsica, as well as its cultural centre. The city is skirted by a region of tall, rugged mountains forming the very backbone of the island: Monte Rotondo, Monte d'Oro and Monte Renoso stand southwest of Corte, while Monte Cinto and Capo Tafonato are northwest of the city. To the northeast, descending towards the coast, are the hilly regions of Bozio and Castagniccia, where, from the period of Genoese domination (late 12th century) onwards, the less harsh terrain favoured the birth of many small villages. The area surrounding Corte is also known for its gastronomy, which includes game, wild boar and traditional cheeses.

KEY

▦	Major road
▧	Minor road
▨	Scenic route
▬	River

L'Île Rousse

ST-FRANÇ DE CACC

Melaja   *Tartagine*

VALLÉE DE L'ASCO ❶

L'Asco

D147

● *HAUT-ASCO*

SCALA DI S. RE

Golo

❷❷ *CALACUCCIA*

CASAMACCIOLI ❷❸

FORÊT DE VALDU-NIELLU

COL DE VERGHIO ❷❺   *D84* ❷❹

❿ *GORGES DU TAVIGNANO* D

Tavignano

Res

GO L

RESTO

Vec

Porto ←

P A R C   N A T U R E L
R É G I O N A L
D E   L A   C O R S E

FORÊT DE VIZZAVON
❹

Cruzini

CASCADE DES ❻
ANGLAIS

❺

N193

COL DE VIZZAVONA

Soveria, a village in the vicinity of Corte, with a
view of the magnificent mountains in the background

Ajaccio

Prunelli

Sart

GETTING AROUND

Corte lies on the N193 road, which, coming from Ajaccio, crosses the Col de Vizzavona in the inland valleys. North of Corte, at Ponte Leccia, the N193 divides, going either northeast in the direction of Bastia (N193) or north to L'Île Rousse and Calvi (N1197 and N197). Other roads branch off from this main artery, traversing the splendid side valleys both west, towards the mountains, and east, towards Bozio and Castagniccia. An enjoyable way to travel to Corte from Bastia or Ajaccio is to take the small train – jokingly called the TGV, or Train of Great Vibrations – which stops at almost all the stations along the way.

Bastia ↑

LA CANONICA 16

N193

Golo

18 PONTE-NOVO

VESCOVATO 17

● PONTE LECCIA

N197

D71

D41

D506

LA PORTA 13

CASTAGNICCIA

12

D71

D330

VALLÉE DE ALESANI 14

CERVIONE 15

D71

N198

TE

D41

D14

2 BOZIO

N200

D314

D14

ENACO

N200

VALLÉE DU TAVIGNANO 9

Bravona

Tavignano

RIO

Tegnone

N200

Arena

Étang de Diane

 GHISONI

D69

D344

8 ALÉRIA

D343

Varagno

Étang d'Urbino

Fium'Orbu

D344

D345

7 FIUMORBO

N198

Travo

Bonifacio ↓

0 kilometres   10

0 miles   5

Horses in high pastures near Calacuccia, in the valley of the Verghio

Corte ❶

L OCATED IN THE HEART OF CORSICA, Corte was fortified in 1419 by the viceroy of Aragón, Vincentello d'Istria. Later, it was ruled intermittently by the Genoese and the French. In 1735 it became the cradle of Corsican patriotism when the constitution for an independent state was drafted here. In 1755, when Corsica was liberated by Pascal Paoli, Corte became its capital. Ten years later Paoli founded the island's first university here.
Corte still maintains a proud spirit of nationalism. It is part of the city's charm and can be discovered through a walk in the old town and a tour of the Citadelle. The latter, the symbol of the military power of past ages, is now home to the Musée de la Corse, one of the leading centres of Corsican culture. A hike to the Belvedere overlooking the Gorges du Tavignano and the Gorges de la Restonica reveals the natural beauty of the area.

The nave in the Église de l'Annonciation

Place Gaffori and the monument to the hero of the taking of Corte

🏛 Place Paoli

At the foot of the upper city (*haute ville*) is a large and lively square named after Pascal Paoli (*see p47*). Laid out in the early 20th century by Huguenin, the centre of the square features a large monument to the patriot and hero of Corsican independence.

🏛 Place Gaffori

West of Place Paoli are the ramps of Rue Scoliscia, which lead to the heart of the city and Place Gaffori. In the middle of this square is the statue commemorating General Jean-Pierre Gaffori. On the pedestal are two bas-reliefs depicting his feats and those of his brave wife Faustina (*see p46*). Also on the square are the Église de l'Annonciation and the house where Gaffori was born.

🔒 Église de l'Annonciation

Place Gaffori. ◯ *daily.*
Founded around the mid-15th century, this church is one of the oldest buildings in Corte. However, the façade as it stands today dates from the 18th century. Commissioned by Alexandre Sauli, who later became bishop of Aléria, it has five pilasters with Corinthian capitals. The tall, slender bell tower that dominates the entire quarter is Baroque. Inside the church is a series of Baroque statues and an altar made of the local grey marble.
A short, steep descent along Rue Feracci leads to a pretty Baroque mansion known as Maison Palazzi.

🔒 Ste-Croix

Rampe Ste-Croix. ◯ *daily.*
Past the Maison Palazzi is the austere façade of the 17th-century church of Ste-Croix. The pillarless nave has a barrel vault and an aisle paved in grey marble. By the altar is a colourful Baroque retable and a large medallion with a relief of the *Madonna of the Apocalypse.*
This church is also the home of the Ste-Croix Confraternity, which has always played a leading role in the religious life of the city.

JEAN-PIERRE GAFFORI

The hero of the Corsican independence movement along with Pascal Paoli, Jean-Pierre Gaffori was born in 1704 in Corte and studied medicine. In 1745, during the armed revolt against the Genoese occupation, he was elected as one of the triumvirate of the "Protectors of the Nation".
One of his exploits was the taking of Corte in 1746. According to local lore, during the battle against the Genoese troops, Gaffori realized that his enemies were using one of his sons as a shield. He was uncertain about what to do, but his courageous wife Faustina urged the Corsican patriots to continue attacking, allegedly shouting: "Don't think about my son, think about your country!" Made a general, Gaffori managed to conquer most of the island but was assassinated in an ambush organized by his brother, who was in the service of the Genoese. In the square named after him is his statue, and on the façade of his house, opposite the Église de l'Annonciation, there are still marks of the shots fired by the Genoese during the 1746 siege of Corte.

Statue of Jean-Pierre Gaffori

Fontaine des Quatre-Canons

A short descent along a ramp in front of the church leads to the square and the Fontaine des Quatre-Canons.

⊞ Fontaine des Quatre-Canons
Place des Quatre-Canons. Commissioned by Louis XVI, this fountain ("of the four cannons") was completed in 1778. Its purpose was to channel water from the Orta torrent to the city to furnish the local garrison with a sorely needed supply of water. From the square

ramps go up to the massive walls of the Citadelle (see pp136–7).

⊞ Place du Poilu
In front of the entrance to the bastions of the Citadelle is Place du Poilu, with the house where General Arrighi di Casanova, one of Napoleon Bonaparte's generals, was born. It was here that Napoleon's father lived and that his brother Joseph, who was to become king of Spain, was born in 1768.

The 17th-century Palais National, once the residence of the Genoese governors and then of Pascal Paoli, is where Corsican independence was declared. For 14 years (1755–69, see pp46–7) this palace was the home of the new Corsican parliament. It now houses the University Institute of Corsican Studies, a separate branch of the University of Corte, which is based in the Citadelle.

Plaque on the house where Joseph Bonaparte was born

VISITORS' CHECKLIST

Road map C3. 🏠 *5,700.*
🚌 🚉 *04 95 46 00 97.*
ℹ *Station Touristique de l'Intérieur, Citadelle (04 95 46 26 70).* 🎭 *Easter Procession (Thu–Good Fri); St Theophilus's Procession (19 May); Festival des Arts Sonnés (second weekend in May).*
🌐 *www.corte-tourisme.com*

⊞ Belvedere
Before visiting the Citadelle, it is worth making time for a walk along the uphill road that skirts its walls. This road leads to the platform of the Belvedere, which offers a magnificent view of the castle, the Nid d'Aigle ("eagle's nest") tower and, below this, the city and the confluence of the Tavignano and Restonica rivers.

From the Belvedere a steep path leads to the banks of the Tavignano river. The reward for making this trek is an impressive panoramic view over the rocky cliffs of the Citadelle.

CORTE TOWN CENTRE

0 metres   175
0 yards   175

KEY

ℹ Tourist information

🔆 Viewpoint

Corte: the Citadelle

ALREADY FORTIFIED before the Genoese conquest in the 13th century, the Citadelle was transformed into a true fortress in 1419. After many years of foreign rule, the Citadelle became the symbol of the islanders' struggle for independence, a struggle that took a giant leap forwards when Pascal Paoli established Corsica's first university here. When the French took control of Corsica in 1769, the Citadelle became a military zone. Today it houses part of the university, the Musée de la Corse and many historic archives, located in the old barracks on the lower level. On the upper level is the castle, with the Nid d'Aigle, the tallest tower, overlooking the Restonica and Tavignano valleys.

Moor's Head, Musée de la Corse

★ Castle
Built in 1419 on the southern tip of the rocky spur by Vincentello d'Istria, the castle is the oldest part of the Citadelle.

Upper level

The Fond Régional d'Art Contemporain is an institute that organizes shows of modern art of the region.

Nid d'Aigle
On top of the bastions, the Nid d'Aigle (eagle's nest) tower offers an impressive view of the precipitous walls of the Citadelle.

Entrance to the Citadelle
Austere and fortified, as befits a military structure, the entrance portal to the Citadelle is a simple arch surmounted by a tympanum.

STAR SIGHTS

★ **Musée de la Corse**

★ **Castle**

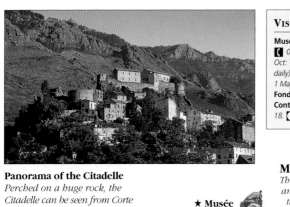

Panorama of the Citadelle
Perched on a huge rock, the Citadelle can be seen from Corte and the surrounding area. Many people consider it one of the symbols of Corsica.

VISITORS' CHECKLIST

Musée de la Corse & Citadelle
04 95 45 25 45. Apr–Oct: Tue–Sun (mid-Jun–mid-Sep: daily); Nov–Mar: Tue–Sat.
1 May, public hols.
Fond Régional d'Art Contemporain 04 95 46 22 18. Mon–Sat pm only.

EXPLORING THE MUSÉE DE LA CORSE

This museum houses a fine anthropological collection, the core of which consists of the objects gathered from the 1950s onwards by abbot Louis Doazan. On display are various relics of the island's past, from the costumes of the confraternities of Corte, Bonifacio and other towns, to farmers' work tools. An interesting feature are the booths where visitors can listen to the traditional religious and secular music of the region. The first floor hosts temporary exhibits, and the museum also organizes concerts of traditional Corsican music here. The Nid d'Aigle tower and its spectacular views can be reached by a short walk after exiting through the first-floor doors.

★ Musée de la Corse
The exhibition rooms are in the former Sérurier barracks, once used by the Foreign Legion.

Entrance to Musée de Corse

Sérurier barracks

Lower level

The bastions are in keeping with late 18th-century military architecture. The large casemates and terracing accommodated pieces of artillery that made the Citadelle virtually impregnable.

Padoue barracks

LINGUA DOPPIA MONDU DOPPIU
BILINGUISME
BISLINGUISIMU
DOUBLE LANGUE DOUBLE CULTURE

The University
The University of Corsica is the expression of the island's cultural distinctiveness, which is manifested especially in the language (see p30).

A Tour of Bozio ❷

THE HILLY REGIONS of Bozio and Castagniccia (*see pp146–7*), respectively east and northeast of the town of Corte, have many surprises in store for art lovers. Do not expect grandiose basilicas or majestic bell towers, however. The art in these areas consists of a series of chapels – sometimes in a tiny hamlet, sometimes in open countryside – that require a degree of patience to find, and just as much patience to track down the person with the keys (who is always quite courteous). The Bozio tourist office organizes tours of the chapels with frescoes in the area. The regions east of Corte are also worth exploring for their natural landscape, which features hills, gorges and winding valleys. The constant curves and hairpin turns make the average speed on these roads extremely low. However, those who are not deterred by this will be rewarded with beautiful views.

Omessa ②
This hamlet overlooks the Vallée du Golo. Its Chapelle de l'Annonciade, built in 1596, has a marble statue of the Virgin Mary. The Baroque bell tower of the church of St-André rises above the village roofs.

Chapelle St-Michel de Castirla ①
This pre-Romanesque chapel in the middle of the cemetery of Castirla, a village near Corte, houses the beautifully preserved symbols of the Evangelists, which flank the fresco of the *Majesty of Christ*, seen above.

Chapelle St-Nicolas ③
Just after Sermano, on the D41 road, is the dark-schist chapel of St-Nicolas. Built in the 7th century, this church boasts some of the best-preserved frescoes in the entire region.

PONTE LECCIA

Francardo

PORTO
Golo
D84

Castirla

Soveria

Tralonca

Ellerato

D818

N193

D41

D18

N193

CORTE

Santa Lucia di Mercurio

Castellar di Mercur

Sermano

N200

D39

D341

D41

ALERIA

0 kilometres 3

0 miles 3

Visitors' Checklist

🛈 Station Touristique de l'Intérieur, Citadelle, Corte (04 95 46 26 70); Bozio tourist office (04 95 48 69 23; open Apr–Oct).
Length of tour: about 60 km (37 miles), including the return to Corte; longer with detours.
Duration: one day, including the visits to the churches.
Stopping-off points: in the villages along the route.

Chapelle Ste-Marie ④
Near the town of Favalello, on a curve along the road, is this tiny chapel. Its noteworthy frescoes reflect the faith of the Corsican artists who lived five centuries ago.

D441
BUSTANICO
rmano
ulello ④

EY

▌ Tour route
▌ Other roads

Gorges de la Restonica ❸

Road map C3. 🚌 free bus across the length of the valley (Jul–Aug); at these times the last stretch of the D623 might be closed to private cars due to congestion. 🛈 Station Touristique de l'Intérieur, Citadelle, Corte (04 95 46 26 70).
Tuani Camping 📞 04 95 46 11 65.

THE NARROW VALLEY that descends from the seven lakes of Monte Rotondo (see p22) towards Corte lies between steep slopes, creating a series of awesome gorges. Despite the terrible fires that, in 2000, damaged the centuries-old forest covering its slopes, this fascinating valley is still very popular among hikers who, from spring onwards, look for relief from the heat along the pebbled shores of the torrent.

After leaving Corte, the Restonica road (D623) goes past the small Hotel Dominique Colonna and up the hills. For certain stretches the gorge becomes deep and seems to be hewn out of the rock. After about 14 km (9 miles) are the Bergeries de Grottelle, which lie 1,375 m (4,511 ft) above sea level. These typical stone-hut complexes house shepherds and sheep in the summer (see p29). This is where the motorable road ends and there are some kiosks open in spring and summer.

From the Bergeries de Grottelle, a steep path goes over a rocky crest. Here the hardest stretches have metal

The Restonica, flowing quickly down through the rocks

ladders; should it rain, be careful of the slippery rocks. After about an hour's walk is the first of the small lakes in this area, the Lac de Mélo, at an altitude of 1,711 m (5,613 ft). From the shore of the lake the views are wonderful and encompass the surrounding mountains and the Vallée de la Restonica. Further along the path, at 1,930 m (6,331 ft), is the Lac du Capitellu, a glacial lake surrounded by steep cliffs.

A *Vanessa* butterfly, typical of this zone

At an altitude of about 2,000 m (6,500 ft), where the forest ends, the landscape is open and impressive: to the left is the 2,622-m (8,602-ft) high Monte Rotondo, and to the right the crest of Capo Chiostro, which reaches 2,295 m (7,529 ft).

The two sides of the valley have many paths leading to lakes and *bergeries*. In summer it is possible to stay at the Tuani camp site, midway along the D623.

A breathtaking view of the Gorges de la Restonica

One of the many swiftly flowing torrents of inland Corsica ▷

Panoramic view of the large Forêt de Vizzavona

Forêt de Vizzavona ❹

Road map C4. 🚉 *Vizzavona.*
ℹ *Station Touristique de l'Intérieur, Citadelle, Corte (04 95 46 26 70).*

OF ALL THE FORESTS in the large green heart of the island, the Forêt de Vizzavona is one of the most famous and popular. This partly depends on the fact that the area is traversed by the GR20 long-distance path *(see p23)*, and in spring and summer groups of hikers disembark at the small railway station of Vizzavona, 3 km (2 miles) away.

Delicious hazelnuts

The forest is the home of hazelnut and chestnut trees as well as Corsican pines and other conifers. Along the road that crosses it is a Foreign Legion camp.

The Forêt de Vizzavona is also crossed by the N193 road linking Ajaccio and Bastia and by the railway line inaugurated in 1894.

Col de Vizzavona ❺

Road map C4. 🚉 *Vizzavona.*
ℹ *Station Touristique de l'Intérieur, Citadelle, Corte (04 95 46 26 70).*

THE ROAD LINKING Bastia and Ajaccio (the N193, one of the main roads on the island) crosses Corsica's inland mountain ranges at the pass of Col de Vizzavona. This mountain, at an altitude of 1,161 m (3,809 ft), marks the border between Haute-Corse and Corse-du-Sud *(see p49)*. The pass has tables and benches for a stopoff and picnic and is populated by wild pigs that are not disturbed by visitors.

From Col de Vizzavona, which is often quite windy, there is a fine view of the impressive silhouette of the 2,389-m (7,838-ft) high Monte d'Oro. An easy, uphill path leading north off the N193 road to Bastia stretches for about 400 m (1,300 ft) to the ruins of a Genoese fortification. Many other footpaths cross this area, including the GR20 long-distance path *(see pp20–25)*.

Cascade des Anglais ❻

Road map C4. 🚉 *Vizzavona.*
ℹ *Station Touristique de l'Intérieur, Citadelle, Corte (04 95 46 26 70).*

ONE OF THE MOST popular walks in this area is the hike along the GR20 long-distance path *(see pp20–25)*, which goes from the road near the hamlet of La Foce to the Cascade des Anglais ("waterfall of the English"), a beauty spot much admired by early English visitors to this area. This trip, which is on an easy and well-marked path, takes less than two hours up and back, and follows the course of the Agnone torrent.

Beyond the Cascade des Anglais, which stands 1,100 m (3,600 ft) above sea level, the water has carved a series of deep potholes that are ideal for a swim.

In fair weather, and with adequate equipment, it is possible to continue up to the head of the valley towards the summit of Monte d'Oro. However, this is a strenuous round hike of around 7–8 hours from Vizzavona and is only recommended for fit and experienced hill walkers.

The summit of Monte d'Oro overlooks all the main Corsican peaks and from there it is even possible to see the Italian coast.

THE GENOESE BRIDGES

The architectural works that the Genoese bequeathed to the island of Corsica comprise not only buildings, squares, citadels and watchtowers *(see pp27 and 93)*, but also a great many bridges. Over the centuries, these have facilitated communications with the interior, which is traversed by numerous watercourses that more often than not are quite swift. Many of these bridges, which were built from 1284 onwards, are intact and still in use today. They are made of dry-stone, have a single arch and are never more than 20 m (65 ft) long. The bridges are usually supported by two piers that are often reinforced with corner brackets on the upper part; there may be circular openings on the sides of the arch to let the water pass through in case of a flood. Originally quite simple, the bridges began to be decorated only after the Renaissance.

The Genoese bridge in the Vallée de l'Asco

Tour of the Fiumorbo 🕖

THIS AREA IS NAMED AFTER the Fium'Orbu ("blind river" in Corsican). The river starts from the slopes of Monte Renoso and winds its way down through the deep Strette and Inzecca gorges to the east coast, a short distance south of the archaeological site of Aléria. This wild region was one of the last in Corsica to agree to abide by French law, and tales of the battles between the French army and the locals have become legendary. The small villages have not changed much in the last two centuries and are not famous tourist attractions, but a tour of the rugged scenery and isolated hamlets is certainly worthwhile.

TIPS FOR DRIVERS

ℹ️ *Route Nationale 198, Ghisonaccia (04 95 56 12 38).*
Length of tour: *90 km (56 miles).*
Duration: *one or two days, depending on the stops.* **Stopping-off points**: *in the villages.*

Auberge Vecchia Mina ⑤
A short distance from Ghisoni is this charming little hotel. To its left is a path that descends towards Ponte a Mela, a lovely Genoese bridge.

Defilé de l'Inzecca ④
The D344 road, going from the coast to the village of Ghisoni, crosses the narrow gorge known as Defilé de l'Inzecca, followed by Lac de Sampolo and the Defilé des Strette.

Pietrapola ②
Near the village of Pietrapola are the hot springs that were frequented by the ancient Romans who lived in Aléria. They are still in use today.

Prunelli-di-Fiumorbo
The main village in this region is dominated by an austere fortified church. From here there is a great view of the region and the coast.

```
0 kilometres        3
0 miles             2
```

KEY

 Tour route

═ Other roads

Serra-di-Fiumorbo ①
Overlooking the Abatesco river valley, parallel to the Vallée du Fium'Orbu, the village of Serra-di-Fiumorbo offers a fine view towards the coast, the ancient site of Aléria and the small Étang di Palo.

Aléria

Road map D4. 🏚 *2,500.* 🛈 *Route Nationale 198 (04 95 57 01 51).*

THE HISTORY of the ancient settlement of Aléria, on the marshy east coast of Corsica, began when the Greek colonists from Phocaea set up a commercial outpost here around the middle of the 6th century BC. The outpost, then known as Alalia, served as a strategic base for trade with the populations on the nearby Italian and southern French coasts. For the Greeks, Corsica was also a vital source of raw materials, from timber to lead and copper from the mines inland.

After a period of Carthaginian domination, in 259 BC Alalia was invaded by the Roman troops of consul Lucius Cornelius Scipio. The Romans renamed the settlement Aléria and initiated the conquest of the island, which lasted for more than a century. Aléria was the capital of Corsica in the Imperial Age, and Augustus, Hadrian and Diocletian beautified it with large public works.

Courtyard of Fort Matra, home of the Musée Jérôme Carcopino

In the 5th century AD, the increase of malaria and invasion by the Vandals led to the abandonment of the city.

Visits to the archaeological site begin at a Genoese fort, Fort Matra. Built in 1484, it is now the home of the **Musée d'Archéologie Jérôme Carcopino**, named after the great scholar of Corsican origin. The items on display in this archaeological museum illustrate the historic continuity of Aléria and the great

number of trade relations it had with the entire Mediterranean region. Greek, Phoenician, Roman, Apulian and Etruscan vases and ceramics were found on the hill where the city rose up. Among the most interesting works are two rhytons (wine vessels) that were made in Attica, Greece, one in the shape of a mule's head, the other representing a dog.

Outside the museum are the ruins of the Roman city. To the left of the Forum is a large temple flanked by two porticoes and, to the right, the Praetorium – the official residence of the governor of the island – and the Capitol. Everything gives the impression of an efficient city with all the typical Roman amenities. In addition, tombs and traces of past civilizations dating as far back as the 6th century BC have been found throughout the area.

🏛 **Musée d'Archéologie Jérôme Carcopino & site of Aléria**
Fort Matra. 🛈 *04 95 57 00 92.* ⏰ *daily.* ⏰ *mid-Oct–mid-May: Sun.* 🏷

THE RUINS OF ALÉRIA

Balneum (baths) ⑨	Domus cum Impluvium (water storage) ④	Praetorium (governor's residence) ⑭
Bastions ⑲	Forum ①	Shops ⑤
Calidarium (steam rooms) ⑩	Industrial edifices ⑫	South arch ⑰
Capitol ⑮	North arch ⑯	South portico ⑥
Chambers ⑪	North portico ⑦	Temple ②
Decumanus ⑱	Pools ⑬	Thermae (warm baths) ⑧
Domus cum Domus (town house) ③		

Entrance *(cardo)*

↓ *Aléria*

0 metres   30

0 yards   30

The Genoese bridge of Altiani, decorated with a series of small blind arches

Vallée du Tavignano ❾

Road map C3. ℹ️ *Station Touristique de l'Intérieur, Citadelle, Corte (04 95 46 26 70).*

THE VALLÉE du Tavignano is traversed by one of the oldest roads on the island, the N200, connecting Aléria and Corte.

Travelling from Aléria along the course of the Tavignano river, which begins at Lac de Nino, in the middle of Corsica, there are many narrow gorges.

On the north side of the valley, the narrow D14 road leads to villages typical of the region, perched halfway up the hills in panoramic positions. One of these, **Piedicorte di Gaggio**, offers a fine view towards the coast and has an ancient Roman architrave in the wall of the parish-church bell tower.

A Genoese bridge still stands at **Altiani**, as promised by its engineers, who guaranteed the bridge would remain standing in all circumstances "save a deluge".

The village of **Erbajolo**, towering over the canyon

The village of Piedicorte, in the Vallée du Tavignano

carved by the Tavignano river, offers a breathtaking view of the profiles of Monte Renoso and Monte d'Oro. On the belvedere square is a plaque indicating interesting natural and historic attractions.

Gorges du Tavignano ❿

Road map C3. ℹ️ *Station Touristique de l'Intérieur, Citadelle, Corte (04 95 46 26 70).*

WHILE, EAST OF Corte, the lower course of the Tavignano river extends to Aléria and the sea, its upper course consists of a narrow valley. Here are fascinating gorges that can be reached only by walking along easy paths paved for much of their length in original medieval cobbles and steeped in nature.

One of these paths starts off from below Corte's Citadelle and leads to the Arche de Corte (also known as Arche de Padule), a rocky crest surrounded by *bergeries* (*see p29*) lying at an altitude of 1,500 m (4,921 ft). The path passes through chestnut groves in the hilly zone and then, above 1,000 m (3,300 ft), through conifer woods. Strenuous rather than difficult,

Niche with statue, Santa Mariona

it entails a walk of over five hours each way. Looking back from the gorges, the impressive rock of the Citadelle can be seen, still seeming to have control over the entire region.

Sovéria ⓫

Road map C3. 🚉 *Sovéria.* ℹ️ *Station Touristique de l'Intérieur, Citadelle, Corte (04 95 46 26 70).*

NOT FAR FROM Corte is the pretty village of Sovéria, located high over the Vallée du Golo, a stone's throw away from the Vallée de l'Asco and the regions of Bozio and Castagniccia. Sovéria is appreciated for the harmonious architecture of its houses.

In antiquity the countryside around Sovéria was given over to vineyards and winemaking. The landscape has changed, however, and today the soft hills are covered with chestnut and oak groves.

Along the D18 road, just outside Corte, the 10th-century Romanesque church of **Santa Mariona** can be found. The only remaining original parts of this church are the twin apses made up of grey stone extracted from the schist mountains in this area.

A Tour of Castagniccia ⑫

W ITH ITS ROLLING GREEN HILLS, the region east of Corte offers quite a different landscape from Corsica's mountainous interior. Named after its numerous chestnut (*castagna*) groves, Castagniccia was one of the first areas on the island to be inhabited. The highlights of a journey through this region include small villages, 16th-century Baroque chapels with impressive frescoes and the complex 18th-century architecture of the churches of La Porta and Piedicroce. Castagniccia also played a significant role in the history of Corsica – Morosaglia was the birthplace of independence hero Pascal Paoli, and the region became the centre of a thriving arms industry during the Corsican revolution.

San Tommaso di Pastoreccia ①
This chapel has survived excessive restoration that, in the 1930s, destroyed half of its original structure. In the apse, above the hieratic image of *Christ Pantocrator*, is an *Annunciation*; on the walls are the remains of a *Last Judgment*.

Morosaglia ②
Corsicans attach special importance to this village where Pascal Paoli, the national hero during the period of independence (*see pp46–7*), was born. His ashes are interred here. A short walk from Paoli's house-museum is the small church of Santa Reparata, decorated with sculptures that reveal its Romanesque origin.

San Pantaleo ③
The small church of San Pantaleo is on the D15 road going down from Morosaglia in the direction of the village of Saliceto. It is worth a visit for the splendid apse that was frescoed in the 15th century.

San Quilico ④
On the D639 road is the Pisan chapel of San Quilico, the lovely tympanum of which is sculpted with Adam and Eve being tempted by the serpent, and a bas-relief of a man fighting a dragon with his bare hands.

KEY

▬ Tour route

═ Other roads

0 kilometres   5

0 miles   3

VISITORS' CHECKLIST

Tourist office, Piedicroce-Castagniccia (04 95 35 82 54).
www.en-castagniccia.com
San Pantaleo: ask for the keys at the only house in the hamlet of Pieditermini.
Sts-Pierre-et-Paul: *Piedicroce.*
04 95 35 81 86. *daily.*
Length of tour: *120 km (75 miles).* **Duration:** *from two to three days, depending on your pace.* **Stopping-off points:** *in the localities along the route.*

La Porta ⑤
A masterpiece of Corsican Baroque architecture, the church of St-Jean-Baptiste towers over the hamlet of La Porta with its tall bell tower, to the left of the façade.

Piedicroce ⑥
At Piedicroce, the Baroque church of Sts-Pierre-et-Paul dominates a soft landscape of rolling green hills. Built in 1691, its light-coloured façade is decorated with white pilasters and friezes. Inside are frescoes and Rococo decorations.

Couvent d'Orezza ⑦
An assembly met in this large monastery in the outskirts of Piedicroce in 1751 and conferred military and executive power on Jean-Pierre Gaffori *(see p134).* The monastery was reduced to ruins during World War II.

La Porta ⑧

Road map D3. 250.
Mairie (04 95 39 21 48).
St-Jean-Baptiste *daily.*

SITUATED IN a fertile area covered in woods, the village of La Porta ("the door") owes its name and prosperity to its location – in the past this village was the only access route to the region of Castagniccia.

Today La Porta is famous because of the beautiful church of **St-Jean-Baptiste** which, together with its imposing bell tower, stands out among the slate roofs of the village. It is considered to be the most complete work of Baroque architecture in Corsica. Construction of the church began in 1648 and continued for nearly half a century under the Italian architect Domenico Baina. The façade was completed in 1707, although it had later alterations. It has recently been restored to its original ochre colour, which, combined with the vertical white pilasters, gives quite a spectacular impression.

The lower part of the façade is rather austere, with tall pilasters forming a strict pattern. This is broken up by the upper level's elaborate Baroque elements with hints of Rococo, in the shape of pilaster strips,

Pulpit, St-Jean-Baptiste

swirly volutes and cartouches. The Baroque influence is also predominant around the entrance, which is surmounted by friezes. The excesses of the Italian Baroque style have been avoided through this juxtaposition of the plain base with detailing on the higher parts, while the overall harmony of the building has been maintained. The 45-m (147-ft) bell tower next to it shares the same pattern of design: simpler at the base and growing more elaborate for each of its five storeys.

The interior has a single nave flanked by side chapels separated from one another by columns with Corinthian capitals. The walls and ceiling are decorated with late 19th-century stucco work and trompe l'oeil by the artist Girolamo da Porta. Above the entrance is a magnificent monumental organ used in concerts. Other interesting works here include the high altar, made of white Carrara marble, with the altarpiece framed by two small columns, and the pulpit.

The interior contains many fine works of art. Among these are a *Decapitation of St John the Baptist*, to the right of the choir, and two 17th-century wooden sculptures representing Christ and the Virgin Mary.

The village of La Porta, dominated by the Baroque bell tower

Vallée d'Alesani 🄔

Road map D3. 🏠 *190*.
🛈 *Tourist office, Piedicroce-Castagniccia (04 95 35 82 54).*

THIS AREA CONSISTS of a group of hamlets scattered on the upper course of the Alesani river. The region is known for the circumstances linked to the rise and fall of Theodor von Neuhof, the first and only king of Corsica *(see p46)*, who was crowned in the **Couvent St-François d'Alesani** in 1736 at Perelli. The monastery was founded in 1236, but the current Baroque building dates to 1716. One of the side chapels has the *Virgin of the Cherry* (1450), an oil painting on a wooden panel attributed to Sano di Pietro, an artist from Siena.

This hamlet was also the home of the legendary Grosso-Minuto.

The bell tower of Ste-Marie-et-St-Erasme at Cervione

Cervione 🄕

Road map D3. 🏠 *1,350*.
🛈 *Tourist office, Piedicroce-Castagniccia (04 95 35 82 54).*

AT THE FOOT of Monte Castello and in the easternmost part of Castagniccia, Cervione lies in a beautiful location surrounded by vineyards, olive orchards and chestnut groves. After the destruction of Aléria, Cervione became a bishopric and, for that occasion, the cathedral of St-Erasme was

GROSSO-MINUTO'S WITTICISMS

A famous figure in Castagniccia folklore, Grosso-Minuto's real name was Pietro Giovanni Ficoni. He was a poor travel-ling vendor born in Perelli-d'Alesani in 1715. Because of his frail body, he was nicknamed Minuto (tiny), to which Grosso (fat) was added when he became fat in his old age. Ficoni, who was at Pascal Paoli's side for many years, was famous for his sarcastic witticisms, one of the best-known of which concerned a donkey. A woman heard Minuto's donkey bray and asked him if the animal was in love. His reply was: "You're mistaken, Madame, it probably smelled a female donkey."

A Corsican donkey

built. In 1714 the original church was replaced by a new complex, **Ste-Marie-et-St-Erasme**, the present-day cathedral. The Bishop's Palace and the seminary – now the home of a small ethnographic museum – were also built in this same period. Cervione is the starting point of the panoramic D330 road, also called **Corniche de la Castagniccia**. About 2 km (1 mile) from the town, along this route, is the 9th-century Chapelle Ste-Christine, with twin apses and some frescoes.

La Canonica 🄖

Road map D2. 🛈 *Rue Notre-Dame-de-Lourdes, Bastia (04 95 38 43 40).*
🕐 *Summer: daily.*

DURING THE PERIOD of the Roman conquest (c.259 BC), various colonies were founded in Corsica. While the main colonial city was Aléria *(see p144)*, another one, Mariana, lay nearer to present-day Bastia. It was named after the Roman general Marius, who in 100 BC founded a colony for the veterans of his army near the waters of the Étang de Biguglia.

Mariana, where Augustus had a port built on the Golo river, was the base for the conquest of nearby Cap Corse and for the reclamation and cultivation of the entire plain surrounding the city.

Destroyed by the Vandals in the 5th century AD, as was Aléria, Mariana was dealt its final blow by the malaria epi-demics that struck the inhabitants of the coastal plains in medieval times.

Detail of a frieze, La Canonica

The Pisans built one of their cathedrals nearby, La Canonica, which was consecrated in 1119 by the archbishop of Pisa. He resided in the nearby bishop's palace, of which only traces of the foundations remain. Known by its original name, even though it was dedicated to Santa Maria Assunta, this church was abandoned for reasons of health and security two centuries later, when the bishop moved to the hills of nearby Vescovato. This church is considered the prototype of

The austere Romanesque church La Canonica

all the Pisan churches in Corsica. The nave is divided into three sections and ends in a semicircular apse; its elegance is created by the colours of the stone (from the Cap Corse quarries) and by few architectural decorative elements. Above the main portal are friezes representing griffons, a lamb, a wolf and a deer being chased by a dog. The series of holes on the outer walls of the church have sometimes been said to have originally contained multicoloured stone inlays, but they are in fact damage caused by scaffolding.

Vescovato ⑰

Road map D2. 🏘 *2,350.*
ℹ *Mairie (04 95 38 93 12).*

O**N A MOUNTAINSIDE** at the northern end of the Castagniccia region, the town of Vescovato was founded by refugees who had abandoned the city of Mariana, which had proved too vulnerable to invasions and malaria.

For centuries, Vescovato was the capital of the small hilly region of Casinca, which lies between the Golo river and the Vallée du Fium'Alto and which, thanks to its fertile soil, for a long period had the largest population on the island. Formerly called Belfiorito, it was later renamed Vescovato ("bishopric") because it was the bishop's seat from 1269 to 1570, when it was replaced by Bastia.

The famous Ponte-Novo, site of a battle between Corsicans and French

To make the best of a visit here, it is advisable to park at the only tree-lined square and walk through the alleys. In the middle of the village is the Baroque church of **San Martino**, with a 16th-century tabernacle sculpted by the Italian Antonello Gagini. Next to the church, a vaulted passageway leads to the main square, which has a handsome fountain guarded by an eagle.

There are three other churches in town, reminders that this was once a bishopric: the church of the Capuchin monastery, the chapel of the Ste-Croix Confraternity and the Romanesque Chapelle San Michele.

The coast east of Vescovato is lined by increasingly popular sandy beaches and tourist resorts.

The fountain in the square of Vescovato

View of Vescovato, formerly a bishopric

Ponte-Novo ⑱

Road map D2. Along the N193 road, 8 km (5 miles) northeast of Ponte Leccia. ℹ *Station Touristique de l'Intérieur, Citadelle, Corte (04 95 46 26 70).*

T**HIS LOCALITY** was named after a bridge built by the Genoese, but its fame throughout the island is due to the battle fought on the banks of the Golo river between the French troops commanded by Count de Vaux and the Corsican patriots led by Pascal Paoli *(see pp46–7).*

On 8 May 1769 the invading French troops, who had been defeated the year before at Borgo, were trying to find an entry point to the interior of the island, which was under the control of the independence fighters. The 2,000 Corsican patriots were driven back by the French and retreated along the bridge, where they were quickly overcome. After this defeat, Paoli was forced to abandon the struggle against the French and, in June 1769, left the island for England. Thus ended the Corsicans' dream of independence and freedom.

Today the original bridge is in ruins because of bombardments during World War II. A new bridge was built over the river, but the battle is commemorated by a monument and a plaque, accompanied by flags with a Moor's head, the symbol of the Corsican nation *(see p47).* A visit here offers a great insight into the spirit of the Corsicans.

Cirque de Trimbolocciu, in the Haut-Asco region

Vallée de l'Asco ⑲

Road map C2–C3.
🛈 *Station Touristique de l'Intérieur, Citadelle, Corte (04 95 46 26 70).*

THE LONG, DIAGONAL Vallée de l'Asco – which runs for 30 km (18 miles) southwest of Ponte Leccia – is one of the most isolated areas in Corsica. The road that traverses it follows the winding course of the river Asco up to Corsica's most striking range of mountains, dominated by the dark profile of **Monte Cinto**, the highest peak on the island at 2,706 m (8,878 ft). Along the road is the spectacular **Cirque de Trimbolocciu**, near Monte Cinto, at the head of the Vallée de l'Asco.

In an open area of the valley is the village of **Asco**, which in the 16th century was one of the centres of the Corsican resistance against the Genoese troops. An unsurfaced road full of hairpin bends drops down from Asco towards the banks of the river and then to a marvellous Genoese bridge with the typical arched span.

As the valley rises, the vegetation changes, and the shrubs give way to the pines and larches of the **Forêt de Carozzica**. After this forest, the road ends in the small ski resort at **Haut-Asco**. At an altitude of 1,450 m (4,757 ft), this resort is one of the favourite starting points for hikers on their way towards Monte Cinto (eight hours up and back) or for those who

follow the GR20 long-distance path *(see p20)*, which crosses the Haut-Asco area, passes near the 2,556-m (8,385-ft) high Punta Minuta and arrives at the Tighjiettu refuge *(see p21)*.

The Genoese bridge crossing the river near Asco

St-François de Caccia ⑳

Road map C2. Castifao.
🛈 *Office de Tourisme, Ghjunssani (04 95 47 22 06).*

AT THE BEGINNING of the Vallée de l'Asco, leaving the D47 road in the direction of Moltifao, a detour of about 4 km (2 miles) leads to the ruins of the monastery of St-François de Caccia, near the village of Castifao.

Founded in the early 16th century and destroyed by the Genoese in 1553, the monastery and its church were reconstructed thanks to the efforts of friar Augustinu da Populasca and then entrusted to a group of Franciscan monks. The church, built

in 1569 and rebuilt in 1750, collapsed in 1782. Here, in 1755, Pascal Paoli *(see p47)* took part in the assembly of Corsican deputies who drew up the island's constitution.

Scala di Santa Regina ㉑

Road map C3.
🛈 *Office de Tourisme, Niolu (04 95 47 12 62).*

THE VALLÉE DU GOLO has always been an important communication link between the interior and the west coast of Corsica.

Following the course of the Golo river leads to the highest motorable pass on the island, the Col de Verghio, at 1,464 m (4,803 ft) above sea level. From here one can descend towards Porto and Ajaccio.

Along the valley, on the right-hand side of the road, is the Scala di Santa Regina gorge, which, according to popular tradition, was created thanks to the intervention of the Virgin Mary at the end of a fierce battle between St Martin and Satan. With the brilliant reddish hues of the local granite, this narrow gorge is an impressive sight from the road, stretches of which are often cut from the steep rock.

Parts of a narrow mule track along which commercial traffic travelled in the past are still visible from the paved road on the opposite slope of the valley.

The impressive gorges known as Scala di Santa Regina

151

Wild horses near Calacuccia

Calacuccia ㉒

Road map C3. 🏠 *350.*
ℹ️ *Office de Tourisme, Niolu
(04 95 47 12 62).*

THE MAIN TOWN in the Niolo
mountain region and in
the pass that leads to the Col
de Verghio, Calacuccia stands
1,000 m (3,300 ft) above sea
level. It is famous for its
superb position on the banks
of the lake created by a dam
that blocks the flow of the
Golo river. Small hotels and
restaurants that are quite
crowded in summer provide
relaxation and magnificent
views of Monte Cinto to the
northwest (*see p21*) and
Capo Tafonato, which rises
up next to Col de Verghio.

From Albertacce, 5 km
(3 miles) southwest of
Calacuccia, orange waymarks
lead from opposite a large
white crucifix on the western
edge of the village to the
Pont de Muricciolu, an old
Genoese footbridge
overlooking natural pools that
are popular bathing spots.

On the south bank of the
artificial lake is the hamlet of
Casamaccioli, and going up
towards the 1,592-m (5,223-ft)
high **Bocca di l'Arinella**
pass, an unpaved road offers
breathtaking views of the lake
and surrounding mountains.

Casamaccioli ㉓

Road map C3. 🏠 *90.* ℹ️ *Station
Touristique de l'Intérieur, Citadelle,
Corte (04 95 46 26 70).* 🎪 *Nativity
of the Virgin (7–10 Sep).*

OPPOSITE Calacuccia, across
the artificial lake and at
an altitude of 850 m (2,800 ft),
is Casamaccioli, a hamlet with
fewer than 100 permanent

inhabitants.
Besides offering a
marvellous view of
the lake, the Monte
Cinto massif and
the surrounding
chestnut forests,
this village has an
interesting tradition
that always attracts
visitors. In the
Nativité parish
church, beside a
wooden statue of St Roch,
there is one of the Virgin Mary,
or "La Santa", as she is called
in Corsica. On 7–10 September
this statue is carried in the
Nativity of the Virgin
procession (*see p34*) during
the festivities in her honour.

Forêt de
Valdu-Niellu ㉔

Road map C3.
ℹ️ *Office de Tourisme, Niolu
(04 95 47 12 62).*

SOUTHWEST of Casamaccioli,
on the left-hand side of the
road is this forest, the largest
in Corsica. Although severely
damaged by fires over the
past decade, this forest covers
a surface area of more than
46 sq km (18 sq miles) in a
mountain zone at an altitude
of about 1,000–1,600 m
(3,300–5,250 ft). The forest is
dominated by birch and beech
trees as well as Laricio pines,
trees found only on the island
of Elba, in parts of the Italian
region of Calabria and here in
Corsica. At Valdu-Niellu there
are Laricio pines as much as
500 years old.

The forest offers many
activities, including hiking
paths of several levels of
difficulty. There is one that
takes an hour, going from the
Popaja rangers' house to the
heart of the forest and then
to the Bergeries de Colga. A
harder path goes to the 1,743-
m (5,718-ft) high glacial Lac
de Nino (a walk of 3½ hours),
the source of the Tavignano
river (*see p22*). The descent
to the Cascades de Radule
takes a further 90 minutes.

Col de Verghio ㉕

Road map C3.
ℹ️ *Station Touristique de l'Intérieur,
Citadelle, Corte (04 95 46 26 70).*

THE ROAD TOWARDS Porto
(D84) passes over the Col
de Verghio, the highest point
in the island's road network.
Just east of the Col de Verghio
pass, along this route is the
small winter sports resort of
Verghio, which is a favourite
with hikers in the summer.

Here it is possible to make
the ascent to the small Lac
de Nino (*see p22*), the grassy
basin of which is grazing
land for small herds of wild
horses during the summer.

Beaten by the wind and
extremely wild, Col de Verghio
is part of the itinerary of the
GR20 long-distance path (*see
p20*), which, heading north,
passes by the Cascades de
Radule and then heads up to
the Ciuttulu di i Mori refuge at
the foot of the majestic Capo
Tafonato mountain and the
nearby peak of Paglia Orba.

A humid meadowland area near the Col de Verghio

TRAVELLERS' NEEDS

WHERE TO STAY 154–161

WHERE TO EAT 162–171

SHOPPING IN CORSICA 172–175

ENTERTAINMENT IN CORSICA 176–179

SPORTS AND OUTDOOR ACTIVITIES 180–185

WHERE TO STAY

FROM HOLIDAY VILLAGES along the coast to farm holiday establishments in the mountains, Corsica has about 400 places to stay. They are mostly concentrated in the gulfs of Ajaccio, Calvi, Porto-Vecchio and Bonifacio, and on the coast. Luxury establishments with a swimming pool or private beach tend to be located near the main seaside resorts. It is also possible to rent flats in residences or holiday homes, most

The Gîtes de France logo

of which are located in the southern part of the island. The many camp sites both in the interior and on the coast offer an economic alternative for those who prefer to stay in contact with nature. Another accommodation option consists of the *gîtes ruraux*, or farm holidays. These are small, family-run establishments that enable visitors to become better acquainted with Corsican people and their customs.

GRADING

As IN THE REST of Europe, hotels in Corsica are graded with a star-rating system. One star is for inns with only the most essential comforts and service, while four stars are awarded to first-class hotels that offer high-quality service.

The highest rating bracket is reserved for luxury hotels such as La Villa *(see p158)* in Calvi, the Dolce Vita *(see p159)* in Ajaccio, the Sofitel Thalassa *(see p160)* in Porticcio and the Genovese *(see p160)* in Bonifacio.

Three-star hotels often offer surprisingly good value for money. They include the Centre Nautique *(see p160)* in Bonifacio, the Castel Brando *(see p158)* in Erbalunga and the Dolce Notte *(see p159)* in St-Florent.

Main entrance to the Hostellerie de l'Abbaye *(see p158)* in Calvi

All the four-star and most of the three-star hotels in resorts along the coastline have either a swimming pool or, when they are located on the seaside, private access to a beach.

Pleasant accommodation can also be found in two-star establishments such as the Mare e Monti Hotel *(see p158)* in Felicetto or the Auberge Patrizi *(see p159)* in Nonza.

Rarely will you find single rooms in the hotels so, should you be travelling alone, you will probably have to pay the price for a double room. Conversely, any extra bed in your room must be paid for separately.

Only in the recently built or remodelled hotels has attention been paid to the needs of the disabled so, if you have any special requests, it is advisable to make enquiries beforehand.

A good number of hotels in Corsica welcome pets.

PRICES

FRENCH LAW REQUIRES hotels to post, both outside the premises and in each room, a price list. This list shows the maximum prices TTC, or *Toutes Taxes Comprises* ("including all taxes"), for each season. The prices shown (or quoted when you book a room) also include service. It is illegal to exceed the listed prices.

In the summer, hotels along the coast often quote a rate for obligatory half board.

Not all hotels have their own restaurant, and usually breakfast is not included in the price. The same applies for drinks during your meal, food or drinks served in your room, beverages taken from the minibar and telephone calls. Phone calls are usually quite expensive, so, unless it is absolutely necessary, it is better to use public phones.

The pool in the Hotel Pietracap *(see p158)* in Bastia

◁ **Outdoor cafés and restaurants, a feature of Corsican towns**

THE HOTEL SEASON AND BOOKING

MOST HOTELS in Corsica are run on a seasonal basis and are open from April to October. High season corresponds to the summer months, in particular July and August. Should you decide to visit the island's seaside resorts during these months, it is vital that you arrange accommodation well in advance since many hotels are booked up for the high season.

From November to March, finding any accommodation at all, especially in the smaller tourist resorts, may also prove difficult. However, hotels in the main cities tend to stay open all year round.

When you book your room, you may be asked either to send a certain amount of money as a deposit or to supply your credit card details.

A panoramic terrace at the Dolce Vita (see p159) in Ajaccio

HOLIDAY VILLAGES AND RÉSIDENCES

ALONG THE SEASIDE, holiday villages and *résidences* (holiday homes) offer visitors a less formal atmosphere than that found in a hotel. The level of accommodation in these establishments varies according to the needs of the guest: from simple rooms in a bungalow with restaurant service and entertainment, to self-catering apartments.

All the holiday villages offer entertainment, one or more pools and a wide range of

A room in the Casa Musicale (see p159) in Pigna

sports activities, including tennis, windsurfing, diving or sailing. Some clubs even provide the option of using a baby-sitting service.

Among the best such complexes are the Club Med holiday villages at Cargèse and Sant'Ambroggio, both not far from Calvi.

Some villages offer all-inclusive packages, in which everything, even drinks at the bar, is included in the price. The prices of these packages are quoted on a weekly basis. Other clubs allow you to rent an apartment and leave you free to choose whether you want to make use of the services, activities and entertainment.

Those staying in Corsica for one week or longer could consider renting a house, an option that affords the convenience of modern facilities while maintaining a degree of independence.

For information on holiday villages, contact your travel agency or the tour operator who manages the establish-

ments. For information on residences, call the **Syndicat National des Résidences de Tourisme** in Paris, or ask the **Agence de Tourisme de la Corse** for a brochure. Local tourist offices also publish lists of private houses and apartments to let in their areas.

CAMPING

STAYING AT a camp site is an inexpensive way to spend your holiday. There are about 200 camp sites in Corsica, most of which are between Bonifacio and Porto-Vecchio, along the coast of the Balagne region and in the Golfe d'Ajaccio. Most sites are open from Easter to October, while very few are open all year round.

The standard of services and facilities varies quite a lot. Some camp sites are mere plots of land with modest facilities, few bathrooms and some trees for shade. Others have swimming pools, organize sports activities and have many facilities, including food stores, pizzerias (and, occasionally, restaurants) and laundry rooms. Some even rent bungalows for two to four people, with a private bathroom and kitchenette.

For a small fee, some farmers allow tents to be pitched in their farmyards. This type of camping also includes the use of the farm's bathing facilities.

It is forbidden to pitch tents outside camp sites or sleep on the beach. To camp on private land, you must ask the owner's permission.

As with hotels, it is best to book well in advance, especially for long stays.

Staying at a camp site: an economic way to spend a holiday

SELF-CATERING

WHETHER IT IS a mini-apartment in Bonifacio, or a villa with a garden and swimming pool in Balagne, a self-catering apartment (*location saisonnière*) is an inexpensive solution for a family or a group of friends, and certainly an option worth considering when there are small children in your party.

This type of accommodation is particularly convenient for holidays of two weeks or more. Self-catering for only one week is a less valid option, partly because fixed expenses, such as cleaning, may be the same for a short or long period.

Corsica offers a great many houses and apartments for rent, but it is always advisable to make your reservations in advance. Local tourist offices provide lists of houses for rent; alternatively estate agents sometimes offer flats and villas for short periods as well.

Before agreeing to rent a place, ask for a detailed description of the house or apartment, its location and amenities, as well as the services and facilities in the area. Sometimes one discovers too late that the sea is quite a distance from the house or that some beds in the house are mere makeshift arrangements. It is a good idea to find out whether the

One of the many mountain refuges offering shelter to hikers

gas and electricity expenses are included in the rent or are considered extras. Enquiries should also be made about all the amenities, even the swimming pool or garden, in order to avoid having to pay for unexpected maintenance expenses.

CHAMBRES D'HÔTES

MUCH LIKE the British bed and breakfast, *chambres d'hôtes* are rooms rented in private homes. They include breakfast and are ideal for visitors who plan to travel a lot. They are also a good way to get to know Corsican people first-hand. To find a *chambre d'hôtes* in Corsica, contact a local tourist office.

REFUGES AND HOSTELS

CORSICA OFFERS 16 mountain refuges and many more *gîtes d'étapes* (shelters). They are located mostly along the GR20 long-distance path (*see pp20–25 and 180*) and all are marked on IGN maps. Both refuges and *gîtes d'étapes* tend to be small, with 20–50 bed spaces, often in a dorm, and with only one communal shower room. *Gîtes d'étapes* also have self-catering facilities.

Refuges are staffed from June to September. In the high season it may be hard to find a place to stay, since it is not possible to book in advance, but for those who cannot find a bed there is always an area with facilities for camping.

A comfortable, family-run farm-holiday establishment in the Corsican interior

A handful of refuges also have food available, such as cheese and charcuterie, and drinks.

There are only two youth hostels (*relais de jeunesse*) in Corsica providing beds at low prices; both are in Calvi.

FARM HOLIDAYS

FOR SIMPLE accommodation in exceptionally beautiful settings try the *gîtes ruraux*. Although there are not many of these farms on the island, they are a pleasant and economic solution allowing an opportunity to become acquainted with the local traditions and life.

The grading of the *gîtes* is based not on stars, like hotels, but on ears of wheat (from one to four), and they are guaranteed by the **Maison des Gîtes de France**.

As well as rooms, which usually have a private bathroom and include breakfast, there are many small flats with a kitchenette and private bathroom, usually in converted stables or rooms where wine was once made.

All the guests eat at the same table, so if you like your privacy this is not the solution for you. However, it is ideal for those who want to relax without being tied down to a hotel routine, and for families with children, who will have plenty of space to play in. The price categories you will be quoted indicate the maximum price for a double room with breakfast, including tax and service.

DIRECTORY

TOURIST OFFICES

Agence de Tourisme de la Corse
17 Blvd du Roi Jérôme, Ajaccio.
04 95 51 00 00.
w www.visit-corsica.com

RESIDENCES

Arinella
Route du Bord de Mer, Lumio.
04 95 60 60 60.

Baies des Voiles
Santa Manza, Bonifacio.
04 95 73 03 55.

Belvédère de Palombaggia
Route de Palombaggia, Porto-Vecchio.
04 95 70 95 70.

Les Pins
Route de Porto, Calvi.
04 95 65 28 20.

Sarl Immobilière de Balagne
Cocody Village, Baie de Sant'Ambroggio, Lumio.
04 95 60 72 76.

Syndicat National des Résidences de Tourisme
Paris.
01 47 38 35 60.
w www.snrt.fr

Le Thyrrénéen
Solenzara.
04 95 57 47 59.

CAMPING

Arinella Bianca
Ghisonaccia.
04 95 56 04 78.

Barbicaja
Route des Sanguinaires, Ajaccio.
04 95 52 01 17.

Belgodère
Les Campéoles, Lozari.
04 95 60 20 20.

Benista
Pisciatello, Porticcio.
04 95 25 19 30.

Le Clos du Mouflon
Route de Porto, Calvi.
04 95 65 03 53.

Dolce Vita
Route Nationale 197, Calvi.
04 95 65 05 99.

Kallisté
Route de la Plage de la Roya, St-Florent.
04 95 37 03 08.

Kalypso
Route Nationale 198, Santa Maria, Poghju.
04 95 38 56 74.

Marina d'Aléria
Boite Postale 11, Aléria.
04 95 57 01 42.

Les Oliviers
Porto (Ota).
04 95 26 14 49.

Ostriconi
Palasca.
04 95 60 10 05.

La Pinède
Lieu-dit Serrigio, St-Florent.
04 95 37 07 26.

Torraccia
Baghiuccia, Cargèse.
04 95 26 42 39.

U Prunelli
Pont du Prunelli, Porticcio.
04 95 25 19 23.

ESTATE AGENCIES

Agence du Golfe
111 Cours Napoléon, Ajaccio.
04 95 22 19 09.

Agence Immobilière Insulaire
4 Rue Camille Pietri, Propriano.
04 95 76 08 84.

Bastia Immobilier
45 Blvd Paoli, Bastia.
04 95 31 48 05.

Calvi Balagne
8 Blvd Wilson, Calvi.
04 95 65 11 40.

Immobilier Alias
Marina di Fiori, Porto-Vecchio.
04 95 70 21 30.

Millénaire Immobilier
12 Rue St-Jean-Baptiste, Bonifacio.
04 95 73 59 51.

CHAMBRES D'HÔTES

Alberte Bartoli
L'Orca di San Gavinu, Figari. 04 95 71 01 29.

A Pignata
Route du Pianu, Levie.
04 95 78 41 90.

A Tinedda
Sartène.
04 95 77 09 31.

Carole Leandri
Ferme Equestre du Baracci, Propriano.
04 95 76 19 48.

Jean-Jacques Bartoli
Tasso.
04 95 24 50 54.

Kyrn Flor
Route Nationale 193, U San Gavinu, Corte.
04 95 61 02 88.

Stéphane Natalini
Altu Pratu, Erbajolo.
04 95 48 80 07.

YOUTH HOSTELS

BJV Corsotel
43 Ave de la République, Calvi. 04 95 65 14 15.

U Carabellu
Route de Pietramaggiore, Calvi.
04 95 65 14 16.

FARM HOLIDAYS

Maison des Gîtes de France et du Tourisme Vert
Paris.
01 49 70 75 75.
w www.gites-de-france.fr

Relais Régional des Gîtes Ruraux
77 Cours Napoléon, Boite Postale 10, Ajaccio.
04 95 10 06 14.
w www.gites-corsica.com

Choosing a Hotel

THESE HOTELS have been selected across a wide price range for their quality, service and location. The chart lists the hotels according to the area chapters in this guide; the colour-coded thumb tabs indicate the areas covered on each page. The map references for the hotels refer to the road map of Corsica on the back endpaper.

	Credit Cards	Number of Rooms	Swimming Pool	Beach	Restaurant
BASTIA AND THE NORTH					
BASTIA: *Les Sablettes* €€€ 42 Route du Bord de Mer, Miomo, 20200. **Road map** D2. 📞 04 95 58 50 20. 📠 04 95 33 95 97. 🌐 www.lessablettes.com This recently renovated hotel stands by the seaside. The rooms are large and quiet, with a view of the sea or the hills. ● *Nov–Mar.* �')	AE MC V	52	●	■	●
BASTIA: *Les Voyageurs* €€€ 9 Avenue Maréchal Sébastiani, 20200. **Road map** D2. 📞 04 95 34 90 80. 📠 04 95 34 00 65. 🌐 www.hotel-lesvoyageurs.com A comfortable hotel in an advantageous position in the heart of town. All the rooms have been completely renovated. ● *25 Dec–3 Jan.* 🚀	AE DC MC V	24			
BASTIA: *Hotel Pietracap* €€€€ Route de San Martino di Lota, 20200. **Road map** D2. 📞 04 95 31 64 63. 📠 04 95 31 39 00. 🌐 www.hotel-pietracap.com A short drive from the town centre and the beach, this comfortable hotel stands in the middle of an olive grove. ● *Dec–Apr.* 🚀	AE DC MC V	39	●	■	●
CALVI: *Le Rocher* €€€€ 1 Blvd Wilson, 20260. **Road map** B2. 📞 04 95 65 20 04. 🌐 www.lerocher.com A modern, centrally located hotel. Some rooms have a fine view over the roofs of the Old Town. ● *Nov–Apr.* 🚀	AE DC MC V	20			
CALVI: *Hostellerie de l'Abbaye* €€€€ Route de Santore, 20260. **Road map** B2. 📞 04 95 65 04 27. 🌐 www.hotel-abbaye.com This hotel in the converted 16th-century St-François abbey exudes a timeless atmosphere. ● *Nov–Mar.* 🚀	AE DC MC V	43			
CALVI: *La Villa* €€€€€ Chemin de Notre-Dame de la Serra, 20260. **Road map** B2. 📞 04 95 65 10 10. 📠 04 95 65 10 50. 🌐 www.hotel-lavilla.com This luxurious oasis of peace boasts colourful mosaics in the patio, a Turkish bath and a masseur. ● *Nov–Mar.* 🚀	AE DC MC V	52	●		●
CENTURI: *Le Vieux Moulin* €€€ Port, 20238. **Road map** D1. 📞 04 95 35 60 15. 🌐 www.le-vieux-moulin.net Though close to the busy harbour, this quiet hotel is ideal for getting away from the bustle. Half board compulsory. ● *Nov–Feb.* 🚀	AE DC MC V	14		■	●
ERBALUNGA: *Castel Brando* €€€€ Cap Corse, 20222. **Road map** D1. 📞 04 95 30 10 30. 🌐 www.castelbrando.com An elegant hotel that has remained true to tradition, located in an old *palazzo* in the middle of a large palm grove. ● *Nov–Mar.* 🚀	AE MC V	29	●	■	
FELICETO: *Mare e Monti* €€€ Village, 20225. **Road map** D2. 📞 04 95 63 02 00. 📠 04 95 63 02 01. An enchanting hotel in a converted house built in 1870 in the heart of the village. A warm, cordial atmosphere. ● *mid-Oct–Mar.* 🚀	MC V	18	●		
L'ÎLE ROUSSE: *Le Splendid* €€€ Rue Comte Valéry, 20220. **Road map** C2. 📞 04 95 60 00 24. 🌐 www.le-splendid-hotel.com A family-run pension with a beautiful terrace. ● *Nov–Feb.* 🚀	DC MC V	52	●	■	●
L'ÎLE ROUSSE: *Santa Maria* €€€€ Rue du Port, 20220. **Road map** C2. 📞 04 95 63 05 05. 🌐 www.santamaria.com A modern hotel with direct access to the beach. 🚀	AE MC V	56	●	■	
MACINAGGIO: *U Libecciu* €€€ Route de la Plage, 20248. **Road map** D1. 📞 04 95 35 43 22. 🌐 www.u-libecciu.com Situated 100 m (330 ft) from the port and the famous beach. The Sentier des Douaniers path *(see p68)* starts nearby. ● *16 Oct–28 Feb.* 🚀	AE DC MC V	30		■	●

Average prices per night in a double room, tax, service and breakfast included:

€ less than €50
€€ €50–€100
€€€ €100–€150
€€€€ €150–€200
€€€€€ more than €200

CREDIT CARDS
AE: American Express; DC: Diners Club; MC: MasterCard/Access; V: Visa.

SWIMMING POOL
A pool with facilities for hotel guests.

BEACH
A beach with facilities for hotel guests.

RESTAURANT
A high-quality restaurant on the hotel premises that is also open to non-residents.

	Credit Cards	Number of Rooms	Swimming Pool	Beach	Restaurant
NONZA: *Auberge Patrizi/Casa Lisa* €€ La Place du Village, 20217. **Road map** D1. [04 95 32 72 52. FAX 04 95 37 86 40. A small, cosy hotel offering excellent value for money. ● mid-Oct–Mar. 🛏	MC V	12			●
PATRIMONIO: *Auberge U Lustincone* €€ Route du Cap, 20253. **Road map** D2. [04 95 37 15 28. This charming hotel surrounded by vineyards has a family atmosphere. The terrace affords a spectacular view of the sea and the cliffs, and the restaurant (open May to September) serves fish specialities. ● Oct–Apr. 🛏 P 🛏		9			●
PIETRACORBARA: *Auberge Macchia e Mare* €€ Marine de Pietracorbara, 20233. **Road map** D1. [04 95 35 21 36. FAX 04 95 35 22 35. This hotel facing a beach offers courteous, attentive service. Guests arriving by boat can moor at the hotel's private dock. 🛏 TV P 🛏	AE MC V	8		■	●
PIGNA: *Casa Musicale* €€ Pigna, 20220. **Road map** C2. [04 95 61 77 31. W www.casa-musicale.org With each room named after a voice range and individually decorated, this cultural centre *(see p74)* offers unique and charming accommodation. ● Jan. 🛏 TV 🛏	AE MC V	8			●
ST-FLORENT: *U Liamone* € Route de Treperi, 20217. **Road map** D2. [04 95 37 12 81. W www.hotel-u-liamone.com This hotel stands some distance from town. It has rustic architecture and a family atmosphere. Guests can use the owner's boat for tours. 🛏 P 🐕		15		■	
ST-FLORENT: *Dolce Notte* €€€ Route de Bastia, 20217. **Road map** D2. [04 95 37 06 65. W www.hotel-dolce-notte.com Quality and attention to guests' needs are the features of this quiet hotel on the seaside just outside the heart of town. ● Nov–Mar. 🛏 TV P	MC V	20		■	
SAN MARTINO DI LOTA: *La Corniche* €€ Cap Corse, 20200. **Road map** D1. [04 95 31 40 98. W www.hotel-lacorniche.com A recently renovated hotel in a splendid position from which, on clear days, it is possible to see the the island of Elba. ● Jan. 🛏 TV P 🍴	AE MC V	20	●		●

AJACCIO AND THE WEST COAST

	Credit Cards	Number of Rooms	Swimming Pool	Beach	Restaurant
AJACCIO: *Fesch* €€ 7 Rue Fesch, 20000. **Road map** B4. [04 95 51 62 62. FAX 04 95 21 83 36. Located in the heart of the Old Town, this characteristic hotel has a warm, cosy atmosphere. ● 20 Dec–20 Jan. 🛏 ▤ TV 🛏	AE DC MC V	77			
AJACCIO: *Stella di Mare* €€ Route des Sanguinaires, 20000. **Road map** B4. [04 95 52 01 07. FAX 04 95 52 08 69. W www.hotel-stelladimare.com About 7 km (4 miles) from Ajaccio, Stella di Mare has a great view of both the gulf and the Îles Sanguinaires *(see p92)*. ● Nov–Mar. 🛏 ▤ TV ♿ P 🍴	MC V	60	●	■	●
AJACCIO: *Dolce Vita* €€€€€ Route des Sanguinaires, 20000. **Road map** B4. [04 95 52 42 42. FAX 04 95 52 07 15. W www.hotel-dolcevita.com Great attention is paid to detail in this famous hotel run by the Federici family. Fabulous atmosphere. ● Nov–mid-Mar. 🛏 ▤ TV 🛏	AE DC MC V	32	●	■	●
CARGÈSE: *Beau Rivage* € Plage Chiuni, 20130. **Road map** B3. [04 95 26 43 91. A peaceful hotel on the beautiful beach of Cargèse, with a private aquatic centre and a restaurant serving fish specialities. ● Nov–Mar. 🛏 P 🍴 🛏		15		■	●
EVISA: *Aitone* €€ Rue Principale, 20126. **Road map** C4. [04 95 26 20 04. W www.hotel-aitone.com At an altitude of 850 m (2,800 ft), close to the Forêt d'Aitone *(see p103)*, this hotel is an ideal starting point for excursions. ● Dec–Jan. 🛏 TV P 🛏	MC V	32	●		●

For key to symbols, see back flap

	Average prices per night in a double room, tax, service and breakfast included:
€	less than €50
€€	€50–€100
€€€	€100–€150
€€€€	€150–€200
€€€€€	more than €200

CREDIT CARDS
AE: American Express; DC: Diners Club; MC: MasterCard/Access; V: Visa.

SWIMMING POOL
A pool with facilities for hotel guests.

BEACH
A beach with facilities for hotel guests.

RESTAURANT
A high-quality restaurant on the hotel premises that is also open to non-residents.

	Price	Credit Cards	Number of Rooms	Swimming Pool	Beach	Restaurant
GUAGNO-LES-BAINS: *Hôtel des Thermes* 20160. **Road map** B4. **(** 04 95 26 80 50. **FAX** 04 95 28 34 02. At this hotel with a spa, relaxation, well-being and good food are in perfect harmony. Spacious and comfortable rooms. ● *Nov–Apr.* 🛏 📺 🚻 🅿 🏠 🍴	€€	AE DC MC V	34	●		●
PIANA: *Les Calanches* Entrée Village, 20155. **Road map** B3. **(** 04 95 27 82 08. **FAX** 04 95 26 17 48. A tranquil hotel in the midst of a picturesque natural setting, near the village of Piana. ● *Nov–Mar.* 🛏 🅿 🏠	€€	MC V	17			
PORTICCIO: *Sofitel Thalassa* Domaine de la Pointe, 20166. **Road map** B4. **(** 04 95 29 40 40. **W** www.thalassa.com Opposite the Îles Sanguinaires *(see p92)* is this modern, luxurious complex in a large private park, with direct access to the Thalassotherapy Institute. All the rooms have a view of the sea. ● *2 wks in Jan.* 🛏 🍴 📺 🚻 🅿 🏠 ⚡ 🎾 🍴	€€€€€	AE DC MC V	98	●	■	●
PORTO: *Capo d'Orto* Route de Calvi, 20150. **Road map** B3. **(** 04 95 26 11 14. **W** www.hotel-capo-dorto.com In the Parc Naturel Régional de la Corse *(see p99)*, this simple, comfortable hotel overlooks the Golfe de Porto. ● *Nov–Mar.* 🛏 📺 🚻 🅿	€€	MC V	39	●		
PORTO: *Idéal* La Marine, 20150. **Road map** B3. **(** 04 95 26 14 94. **W** www.hotels-porto.com/ideal Situated in the middle of the Marina, the Idéal has a fine view of the gulf and the Genoese tower. All the rooms have a balcony with a view of the sea or the mountains. ● *mid-Oct–Easter.* 🛏 🍴 🅿	€€	MC V	25		■	
PORTO: *Le Kallisté* Place de la Marine, 20150. **Road map** B3. **(** 04 95 26 10 30. **W** www.hotel-kalliste.com The large, pink-granite complex of Le Kallisté is in a beautiful part of the Marina. Most rooms have a balcony with sea view. ● *Nov–Mar.* 🛏 🍴 📺 🅿 🏠	€€	MC V	58			

BONIFACIO AND THE SOUTH

	Price	Credit Cards	Number of Rooms	Swimming Pool	Beach	Restaurant
BONIFACIO: *Du Golfe* Golfe de Santa Manza, 20169. **Road map** C6. **(** 04 95 73 05 91. **FAX** 04 95 73 17 18. **W** www.corsud.com/golfe.hotel About 5 km (3 miles) from the town, in a magical spot along the coast, is this delightful hotel. Half board only. ● *20 Oct–mid-Mar.* 🛏 🍴 🅿 🏠	€€	MC V	12		■	●
BONIFACIO: *Hotel Restaurant du Centre Nautique* Quai Nord, Port de Plaisance, 20169. **Road map** C6. **(** 04 95 73 02 11. **FAX** 04 95 73 17 47. **W** www.centre-nautique.com Open all year round, this hotel is quite famous, as is its restaurant, which is frequented by the yachting world. ● *Nov.* 🛏 🍴 📺 🅿	€€€	AE DC MC V	10			●
BONIFACIO: *Genovese* Quartier de la Citadelle, Haute Ville, 20169. **Road map** C6. **(** 04 95 73 12 34. **FAX** 04 95 73 09 03. **W** www.hotel-genovese.com In the heart of the Citadelle, the Genovese is located in the ramparts overlooking the sea. The price varies according to whether there is a view of the port or of the Citadelle. ● *Jan–mid-Mar.* 🛏 🍴 📺 🅿	€€€€€	AE DC MC V	18	●		
PORTO-POLLO: *Les Eucalyptus* Serra di Serro, 20140. **Road map** B5. **(** 04 95 74 01 52. **W** www.hotelleseucalyptus.com This modern, peaceful complex, right on the beach and surrounded by a lovely garden, offers great value for money. All the rooms have a balcony and a view of the sea. ● *mid-Oct–Mar.* 🛏 📺 🅿 🏠 🍴	€€	AE MC V	27		■	
PORTO-VECCHIO: *San Giovanni* Route d'Arca, 20137. **Road map** C6. **(** 04 95 70 22 25. **W** www.hotel-san-giovanni.com A park filled with flowers, a heated swimming pool and many sports facilities are the features of the San Giovanni, a hotel with a warm, welcoming atmosphere. ● *Nov–Feb.* 🛏 📺 🚻 🅿 🍴 🍴	€€	AE MC V	30	●		●

PORTO-VECCHIO: *Moby Dick* €€€

Santa Giulia, 20137. **Road map** C6.

📞 *04 95 70 70 00 (to book: 0825 082 506).* 📠 *04 95 70 70 01.*

A famous hotel complex on a sand bar between the sea and the Santa Giulia lagoon. It offers different types of room and mini-apartment.

● *mid-Oct–mid-Apr.* 🛏 🍴 📺 🔆 🅿 🍽 🐾

| | AE MC V | 44 | | ■ | ● |

PORTO-VECCHIO: *U Benedettu* €€€

Presqu'Île Benedettu, Lecci, 20137. **Road map** C6.

📞 *04 95 71 62 81.* 📠 *04 95 71 66 37.* 🌐 www.ubenedettu.com

This seaside hotel is ideal for a relaxing holiday. ● *Feb.* 🛏 🍴 📺 🔆 🅿 🍽 🐾

| | AE MC V | 15 | | ■ | ● |

PROPRIANO: *Grand Hôtel Miramar* €€€€€

Route de la Corniche, 20110. **Road map** B5. 📞 *04 95 76 06 13.* 🌐 www.miramarcorse.com

A luxurious hotel in a unique setting between beaches and mountains.
There are also two suites with jacuzzis and an independent garden.

● *Oct–Apr.* 🛏 🍴 📺 🅿 🍽 🐾

| | AE DC MC V | 28 | ● | ■ | ● |

QUENZA: *Sole e Monti* €€

Monticello, 20122. **Road map** C5. 📞 *04 95 78 62 53.* 🌐 www.solemonti.com

At an altitude of 800 m (2,600 ft), this hotel immersed in greenery also has
a good restaurant. ● *Oct–Apr.* 🛏 📺 🅿 🍽 🐾

| | AE DC MC V | 18 | | | ● |

SARTÈNE: *Les Roches* €€

Avenue Jean Jaurès, 20100. **Road map** C5. 📞 *04 95 77 07 61.* 📠 *04 95 77 19 93.*

In the historic centre of Sartène, this simple, economic
hotel is open all year round. 🛏 🍴 📺 🔆 🅿 🐾

| | MC V | 66 | | | ● |

SOLENZARA: *La Solenzara* €€

Hameau Solenzara, 20145. **Road map** D5. 📞 *04 95 57 42 18.* 🌐 www.lasolenzara.com

In a converted 18th-century Genoese-style building, La Solenzara
is surrounded by a beautiful garden. ● *Nov–Mar.* 🛏 🍴 📺 🔆 🅿 🐾

| | AE DC MC V | 28 | ● | ■ | |

ZONZA: *Aiglon* €€

20124. **Road map** C5. 📞 *04 95 78 67 79.* 📠 *04 95 78 63 62.* 🌐 www.aiglonhotel.com

Situated in the heart of town, this is a charming, old-fashioned hotel.
Regional cuisine is on offer in the restaurant. ● *mid-Jan–Mar.* 🛏 🅿 🐾

| | AE MC V | 10 | | | ● |

CORTE AND THE INTERIOR

CALACUCCIA: *L'Acqua Viva* €

Id Scardacciole, 20224. **Road map** C3. 📞 *04 95 48 06 90.* 📠 *04 95 48 08 82.*

A small hotel open all year round, where you can enjoy the many
natural sights and sports activities in this area. The rooms are simply
furnished and all have a balcony or terrace. 🛏 📺 🅿 🐾

| | MC V | 14 | | | |

CORTE: *De la Paix* €€

Avenue Général de Gaulle, 20250. **Road map** C3. 📞 *04 95 46 06 72.* 📠 *04 95 46 23 84.*

In the heart of town, this economic hotel is useful as a base to
visit the central part of the island. ● *10 days at Christmas.* 🛏 📺 🐾

| | | 64 | | | ● |

CORTE: *Dominique Colonna* €€€

Lieu-dit Restonica, 20250. **Road map** C3.

📞 *04 95 45 25 65.* 📠 *04 95 61 03 91.* 🌐 www.dominique-colonna.com

The excellent Dominique Colonna, outside the town, offers a peaceful stay.
All the rooms have a balcony or terrace. ● *6 Nov–mid-Mar.* 🛏 🍴 📺 🔆 🅿 🐾

| | AE DC MC V | 28 | ● | | |

PIEDICROCE: *Le Refuge* €€

Village, 20229. **Road map** C3. 📞 *04 95 35 82 65.* 📠 *04 95 35 84 42.*

A typical mountain hotel, rustic and simple. It has a good
restaurant offering Corsican specialities. ● *Nov–Mar.* 🛏 📺 🔆 🐾

| | MC V | 20 | | | ● |

VENACO: *Paesotel E Caselle* €€

Lieu-dit Polveroso, 20231. **Road map** C3. 📞 *04 95 47 39 00.* 🌐 www.e-caselle.com

This hotel offers lovely architecture modelled after the mountain
sheepfolds, with chestnut furniture in the local style. There are different
kinds of room and mini-apartments. ● *mid-Oct–mid-Apr.* 🛏 📺 🔆 🅿 🍽 🐾

| | AE MC V | 47 | ● | | ● |

VIZZAVONA: *Monte d'Oro* €€

Col de Vizzavona, Hameau de la Foce, 20129. **Road map** C4.

📞 *04 95 47 21 06.* 📠 *04 95 47 22 05.* 🌐 www.monte-oro.com

In the middle of a forest with centuries-old trees, this establishment
is in the style typical of 19th-century health resorts, with sloping roofs.

● *mid-Oct–Apr.* 🛏 🔆 🅿 🍽 🐾 🐾

| | MC V | 30 | | | ● |

WHERE TO EAT

Tearoom sign in Ajaccio

N APÉRITIF AT SUNSET in front of the small harbour in Ajaccio, or fresh grilled fish on a small beach in Cap Corse, cannelloni stuffed with *brocciu* cheese at a *ferme-auberge* or the elegant refinement of a restaurant in a large hotel – Corsica offers many options when it comes to eating and drinking. The beauty of a trip to this island also depends on its rich cuisine, which blends the flavours of the sea with those of the land. In Corsica the food is generally good and not overpriced. Cafés and bistros are ideal for a quick snack and, if you want to economize, there are pizza parlours, especially in seaside resorts. Even inland, where tourism is less hectic, you can find nice places offering typically Corsican specialities. Indeed, if you are staying along the coast, it is still worthwhile making a trip inland to have a fine meal. At country inns, good regional food is often accompanied by interesting conversations with the locals.

A small beach restaurant in Bussaglia, near Porto

RESTAURANTS

IN CORSICA, restaurants in the coastal towns offer fresh fish, grilled shrimp, lobsters, sardines with fresh *brocciu* cheese, *aziminu* (an elaborate seafood stew) and other seafood specialities. These establishments often have verandas or tables outdoors, along the promenades or in the harbour area.

The more exclusive restaurants in the tourist resorts include Le Floride (*see p169*) in Ajaccio, and Le Troubadour (*see p171*) and L'Orée du Maquis (*see p171*) in Porto-Vecchio. Among the best fish restaurants in Corsica are Le Vieux Port Chez Huguette (*see p168*) in Bastia and Cyrnos (*see p168*) in Calvi.

There are also high-quality hotel restaurants, including the refined Le Belvédère (*see p170*) and the Grand Hôtel Cala Rossa (*see p171*) in Porto-Vecchio, and L'Arbousier (*see p170*) in Porticcio. Other types of hotel, such as Casa Musicale (*see p159*) in Pigna, have fine restaurants that combine tradition and innovation.

The restaurants known as *tables gastronomiques* are a guarantee of quality for the variety of their menu, the careful preparation of the dishes and the excellent service, while the places called *tables du terroir* offer typical Corsican dishes, such as game, charcuterie and home-made cheeses.

Seaside resorts also have bistros, which are ideal for a simple meal, a slice of quiche or a plate of cheese or cold cuts, and pizza parlours, which also offer *crêpes* and local specialities at low prices.

In the villages inland, it is possible to eat at typical restaurants with genuine products such as ham, pork neck salami and *figatellu* (liver sausage).

The restaurants recommended on pages 168–71 are among the best in Corsica.

FERME-AUBERGES

AN EXCELLENT OPTION when it comes to eating consists of the *ferme-auberges* ("farm-inns"). They offer genuine Corsican dishes made with products from the farm itself, such as cheese, vegetables and charcuterie. Among the best, A Pignata (*see p170*), in Levie, features specialities based on chestnut flour, while La Bergerie d'Acciola (*see p171*), near Sartène, serves different cheeses made on the premises.

Most *ferme-auberges* offer half-board accommodation. During the summer, guests can stay on a weekly basis only.

Outdoor dining at a typical small restaurant

Outdoor café in a shaded esplanade

BARS AND CAFÉS

MANY BARS and cafés, especially those in coastal towns, have tables outdoors. They become particularly crowded during the apéritif hour, when people gather at their local bar or café to have a glass of *pastis*, Cap Corse or Corsican beer, accompanied by olives.

These cafés also serve breakfast, and in many pastry shops there are small tables where you can enjoy croissants, biscuits, pastries, cakes and tarts, some of which are made with chestnuts or fruit.

The most characteristic Corsican cafés are located in Place St-Nicolas in Bastia, along the Quai Landry in Calvi, on the main square in Porto-Vecchio and along the yacht harbour in Ajaccio.

BREAKFAST

IN CORSICA, breakfast *(petit déjeuner)* is an important ritual. The day begins with coffee *(café au lait* or *café crème)*, accompanied by fresh bread *(baguette)*, eaten with honey or preserves. There are also croissants and *pains au chocolat*. The large hotels serve continental breakfasts, while on the farms breakfast consists of the farm's own products, such as honey, milk and preserves.

PRICES AND PAYING

BESIDES the à la carte menu, almost all restaurants in Corsica have fixed-price menus *(formule)*, the prices of which differ according to the dishes. These menus offer regional or fish and seafood specialities and sometimes give you the opportunity to try typical dishes that would otherwise be hard to find.

In general, a complete meal in an average-level restaurant costs €20–€25, while in bistros and simple restaurants it is €13–€15. If you do not want to spend much, try the pizzerias – a meal here never costs more than €10–€12.

Restaurants usually accept the most common credit cards used in Europe; smaller establishments in less frequented areas prefer cash.

OPENING HOURS AND RESERVATIONS

OPENING HOURS in Corsica are similar to those in mainland France. Lunch is usually served from 12:30 to 2:30pm and dinner from 7:30 to 10pm, but in tourist resorts many places close later in summer. The villages inland have shorter opening hours. Most establishments close once a week and for their holidays, which usually coincide with the low season.

In the summer, especially in the evening, it is always advisable to book a table.

VEGETARIAN FOOD AND WHEELCHAIR ACCESS

VEGETARIANS will not have too hard a time ordering a meat- or fish-free meal in Corsica. Among the options are omelettes, cheese, pizzas and *cannelloni al brocciu*.

Wheelchair access and other facilities for the disabled may be hard to find, especially in the old historic centres and villages, although many places have conformed to the new regulations. Holiday Care *(see p189)* publishes a guide listing all the establishments with wheelchair access in France and Corsica.

DRESS AND SMOKING

THERE IS NO NEED to dress elegantly in restaurants, unless they are exclusive. However, avoid going to the opposite extreme: it is best not to dine in your bathing costume, even in places along the seaside.

Smoking is permitted in most Corsican restaurants.

The elegant dining room in La Caravelle *(see p170)*, in Bonifacio

What to Eat in Corsica

CORSICAN CUISINE EFFORTLESSLY COMBINES surf and turf and offers genuine products and simple dishes with strong flavours, seasoned with olive oil and aromatic herbs. Inland you can find pork, boar or lamb dishes, either roasted or stewed, and charcuterie, which is often smoked. Along the coast, fish and seafood are cooked on the grill or in soups. As is often the case in the Mediterranean, first courses include pasta with tomato paste and olive oil or seasoned with *brocciu*, a local cheese similar to ricotta. There are also different soups with vegetables, legumes and onions. Another typical ingredient is chestnuts, used as a side dish or in desserts.

Cannelloni al brocciu, *stuffed with the local sheep's-milk cheese, make for a tasty meal. They are oven-baked and served with tomato sauce.*

STARTERS

The variety of Corsican starters is such that there is something for everyone. They can be as simple and rustic as bean soup, or more elaborate, like *cannelloni al brocciu*. The ingredients are locally produced and many Corsican dishes are quite unique. During the chestnut season, make sure you try the hearty chestnut soup.

Suppa corsa *is a thick bean soup also containing onions, potatoes and chickpeas. It is not for vegetarians – smoked bacon is added for flavour.*

Suppa di castagna, *a winter dish based on chestnuts, is seasoned with onions, garlic, aromatic herbs and meat. It is served warm rather than hot.*

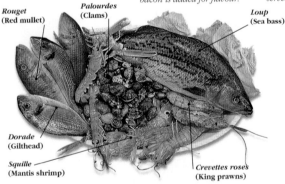

Rouget (Red mullet)
Palourdes (Clams)
Loup (Sea bass)
Dorade (Gilthead)
Squille (Mantis shrimp)
Crevettes roses (King prawns)

Grilled fish: *gilthead, sea bass, mullet and crustaceans are perfect for the scrumptious grilled fish dishes flavoured with maquis herbs.*

FISH-BASED MAIN COURSES

Like all places by the sea, Corsica features fish, crustaceans and molluscs in its cuisine. They are usually very fresh, thanks to the daily catch, and are served in various tasty recipes, some of which have an international flavour, while others are more unusual and reflect the tradition of the island's typical cuisine.

Aziminu, *a classic Corsican seafood soup, is served in the same way as bouillabaisse: the fish on a plate and the bouillon (stock) on the side.*

Grondin aux olives: *gurnard is cooked in the oven and served with a sauce made with eggs, oil and vinegar and flavoured with tomatoes and olives.*

Rouget au fenouil: *red mullet is cooked in the oven with a splash of olive oil and served with a sauce made of onions, fennel and olive oil.*

MEAT-BASED MAIN COURSES

Corsican meat comes from animals living in the wild. It has a strong flavour and is often accompanied by herbs that enhance this quality. The meat is cooked in various ways: it can be roasted, braised or stewed, and it is often also grilled in fireplaces. Meat dishes are part of the winter cuisine more often than fish dishes.

Agnellu (lamb) flavoured with herbs is barbecued and served with piverunata (peppers cooked with tomatoes and onions).

Cingale (wild boar) can be marinated in red wine, brandy and herbs, and cooked with chestnuts and fennel.

Porc rotî aux aubergines is roast pork flavoured with garlic and laurel, and sautéed aubergines (eggplant).

Stifatu is a stew with mixed meats cooked with cubes of smoked raw ham, onions, olive oil, tomato sauce and red wine.

Pulenta made with chestnut flour accompanies figatelli (smoked sausages), brocciu cheese and all meat dishes.

DESSERTS AND FRUIT

Corsican desserts combine genuine flavours with traditional, home-made cooking. They are mostly made with simple, natural ingredients, such as brocciu cheese and chestnuts.

On the island there is no shortage of fruit, which can be combined with other food – for example, figs with cheese or ham – or eaten fresh in the summer as relief from the heat.

Torta castagnina is prepared with chestnut flour mixed with milk, vanilla sugar, grappa, chopped almonds and hazelnuts, and raisins or pine nuts.

Fiadone is made with eggs, sugar, milk and brocciu cheese, and flavoured with orange flowers. It is served cold or warm, or even flambé.

Fresh figs

Chestnuts

Corsican fruit is varied and tasty. It includes produce typical of both sunny areas, such as oranges and lemons, and hilly, wooded areas, such as sweet figs and chestnuts.

CHARCUTERIE AND CHEESE

The wild pigs left to roam free feed on acorns, chestnuts and other natural foods, and their diet lends a special flavour to their meats. There are prisuttu (cured ham), figatellu (smoked liver sausage), pork neck and lonzu (smoked fillet), which are salted, spiced and smoked. There are also many sheep's-milk cheeses, such as niulincu, orezzincu, bastelicaccia, balaninu, sartenese and ghisonaccia, and the more delicate brocciu.

What to Drink in Corsica

CORSICAN WINES date back to the period when the ancient Greeks and Romans colonized the island, as revealed by the amphoras of wine found in galleys that sank off the east coast. Full-bodied, fruity and strong, Corsican wines are made from three local grapes, Sciaccarellu, Niellucciu and Vermentinu, which, over the years, have been combined with others from the Continent that have flourished on the island. The wines are made in nine zones that have the AOC (*Appellation d'Origine Controlée*) designation, which is a guarantee of superior quality and authenticity. In addition, Corsica produces various liqueurs and brandies that are made from maquis plants such as myrtle and strawberry tree and that reflect the strong flavours of the island. There are also local mineral water springs and aromatized beers.

The tables of the Café Napoléon, in Place St-Nicolas, Bastia

LIQUEURS AND APÉRITIFS

As an apéritif, Corsicans drink *pastis*, an aniseed liqueur that in the summer is enjoyed with ice. Other liqueurs are made from myrtle, strawberry tree and citrus fruits like tangerines, oranges and citrons. Castagniccia also produces a chestnut liqueur.

Cap Corse is a real institution also known abroad. Its inimitable bitter and acidulous taste derives from quinine. This Corsican apéritif can be purchased at the Maison Mattei (see p63), the historic house founded in Bastia in 1872.

Citron liqueur

Tangerines

Citrons

WATER AND BEER

Cool mineral water flows from springs in the mountains and is then bottled and sold throughout the island. Beer is also produced on the island. Corsican beer is known for its strong aromas.

Zilia mineral water

Orezza mineral water

St-Georges mineral water

Three brands of beer are produced in Corsica. Pietra is amber-coloured and includes chestnuts among its ingredients; Serena is pale and light; Colomba is a Belgian/German-style wheat beer with a strong taste thanks to the addition of myrtle.

The best-known sparkling (pétillante) mineral water is Orezza, from the Castagniccia area, which is bottled and distributed throughout Corsica and even to fine restaurants in Paris. Other mineral water comes from the Zilia springs, in the Balagne area, and from St-Georges, near Ajaccio.

WINE

Corsican wines usually bear the name of the AOC zone in which they are made on their labels. These zones are: Ajaccio, Calvi, Coteaux du Cap Corse, Figari, Patrimonio, Porto-Vecchio and Sartène. Two other AOCs are called Muscat du Cap Corse and Vins de Corse. Wines also bear the name of the winemaker, preceded by the words *Clos* or *Domaine*, to guarantee the fact that they are made in the winery or estate on the label.

An AOC Cap Corse wine label

Among the best Corsican white wines, there is a good, fruity Malvasia made from grapes grown on the terraced vineyards of Cap Corse. The AOC Patrimonio is famous for its Niellucciu, a dry wine made from a local grape. Other first-rate white wines are those from AOC Muscat du Cap Corse.

AOC Coteaux du Cap Corse   **AOC Vins de Corse**

Rosé is a common wine and the Porto-Vecchio, Patrimonio and Vins de Corse AOCs are among the best. The basic grapes used are the local Niellucciu and Sciaccarellu, which are mixed with many other grapes to produce a tasty wine with a fine bouquet that is ideal for summer consumption.

AOC Patrimonio   **AOC Vins de Corse**

RECOMMENDED AOC WINERIES

The best wines can be purchased directly from the wineries.

AOC Ajaccio
A Cantina, Les Marines, Porticcio.
📞 04 95 25 08 90. 🄵🄰🅇 04 95 24 38 07.
Clos Capitoro, Ajaccio.
📞 04 95 25 19 61. 🄵🄰🅇 04 95 25 19 33.

AOC Calvi
Domaine Balaninu Nobile, Calvi. 📞 04 95 65 37 10.

AOC Figari
Olmu di Cagna, Coopérative de Figari. 📞 04 95 71 87 42. Domaine de Tanella, Figari. 📞 04 95 71 00 25.

AOC Muscat du Cap Corse
Clos Nicrosi, Rogliano.
📞 04 95 35 41 17. 🄵🄰🅇 04 95 35 47 94.
Domaine de Pietri, Morsiglia (for Rappu).
📞 04 95 35 60 93.

AOC Patrimonio
Domaine Gentile, St-Florent.
📞 04 95 37 01 54.

AOC Porto-Vecchio
Domaine de Torraccia, Lecci, Porto-Vecchio.
📞 04 95 71 43 50.

AOC Sartène
Domaine San Michèle.
📞 04 95 77 06 38.

AOC Vins de Corse
Le Clos Lea, Aléria. 📞 04 95 57 13 60.

Red wines, which are full-bodied and have a good bouquet, are mostly made from local grapes. The best reds in Corsica belong to the AOC Patrimonio, thanks to the mild climate and the soil, which is particularly suitable for grape cultivation. Connoisseurs will also enjoy reds from AOC Ajaccio, made from Sciaccarellu grapes, which are every bit as good as Beaujolais. Also worth a try are the reds from Coteaux du Cap Corse, Figari, Porto-Vecchio and Sartène AOCs, the last of which is particularly robust.

AOC Patrimonio

Dessert wines are mostly made in the Cap Corse and Patrimonio areas, and among the best are the white muscat and red aleatico. A rare white dessert wine from Cap Corse is Rappu, which can be purchased only from the wineries that produce it. Rappu makes a perfect accompaniment for all dry desserts.

The label of a wine originating from the AOC Muscat du Cap Corse

Choosing a Restaurant

THESE RESTAURANTS have been selected across a range of price categories for their exceptional food, interesting location and good value for money. The chart lists the restaurants by area; the colour-coded thumb tabs indicate the areas covered on each page. The map references for the restaurants refer to the road map of Corsica on the back endpaper.

	CREDIT CARDS	OUTDOOR TABLES	FIXED-PRICE MENU	GOOD WINE LIST	OPEN LATE
BASTIA AND THE NORTH					
BASTIA: *Hotel Restaurant Chez Walter* €€ Casamozza, 20290. **Road map** D2. **(** 04 95 36 00 09. Sophisticated regional cuisine is on offer at Chez Walter, a favourite with sportspeople, especially footballers and rally drivers. ● *3 wks in Dec.*	AE DC MC V	■	●	■	●
BASTIA: *La Litorne* €€ Casevechie, Ville de Pietrabugno, 20200. **Road map** D2. **(** 04 95 31 41 89. Traditional, good-quality cuisine in this restaurant 2 km (1 mile) from Bastia. ● *Mon; mid-Oct–mid-Mar.*	AE MC V	■			●
BASTIA: *Le Lavezzi* €€ 8 Rue Saint Jean, 20200. **Road map** D2. **(** 04 95 31 05 73. This 70-year-old restaurant facing out to the port is the oldest in Bastia. The red mullet with herbs is highly recommended. ● *Sun; 6 wks Feb–Mar.*	AE MC V	■		■	●
BASTIA: *Le Vieux Port Chez Huguette* €€€ Le Vieux Port, 20200. **Road map** D2. **(** 04 95 31 37 60. This famous restaurant serves first-rate fish specialities. ● *Sun.*	AE DC MC V	■	●		●
CALENZANA: *Le Calenzana/Chez Michel* € 7 Cours Saint Blaise, 20214. **Road map** D2. **(** 04 95 62 70 25. A country inn with dishes such as boar ragout and *agnellu* (lamb). ● *Mon; Jan.*	MC V	■	●		
CALVI: *Le Bout du Monde* €€ Plage de Calvi, 20260. **Road map** D2. **(** 04 95 65 15 41. With fresh fish, creative cuisine and views of the citadel from its beachside terrace, this restaurant is not to be missed. ● *Feb–mid-Mar.*	AE DC MC V	■		■	
CALVI: *Cyrnos* € Quai Landry, 20260. **Road map** D2. **(** 04 95 65 06 10. The speciality of Cyrnos, in the heart of town, is stuffed fish. ● *Tue; Dec–Feb.*	MC V	■	●		●
CORBARA: *A Pyramida* €€ Lieu-dit Spilonca, 20256. **Road map** C2. **(** 04 95 60 70 43. Mediterranean cuisine in a cosy setting, in the shade of weeping willow trees. ● *Mon & Tue.*	MC V				●
ERBALUNGA: *La Piazzetta* €€ Place du Village, 20222. **Road map** D1. **(** 04 95 33 28 69. A charming place in the little town square. Excellent fresh pasta and fish. ● *Tue; Jan–Feb.*		■			
ERBALUNGA: *Le Pirate* €€€€ Place Marc Barobu, 20222. **Road map** D1. **(** 04 95 33 24 20. Quality fish dishes are served in this eatery within the fishermen's harbour. ● *Mon; Nov–Easter.*	AE MC V	■	●	■	
L'ÎLE ROUSSE: *Le Laetitia* €€€ Route du Port, 20220. **Road map** C2. **(** 04 95 60 01 90. Le Laetitia is frequented by VIPs for its seafood specialities, which include sea bass *en croûte* and spaghetti with lobsters. ● *Mon; Jan.*	MC V	■		■	●
MACINAGGIO: *Maison Bellini* €€ Marina, 20248. **Road map** D1. **(** 04 95 35 40 37. This classic fish restaurant featuring traditional dishes faces out directly onto the port. ● *Nov–Feb.*	MC V	■			●
MURATO: *Le But* €€ Lieu-dit Soprano, 20239. **Road map** D2. **(** 04 95 37 60 92. Set in the heart of the village, this rustic restaurant has great charcuterie, fine Corsican wines and generous-spirited owners. ● *Mon; winter: Tue–Fri; Jan.*	AE DC MC V		●	■	●

Average price per person for a three-course meal, including a half bottle of house wine, tax and service. € less than €25 €€ €25–€40 €€€ €40–€55 €€€€ more than €55	**CREDIT CARDS** AE: American Express; DC: Diners Club; MC: MasterCard/Access; V: Visa. **FIXED-PRICE MENU** This may be for lunch, dinner or both. It is generally a three-course meal. **GOOD WINE LIST** A wide variety of good wines, or a selection of particular wines. **OPEN LATE** Establishments that stay open late, with the entire menu available after 10pm.	**CREDIT CARDS**	**OUTDOOR TABLES**	**FIXED-PRICE MENU**	**GOOD WINE LIST**	**OPEN LATE**

	Price	Credit Cards	Outdoor Tables	Fixed-Price Menu	Good Wine List	Open Late
OGLIASTRU: *Morganti* Marina d'Albu, 20217. **Road map** D2. 04 95 37 85 10. Excellent fish restaurant with elaborate dishes such as fillet of dory with mint, and shrimp gratin. A high-quality wine list. ● 3 wks in Dec.	€€€	MC V	■	●	■	●
OLMI CAPPELLA: *La Tornadia* Route de la Forêt de Tartagines, Pioggiola, 20259. **Road map** D2. 04 95 61 90 93. A rustic restaurant using typical home-made products for its traditional Corsican cuisine. ● 16 Nov–14 Mar.	€	MC V	■	●		●
PIGNA: *Casa Musicale* 20220. **Road map** D2. 04 95 61 77 31. This restaurant lies in a panoramic position. It features regional dishes and, after dinner, live Corsican polyphonic and folk music *(see p74)*. ● Jan.	€€	AE MC V	■	●		●
ST-FLORENT: *Le Cabestan* Rue du Fornello, 20217. **Road map** D2. 04 95 37 05 70. A pleasant, cosy setting. A good fish restaurant with more than 20 years' experience. ● Nov–Feb.	€€	MC V		●	■	●
ST-FLORENT: *La Marinuccia* Place de l'Ancienne Poste, 20217. **Road map** D2. 04 95 37 04 36. Offering excellent fish dishes, this restaurant in a characteristic stone building is located on the seaside, in the heart of the Old Town. ● Oct–Mar.	€€	MC V	■		■	●
ST-FLORENT: *La Rascasse* Le Port, 20217. **Road map** D2. 04 95 37 06 99. La Rascasse is one of the best fish restaurants in Corsica, with a terrace overlooking the sea.	€€€	AE DC MC V	■		■	●

AJACCIO AND THE WEST COAST

	Price	Credit Cards	Outdoor Tables	Fixed-Price Menu	Good Wine List	Open Late
AJACCIO: *Auberge Colomba* 3 Rue Trois Marie, 20000. **Road map** B4. 04 95 51 30 55. Quality regional cuisine at very reasonable prices. ● Sun; Nov.	€	MC V	■	●		
AJACCIO: *L'Estaminet* 7 Rue du Roi de Rome, 20000. **Road map** B4. 04 95 50 10 42. This authentic French-style bistro is a must for visitors. ● Wed (Nov–Mar).	€€	MC V	■	●	■	●
AJACCIO: *Altru Versu* 16 Rue Jean-Baptiste Marcaggi, 20000. **Road map** B4. 04 95 50 05 22. The young chef at this restaurant facing the port produces Corsican food with an original twist, such as chesnut tagliatelli. ● Sun; Feb.	€€	MC V	■	●		
AJACCIO: *Le Floride* Port Charles Ornano, 20090. **Road map** B4. 04 95 22 67 48. Spacious restaurant with a fine view of the Golfe d'Ajaccio. The fish-only menu is based on the day's catch. ● lunch Sat & Sun; mid-Sep–mid-Jun: Sun dinner.	€€	AE DC MC V	■	●	■	●
AJACCIO: *U Cinnaronu* 3 Maréchal d'Ornano, 20000. **Road map** B4. 04 95 21 49 37. U Cinnaronu offers savoury Corsican dishes. Be sure to try the local ham, which is marvellous. ● Sun; Aug.	€€	MC V	■		■	●
BOCOGNANO: *A Funtanella* Lieu-dit Colletta, 20136. **Road map** B3. 04 95 27 40 77. A restaurant/pizzeria open all year round, with typical dishes such as the local village soup, prepared in the fireplace in winter. ● Mon (winter).	€€					
COTI CHIAVARI: *Chez Francis* Plage du Cala d'Orzo, 20138. **Road map** B5. 04 95 27 10 39. Regional cuisine with fine fish, lobster and mixed-grill dishes, as well as the ever-present bouillabaisse. ● mid-Oct–Apr.	€€€	MC V	■		■	●

For key to symbols, see back flap

Average price per person for a three-course meal, including a half bottle of house wine, tax and service.

€ less than €25
€€ €25–€40
€€€ €40–€55
€€€€ more than €55

CREDIT CARDS
AE: American Express; DC: Diners Club; MC: MasterCard/Access; V: Visa.

FIXED-PRICE MENU
This may be for lunch, dinner or both. It is generally a three-course meal.

GOOD WINE LIST
A wide variety of good wines, or a selection of particular wines.

OPEN LATE
Establishments that stay open late, with the entire menu available after 10pm.

	Price	Credit Cards	Outdoor Tables	Fixed-Price Menu	Good Wine List	Open Late
CUTTOLI CORTICCHIATO: *A Casetta* Lieu-dit Cantege Canale, 20167. **Road map** B3. 04 95 25 66 59. A restaurant with unusual dishes and a lovely terrace. ● Sun pm, Mon (Sep–Jun).	€€€	AE MC V	■	●		●
EVISA: *La Châtaignerie* Lieu-dit A Rimpianata, 20126. **Road map** C4. 04 95 26 24 47. Authentic regional cooking in a typical stone house. ● Nov–Mar.	€€	DC MC V	■	●		
PIANA: *Le Neptune* Route des Calanches, 20115. **Road map** B3. 04 95 27 82 40. Part of a hotel, Le Neptune has a splendid view of the Calanques and offers three menus: regional, refined and with lobsters. ● Tue; 16 Oct–Mar.	€€	AE MC V	■	●	■	
PISCIATELLO: *U Prunelli* Bastelicaccia, 20129. **Road map** C4. 04 95 20 02 75. A small restaurant along the riverside with carefully prepared, authentic cuisine, local charcuterie and sausages and superb Corsican wine. ● Tue; Apr.	€€	MC V	■	●		●
PORTICCIO: *L'Arbousier* Hotel Le Maquis, 20166. **Road map** B4. 04 95 25 05 55. This splendidly located restaurant offers fish dishes (monkfish with curry and bass with bacon) and great desserts. ● Jan–mid-Feb.	€€€€	AE DC MC V	■	●	■	
PORTO: *Le Maquis* Porto par Ota, 20150. **Road map** B3. 04 95 26 12 19. In the countryside, with a beautiful terrace overlooking the gulf and city of Porto, Le Maquis offers fish and seafood dishes. ● Nov–Jan.	€€€	MC V	■	●		●
TIUCCIA: *U Taravu* Résid Castello, 20111. **Road map** B4. 04 95 52 22 40. Molluscs, crustaceans and seafood are the specialities of this restaurant.	€€	MC V	■	●		●

BONIFACIO AND THE SOUTH

	Price	Credit Cards	Outdoor Tables	Fixed-Price Menu	Good Wine List	Open Late
BONIFACIO: *A Manichella* Place du Marché, 20169. **Road map** C6. 04 95 73 12 75. A convenient *crêperie* in the upper city for a quick snack and good-quality main courses. ● mid-Nov–Easter.	€	MC V	■			●
BONIFACIO: *La Stella d'Oro – Chez Jules* 7 Rue Doria, 20169. **Road map** C6. 04 95 73 03 63. This restaurant in the Old Town offers typical savoury dishes and super-fresh fish. Be sure to try the aubergines (eggplant) "à la Bonifacienne". ● Oct–Easter.	€€€	AE DC MC V		●	■	●
BONIFACIO: *La Caravelle* Quai Comparetti, 20169. **Road map** C6. 04 95 73 06 47. The specialities here are crustaceans and seafood. Wide-ranging wine list. ● mid-Oct–Easter.	€€€€	AE DC MC V	■	●	■	
LEVIE: *A Pignata* Route du Pianu, 20170. **Road map** C5. 04 95 78 41 90. Between Levie and Cucuruzzu, this is a veritable paradise surrounded by greenery, featuring only local products. Book ahead. ● Nov–Mar.	€€		■	●	■	
PORTO-VECCHIO: *Le Plaisance* Quai Pascal Paoli, Port de Plaisance, 20137. **Road map** C6. 04 95 70 07 50. This eatery has a terrace overlooking the port and is a pleasant place for a snack, *crêpes* or just an ice cream. ● Nov.	€	MC V	■	●		●
PORTO-VECCHIO: *Le Belvédère* Route de Palombaggia, 20137. **Road map** C6. 04 95 70 54 13. A refined, famous restaurant in the Hôtel Belvédère, with a great wine list. ● Jan–Feb.	€€€€	AE DC MC V	■	●	■	

PORTO-VECCHIO: *Le Troubadour* €€€
13 Rue de Général Leclerc, 20137. **Road map** C6. **[** *04 95 70 08 62.*
In the heart of town, Le Troubadour serves Corsican and Mediterranean
specialities. It also features a piano-bar. ● *lunch (Jul–Aug); Sun (Sep–Jun).*

MC V

PORTO-VECCHIO: *Grand Hôtel Cala Rossa* €€€€
Lecci, 20137. **Road map** C6. **[** *04 95 71 61 51.*
This superb restaurant is part of the Relais & Châteaux chain,
and features sophisticated cuisine and first-rate lobsters. ● *Jan–Easter.*

AE DC MC V

PORTO-VECCHIO: *L'Orée du Maquis* €€€€
La Trinité, Route de la Lézardière, 20137. **Road map** C6. **[** *04 95 70 22 21.*
L'Orée du Maquis offers diners only a set menu, which changes daily. Fish
and foie gras are the specialities. ● *lunch; Sun; Mon–Thu (mid-Oct–Easter).*

MC V

SARTÈNE: *La Bergerie d'Acciola* €€
Acciola, 20100. **Road map** C5. **[** *04 95 77 14 00.*
A typical farm offering home-made products. ● *Mon (Sep); Oct–mid-Jun.*

MC V

SARTÈNE: *Santa Barbara* €€€
Lieu-dit Santa Barbara, 20100. **Road map** C5. **[** *04 95 77 09 06.*
Linked to the holiday villas of the same name, Santa Barbara is known for
its lobster salad, pigeon with myrtle and many desserts. ● *Mon; mid-Oct–Easter.*

AE MC V

SOLENZARA: *La Calèche* €€
Sari Solenzara, 20145. **Road map** D5. **[** *04 95 57 40 30.*
The ideal place for a quick snack of *crêpes* or pizza.

AE DC MC V

ZONZA: *Auberge du Col de Bavella* €
Col de Bavella, 20124. **Road map** C5. **[** *04 95 72 09 87.*
Home cooking and a magnificent view are on offer here. ● *Nov–Mar.*

AE MC V

CORTE AND THE INTERIOR

CALACUCCIA: *Le Corsica* €
Route du Couvent, 20224. **Road map** C3. **[** *04 95 48 01 31.*
Le Corsica features the area's specialities – cheese and fresh trout. ● *Nov–Mar.*

MC V

CORTE: *Chez Jacqueline* €
Pont de Castiria, 20250. **Road map** C3. **[** *04 95 47 42 04.*
Excellent from all standpoints, starting with the location at the bridge over
the Golo river. The menu features trout, kid goat and local wines. ● *Dec–Feb.*

CORTE: *L'Oliveraie* €
Lieu-dit Perru, 20250. **Road map** C3. **[** *04 95 46 06 32.*
The university crowd gathers in the lovely garden for the typical
cuisine. Try the scrumptious cakes: with aromatic herbs, hazelnut
and chestnut flour. ● *Mon pm (winter).*

AE MC V

CORTE: *U Museu* €
Rampe Ribanelle, 20250. **Road map** C3. **[** *04 95 61 08 36.*
This restaurant has a pleasant atmosphere and a deservedly
good reputation. Do not miss it. ● *Sun (winter); Jan–Mar.*

MC V

CORTE: *U Paglia Orba* €€
1 Avenue Xavier Luciani, 20250. **Road map** C3. **[** *04 95 61 07 89.*
A typical tavern in the heart of town, U Paglia Orba offers AOC
wines and Corsican specialities such as stuffed onions, aubergine with
chestnut and herbs au gratin and cheese. ● *Sun; mid-Dec–early Jan.*

MC V

GHISONACCIA: *L'Oasis* €
Route de la Mer, 20240. **Road map** D4. **[** *04 95 56 21 03.*
Good fish dishes (try the bass with herbs) and pizza are on offer
at this restaurant with a wood-burning stove. ● *Mon; Jan.*

AE MC V

PIEDICROCE: *Le Refuge* €
20229. **Road map** C3. **[** *04 95 35 82 65.*
This hotel/restaurant serves home-style cooking with dishes such
as rabbit and lard, and excellent charcuterie and cheese. ● *Nov.*

MC V

VENACO: *La Place* €
Place du Pont, 20231. **Road map** C3. **[** *04 95 47 01 30.*
Typical and economic Corsican restaurant, offering well-prepared
dishes. ● *Wed; 20 Dec–5 Jan.*

AE DC MC V

For key to symbols, see back flap

SHOPPING IN CORSICA

Corsica offers a great variety of locally produced foods – from honey and a wide range of chestnut-based products, to charcuterie, sausages and cheeses prepared by shepherds with maquis herbs. The best places to buy this produce are the lively, colourful food markets in the main towns. It is also interesting to visit the centres of production, including the alpine *bergeries* and the many wineries

Shepherd's leather bag

throughout the northern part of the island. Handicraft production is quite varied and efforts to revive the ancient arts of knife-making, pottery and stoneware, basket-weaving and glass-blowing are proving increasingly popular. There are handicraft centres in the cities, but it is more enjoyable to go directly to the workshops to see how these objects are made. The most active region for handicraft production is Balagne.

OPENING HOURS

In corsica, shops operate from Tuesday to Saturday (9am to noon; 3 to 6pm). Food shops are open from 8am to noon and from 2 to 6pm, and also on Sunday morning. In the summer, especially in tourist resorts, opening hours are usually extended, and some shops are also open on Monday.

CREDIT CARDS

Credit cards are accepted almost everywhere, but some shop owners might set a minimum purchase of about 15. Workshops and smaller shops inland tend to prefer cash payment.

SHOPPING CENTRES

On the outskirts of Bastia and Ajaccio there are shopping centres and super-markets. They are usually open from 9am to 8pm, except for Monday morning and Sunday. On sale are clothes, shoes, sports accessories, perfumes, books and food, at reasonable prices. These centres also have restaurants and cafés.

HANDICRAFTS

For quality products, try any of the craftsmen's workshops belonging to the Casa di l'Artigiani, a network of about 50 artisans who guarantee the authenticity of their products. You can also try shops that display the sign Association d'Artisans de Corse or Corsic'Arte. The best option, however, may be to go directly to the workshops, such as those in Balagne *(see pp76–7)*.

Among the best souvenirs are objects made of olive and chestnut wood, straw and wicker baskets, handmade scarves and rugs, Orezza's myrtle-wood pipes, blown-glass objects from Feliceto, and wooden music boxes from Pigna.

One of the many wine producers in the Cap Corse area

The most famous Corsican handicraft products are knives, and the leading makers are Jean-Pierre Caggiari and Laurent Bellini of **Atelier du Couteau** in Ajaccio and **Pol Demongeot** in Calvi.

Pottery and stoneware are also widespread, with work-shops throughout the island. Of particular interest are the ateliers of **Jacques Quilichini** in Pigna and of **Christine and Bernard Isarn** in Portigliolo.

Among the now-scarce luthiers is Christian Magdeleine at **Guitare et Cetera** in Bastia *(see p61)*, who specializes in guitars, and **Ugo Casalonga** in Pigna.

Other interesting shops are **Maison du Coral** in Ajaccio, which sells cut minerals (diorite, porphyry and rhyolite) and coral, and **Cyrnarom** in Bastia *(see p62)*, which distils flowers and plants to create typically Corsican perfumes. Wild-flower essences are also sold in the markets.

A stall with an array of tempting products at an Ajaccio market

Browsing at the Sunday market in Bastia

MARKETS AND FAIRS

THE LIVELY, colourful markets are a must for visitors to Corsica. The one in Bastia is held in the Place de l'Hôtel-de-Ville every morning (except Monday), with stalls that sell vegetables, fish, Corsican specialities and even clothes. There are also vendors who make *crêpes* and local snacks. The bric-à-brac market is held in Place St-Nicolas, in front of the outdoor cafés.

The daily food market in Ajaccio, in Place Campinchi, features mostly regional products, such as charcuterie and sausages, wines, sweets, cheese, oil and honey.

In Calvi, greengrocers and vendors of typical products sell their wares under the roof of the covered market, which can be reached by going up a stairway from Rue Clemenceau.

In nearby L'Île Rousse, the covered market facing Place Paoli dates from the 19th century and is classified as an historic building.

In the second week of September a handicraft fair takes place at Porto-Vecchio. On the first weekend of July there is a wine fair at Luri and on the first weekend after 14 July there is an olive fair in Balagne.

REGIONAL SPECIALITIES

THERE ARE MANY Corsican gastronomic delights, first of all honey, which boasts six AOC designations. A range of honeys from different plants can be found at **Franck Dupré** in Calenzana and **U Stazzu** in Ajaccio.

Corsica's famous *canistrelli* (almond, hazelnut, lemon or aniseed biscuits) are for sale at these recommended shops: **Boulangerie A Viletta** and **Mathieu Carlotti** in Ajaccio and **E Fritelle** in Calenzana.

Local charcuterie and cheeses can be found in all food shops, the best of which are **Charcuterie Pantalacci** in Ajaccio and **U Muntagnolu** and **U Paese** in Bastia.

Local wines (*see p167*) are sold at the **Enoteca** in Ajaccio. For apéritifs try the **Maison Mattei** in Bastia (*see p63*).

The only surviving artisan who makes lobster nets at Cap Corse

---

DIRECTORY

SHOPPING CENTRES

Centre Commercial La Rocade
Ajaccio.

Centre Commercial de Santa Devota
Airport Rotunda, Borgo, Bastia.

Centre Commercial de Toga
Port de Toga, Bastia.

Champion
Mezzavia, Ajaccio.

Continent Résidence
Cours Prince Impérial, Ajaccio.

Galerie Marchande de l'Hypermarché
Avenue Sampiero Corso, Bastia.

La Rocade
Route Nationale 193, Furiani. Géant Casino.

HANDICRAFTS

Atelier du Couteau
Port Ornano, Ajaccio.
☎ 04 95 10 16 52.
Knives.

Christine & Bernard Isarn
Portigliolo, Coti-Chiavari.
☎ 04 95 25 59 51.
Pottery.

Cyrnarom
9 Avenue Monseigneur Rigo, Bastia.
☎ 04 95 31 70 60.
Perfumes.

Guitare et Cetera
2 Place Guasco, Bastia.
☎ 04 95 31 78 99.
Stringed instruments.

Jacques Quilichini
Pigna.
☎ 04 95 61 77 25.
Pottery.

Maison du Coral
1 Rue Fesch, Ajaccio.
☎ 04 95 21 47 94.
Coral.

Pol Demongeot
Fort Mozello, Calvi.
☎ 04 95 65 32 54.
Knives.

Ugo Casalonga
Pigna. ☎ 04 95 61 77 15.
Stringed instruments and wooden music boxes.

Verrerie Corse
Feliceto.
☎ 04 95 61 73 05.
Blown-glass objects.

REGIONAL SPECIALITIES

Boulangerie A Viletta
Avenue Beverini, Ajaccio.
Cakes and croissants.

Charcuterie Pantalacci
Boulevard Pugliesi Conti, Ajaccio.
Charcuterie.

E Fritelle
Tiassu Longu, Calenzana.
☎ 04 95 62 78 17.
Biscuits.

Enoteca
Rue Maréchal Ornano, Ajaccio. *Wines & liqueurs.*

Franck Dupré
Hameau de Pelicciani, Calenzana.
☎ 04 95 65 07 74.
Honey and by-products.

Maison Mattei
Place St-Nicolas, Bastia.
☎ 04 95 32 44 38.
Corsican wines & liqueurs.

Mathieu Carlotti
Place Vincetti, Bastia.
☎ 04 95 31 09 93.
Preserves, chocolate.

U Muntagnolu
15 Rue César Campinchi, Bastia. *Charcuterie and cheese.*

U Paese
4 Rue Napoléon, Bastia.
☎ 04 95 32 33 18.
Charcuterie and cheese.

U Stazzu
1 Rue Bonaparte, Ajaccio.
Honey, wines, charcuterie.

What to Buy in Corsica

Terracotta mask

THE FLAVOURS AND SCENTS of Corsica can be enjoyed in the island's gastronomic delicacies – from honey and sweets, to cheese and charcuterie. The result of an age-old tradition, these products are available in all the large towns, especially in the markets, where they can be purchased directly from the producers. There is also a great variety of typical handicraft products that Corsican artisans have adapted to more modern tastes. The Strada di l'Artigiani in Balagne *(see pp76–7)* is where most of their workshops are located.

Corsican knife-making has evolved from old shepherds' tools to elegant knives with manta ray-skin handles and damask-steel blades. Artisans now produce collector's items.

HANDICRAFTS

Wood, sandstone, animal horns and glass are the basic materials for Corsican handicrafts, and indeed are among the earliest ever used by man. Corsican artisans have given free rein to their creativity, without ever losing sight of local traditions. Their craft perfectly combines past and present, making every object unique for visitors from all over the world.

Coral necklaces and pendants are crafted in keeping with the age-old art of the Ajaccio coral carvers. The fresh creativity of young local artisans has produced fine necklaces, earrings, bracelets and pendants.

The art of glass-blowing has produced vases, sculptures, glasses, jugs and many other objects. A master glass-blower in Feliceto, a village on the Strada di l'Artigiani, in the heart of Balagne, makes these items.

Ceramic ashtray

Enamelled shell

Ceramic wares, such as plates, vases, jugs and tiles, are made with a potter's wheel, fired in the oven and enamelled with typical Mediterranean colours. The stoneware and raku ceramics (see p76) are also worth purchasing.

Hand-crafted music boxes are made mostly in Pigna. They are brightly coloured and come in the shapes of donkeys and dancing figures. The musical pieces, such as A Muresca and Ciucciarella, are typical Corsican melodies.

Wooden objects are also a common product of Corsican handicraft. They include pipes made from olive, myrtle and heather wood, musical instruments and small pieces of furniture, often with unusual inlay work.

The essences of lavender, Corsican pine, myrtle and orange blossoms are used to produce perfumes with the scent of the maquis and Corsican forests.

PERFUMES

The fragrant oils extracted from Mediterranean maquis vegetation, including juniper, myrtle, lavender, cistus and mastic, can be found in many essences that bring to mind the land of Corsica. The woods also yield the balsamic essence of pine resins.

Lavender, one of the components of perfumes

GASTRONOMIC DELICACIES

Like all other regions in the Mediterranean, Corsica produces many gastronomic specialities that visitors can take back home as a reminder of their time on the island. These varied local delicacies will satisfy anyone's palate.

Corsican pâtés, charcuterie and sausages are wonderfully tasty. The best ones hail from Bastelica, Castagniccia and Niolo. Boar pâté is also delicious.

Corsican cheeses include the famous brocciu, a sort of ricotta, as well as goat's-milk cheeses and others that are aged and flavoured with maquis herbs.

Liqueurs are among the typical products of the island. Some of the best are the Maison Mattei apéritifs, which are famous throughout the world, and products made from myrtle and other maquis herbs. These liqueurs are distilled by artisans in various regions of Corsica.

Aromatic vinegars made from herbs, apples and honey, and extracts of fruit such as hydromel, which are like the old-fashioned sweet syrups, are other typical Corsican products.

Chestnut cake, typical of Castagniccia, is among Corsica's best-known sweets. Fiadone is a traditional cake made of brocciu cheese scented with orange blossoms. The aromatized nougat is also special.

Citron and honey nougat

Home-made preserves are a speciality. They are made from melon, myrtle, peach, citron, clementine and figs. The fig-with-walnut preserve makes for a superb accompaniment to cheese.

The local honey is another product bearing the flavours and scents of the island. It can be strong and bitter (chestnut), delicate (asphodel) or aromatic (lavender or strawberry tree) and is sold in the markets.

ENTERTAINMENT IN CORSICA

ALTHOUGH CORSICA'S main attractions are the sea and natural scenery, there is no lack of cultural activity and entertainment, especially in the seaside resorts and the main cities, such as Ajaccio and Bastia. For up-to-date information about concerts, theatre productions and cinemas, consult the local newspaper, *Corse-Matin*. In the summer, in addition to the

Passing the time with old friends at a café

numerous traditional festivals *(see pp32–5)*, many outdoor nightspots, discos and concerts ensure an entertaining evening. During the day, there are many organized excursions by boat and a wide range of sports and outdoor activities available *(see pp180–85)*, as well attractions related to the sea, such as an aquatic park and thalassotherapy centres.

Excursion boat moored near the bastions of Bonifacio

EXCURSIONS BY BOAT

LIKE ALL ISLANDS, Corsica offers all sorts of interesting activities related to the sea. For those who do not have their own boat, there are many companies that hire them out *(see p199)*. Also, in the summer, there are numerous organized excursions or cruises along the coast that will allow you to admire the natural marvels of the island from the sea and stop in a secluded cove for a swim.

Among the best-known and most highly recommendable cruises is the one that takes visitors to the beautiful red cliffs of the Scandola Nature Reserve *(see pp104–5)*. The boats depart from various towns, including Calvi, Porto, Cargèse, Tiuccia, Porticcio and other nearby harbours.

Do not fail to take the excursions from Ajaccio to the solitary Îles Sanguinaires

(see p92), and those departing from Propriano *(see p128)* to the Golfe de Valinco and the southwest coast.

The tours of the cliffs of Bonifacio and the Îles Lavezzi and Cavallo *(see pp116–17)* start from Bonifacio, which is also the departure point for trips across the Straits of Bonifacio *(see p113)* to the coast of Sardinia.

In the northern part of Corsica, most of the excursions to the beaches of Lodo, Cap Corse and the Désert des Agriates depart from the port of St-Florent.

Diving cruises on motorboats are organized more or less anywhere in Corsica, even for an entire weekend. Those who want to spend a week on an 18-m (60-ft) boat with daily dives should contact the **Cyrnos Hotel** *(see p179)*, in Sagone. Further information on diving sites and organizers can be found on page 183.

TRAVELLING ON THE PETIT TRAIN

A TYPICAL CORSICAN attraction consists of the small, fairytale-style trains that take visitors on a leisurely tour of the main towns on the island. These vehicles are called *Petits Trains* because they are reminiscent of the train rides in children's amusement parks.

The *Petits Trains* operate in Ajaccio, Porto-Vecchio, Bonifacio, Corte and L'Île Rousse, generally departing from the centre of town – at Corte, for example, from the Citadelle – and following itineraries through the streets to show you the main sights and monuments. *Petits Trains* move quite slowly so that you can take photographs and enjoy the views while comfortably seated on the colourful little carriages.

The delightful *Petit Train* in Corte, at the entrance to the Citadelle

A group performing during the Calvi Jazz Festival

AQUATIC PARKS

ALTHOUGH POPULAR in many seaside resorts all over Europe, amusement parks featuring aquatic activities are still uncommon in Corsica. The only park of this sort on the island is **Aqua Cyrne Gliss** in Porticcio. With its slides, water chutes, boat rides, swimming pools of all kinds and fountains, Porticcio's aquatic park will delight youngsters and adults alike.

THALASSOTHERAPY

THOSE WHO FEEL that holidays are the perfect opportunity to regenerate the body and relax will not be disappointed by what Corsica has to offer.

Like many other French maritime resorts, the island allows the opportunity to undergo sea-water therapy, also known as "thalasso-therapy". This consists of a series of completely natural cures that, through the use of sea water, help the body to eliminate the toxins caused by stress and too much work. As a result of these cures, the body feels considerably reinvigorated.

In Corsica, thalassotherapy is provided by a handful of prestigious hotels along the coast. The packages on offer usually include both board and cures.

As an alternative, you can go to the first-rate spas scattered in the interior of the island.

MUSIC AND DANCE

THE PROGRAMME of cultural events, in particular music, is especially full during the summer months, even though there are concerts and performances in the low season as well.

In the last week of June, Calvi resounds with the notes of the Jazz Festival (see p33), one of the best-known musical events in Corsica, which features some of the leading names on the international jazz scene.

In early July, the Estivoce (see p33) in Pigna is dedicated to traditional Corsican polyphonic music, and many choirs and groups offer a glimpse into authentic island culture.

In Ajaccio, the first two weeks of July are given over to the Blues Festival "Nuits du Blues" (see p33), which features music performed by famous international artists and groups.

In Patrimonio, during the third week of July, folk, jazz and gipsy musicians give exciting performances for the Guitar Nights festival (see p33), while from July to September Ajaccio plays host to Les Estivales (see p33), with concerts and dance performances.

One of the most popular festivals among Corsicans themselves, though relatively unknown to foreign visitors, is Les Musicales de Bastia (see p35), held in October. This is a festival of folk music, jazz and dance.

In late May, the **Kallisté Theatre** and other venues in Ajaccio host Île Danse (see p32), a festival exploring the art of dance featuring leading European companies.

Local tourist offices offer information regarding the programmes of these various festivals and sell tickets. You can alternatively log on to www.visit-corsica.com.

CINEMA AND THEATRE

DURING THE SUMMER, in the main seaside resorts there are many outdoor cinemas that show the latest films every evening, including the one at Porto, which is situated in the eucalyptus grove of the Marina. A film marked VO in listings is in its original language.

The main cinemas are in Bastia (**Le Regent** and **Le Studio**) and Ajaccio (**Empire**, **L'Aiglon**, **Bonaparte** and **Laetitia**).

March sees the Bastia Film Festival (see p32), which features international film productions. During the first week of October the city hosts a British Film Festival; in November the Mediterranean Cultures Film Festival (see p35) is staged here; and in January the Italian Film Festival (see p35) organizes screenings of Italian films, retrospectives of Italian actors and directors, and lectures. Ajaccio is another centre for film, with Italian, Spanish and Asian festivals.

In the winter, there is an important theatre and opera season in Bastia.

A show performed in a Bastia theatre during the winter

NIGHTLIFE

DISCOTHEQUES in Corsica are few and far between compared to other European seaside resorts, and they are concentrated in the main coastal towns.

One of the best-known clubs on the island is **La Via Notte**, in Porto-Vecchio. A favourite with teenagers, this club hosts famous US DJs.

Among the most famous clubs in Bastia are **La Stella**, which is closed in the summer, **Le Velvet**, frequented by people in their early 20s, and **L'Apocalypse**, in Biguglia. Another good club is **Noche de Cuba**, which attracts older crowds into Cuban music.

The biggest club in Ajaccio is **5ème Avenue**, followed by **L'Entracte**. Popular spots in Porticcio are **Le Blue Moon**, which has a large terrace, and **Atlantids**, which features both disco music and techno.

In Calvi, **La Camargue** has an outdoor dance floor and a swimming pool. About 5 km (3 miles) from the centre of town is **L'Acapulco**, also renowned for its restaurant.

Lastly, in Propriano there are two venues for late night dancing: the discotheques **Latino Café** and **Le Midnight**.

Calvi's promenade, illuminated by the neon signs of the nightspots

If clubbing is not your scene and you would rather drink a cocktail or listen to music, Corsican towns have many bars of every kind.

In Bastia the most popular spots are concentrated around the Vieux Port area and the Port Toga quarter, which in the summer becomes a huge pedestrian precinct with shows and entertainment. Here the tables of the disco bars and restaurants almost touch the water. Among the most popular places are **Le Bounty**, **Le Café de la Place**, **Le Cézanne Café**, **Le Cotton Café**, **U Fanale**, **Café Wha!** and **Le Bouchon**, a wine bar with live music

and a fine wine list where you can drink by the glass or the bottle while having salad or canapés.

In Ajaccio the great variety of nightspots includes **Le Pavillon Bleu**, **Le Son des Guitares**, **Le Privilège** piano bar and **Le Temple du Jeu**.

Calvi has **Chez Tao**, an historic piano bar in the converted Bishops' Palace in Sagone, and **Le Rocher**, a piano bar open till 3am.

Among the best spots in Porto-Vecchio are **La Canne à Sucre**, ideal for an ice cream or a drink, and **La Taverne du Roi**, a popular venue that often hosts jazz and cabaret singers.

Café Wha!, one of the best-known nightspots in Bastia, popular with people of all ages

DIRECTORY

EXCURSIONS BY BOAT

A Dieu Vat
Porto-Vecchio.
04 95 70 27 58.

Colombo Line
Port de Plaisance, Calvi.
04 95 65 32 10.

Croisières Grand Bleu
Cargèse.
04 95 26 40 24.

Le Djinn
Porto-Vecchio.
04 95 70 56 61.

I Paesi du Valincu
Port de Plaisance,
Propriano.
04 95 76 16 78.

Nave Va
2 Rue Jean-Baptiste
Marcaggio, Ajaccio.
04 95 21 83 97.
Porticcio.
04 95 25 94 14.

Princesse Impèriale
Rue Fred Scamaroni,
Bonifacio.
04 95 73 13 96.

Thalassa Croisières
Marina, Bonifacio.
06 08 22 22 21.

U San Paulu
Macinaggio.
04 95 35 07 09.

Vedettes Christina
Marina, Bonifacio.
04 95 73 13 15.

PETITS TRAINS COMPANIES

ITT
Imm. Beau site,
Pietralba, Ajaccio
(departure: Place Foch).
04 95 51 13 69.

Le Petit Train
Col de Fogata,
L'Île Rousse (departure:
Place Paoli).
04 95 60 26 79.

TTB
Via Simoni/Sennola,
Bonifacio
(departure: the port).
04 95 73 15 07.

U Trenu
Corte (departure:
municipal car park,
behind the train station).
06 09 95 70 36.

AQUATIC PARKS

Aqua Cyrne Gliss
Porticcio.
04 95 25 04 48.

THALASSOTHERAPY

Hotel Eden Roc
Route des Sanguinaires,
Ajaccio.
04 95 51 56 00.

Hotel Sofitel
Golfe d'Ajaccio, Porticcio.
04 95 29 40 40.

CINEMAS

L'Aiglon
Cours Grandval, Ajaccio.
04 95 70 35 02.

Bonaparte
10 Cours Napoléon,
Ajaccio.
04 95 51 29 46.

La Cinémathèque de Corse
Espace Jean-Paul de Rocca
Serra, Porto-Vecchio.
04 95 70 35 02.

Empire
30 Cours Napoléon,
Ajaccio.
04 95 21 21 00.

Laetitia
24 Cours Napoléon,
Ajaccio.
04 95 21 07 24.

Le Regent
5 Rue César Campinchi,
Bastia.
04 95 31 03 08.

Le Studio
1 Rue Miséricorde, Bastia.
04 95 31 12 94.

THEATRES

Aghja
6 Chemin de Biancarello,
Ajaccio.
04 95 20 41 15.

Kallisté
6 Rue Colonel
Colonna d'Ornano,
Ajaccio.
04 95 22 43 03.

DISCOTHEQUES

L'Acapulco
Calvi. 04 95 65 08 03.

L'An 200
Corte.
04 95 46 17 04.

L'Apocalypse
Biguglia, Bastia.
04 95 33 36 83.

Atlantids
Porticcio.
04 95 25 03 98.

Le Blue Moon
Les Marines,
Porticcio.
04 95 25 07 70.

La Camargue
Calvi.
04 95 65 08 70.

L'Entracte
Casino Municipal,
Ajaccio.
04 95 50 40 65.

Latino Café
Blvd du Général
de Gaulle, Propriano.
04 95 73 26 93.

Le Midnight Express
Blvd du Général
de Gaulle, Propriano.
04 95 76 05 21.

Noche de Cuba
5 Rue Chanoine Leschi,
Bastia.
04 95 31 02 83.

La Stella
Plage de l'Arinella, Bastia.
04 95 58 06 94.

Le Velvet
15 Maison Romieu,
Bastia.
04 95 31 01 00.

La Via Notte
Porto-Vecchio.
04 95 72 02 12.

NIGHTSPOTS

Le Bouchon
4 bis Rue St-Jean,
Vieux Port, Bastia.
04 95 58 14 22.

Le Bounty
Port de Toga, Bastia.
04 95 34 20 34.

Le Café de la Place
Blvd Général de Gaulle,
Bastia. 04 95 32 06 51.

Café Wha!
Bastia. 04 95 34 25 79.

La Canne à Sucre
Porto-Vecchio.
04 95 70 35 25.

Le Cézanne Café
Port de Plaisance, Toga,
Bastia.
04 95 34 16 60.

Chez Tao
Sagone, Calvi.
04 95 65 00 73.

Le Cotton Café
Quai des Martyrs, Bastia.
04 95 31 36 31.

Le Pavillon Bleu
Cabaret, 26 Cours du
Général Leclerc, Ajaccio.
04 95 51 12 90.

Le Privilège
7 Rue Eugène Macchini,
Ajaccio.
04 95 50 11 80.

Le Rocher
Sant'Ambroggio, Lumio,
Calvi. 04 95 60 68 74.

Le Son des Guitares
Rue du Roi de Rome,
Ajaccio.
04 95 51 16 47.

La Taverne du Roi
Porto-Vecchio.
04 95 70 41 31.

Le Temple du Jeu
2 Avenue de la Grande
Armée, Ajaccio.
04 95 22 19 39.

U Fanale
Place Galetta, Vieux Port,
Bastia. 04 95 32 68 38.

SPORTS AND OUTDOOR ACTIVITIES

ORSICA IS AN IDEAL destination for sports and outdoor enthusiasts. Along the coast, those who love the sea will find beaches with fine sand and coves among craggy cliffs that can often be reached only by boat, as well as splendid sea floors. For hiking or trekking buffs, there is no end of possibilities, with hills, mountains and trails of varying degrees of difficulty. Even the best cyclists will have their work cut out for them along the steep hairpin turns of the

Mountain hiker

inland roads that lead to the passes in the central mountain range. Canoeing, kayaking and rafting aficionados will love the swiftly flowing torrents. And horse riding is a fascinating way of visiting the hills of Corsica. In keeping with the French passion for the great outdoors, all sports and other activities in Corsica are organized efficiently and thoroughly. The Directory on page 185 lists a selection of useful addresses.

HIKING

MORE THAN 25 years ago, Corsica inaugurated its longest hiking route, the GR20 (*see pp20–25*), which crosses the entire island along a northwest–southeast axis. Annually, more than 17,000 hikers from all over the world walk through woods, forests and rugged ridges following this long-distance path.

Because the GR20 is now overflowing with hikers, other paths have been created to ease congestion. These are less difficult than the GR20 and are called *Mare e Monti* ("sea and mountains"; *see p25*) if the paths start out from the sea and go inland to the peaks, and *Mare a Mare* ("sea to sea"; *see p25*) if they go from coast to coast via the interior.

Among the latter, there are three main routes from west to east: Cargèse to the beach

Hikers on their way through Corsica's wild landscape

Amazing rock formations along a hiking trail

at Cervione, in Castagniccia; Ajaccio to Ghisonaccia; and Propriano to Porto-Vecchio. These paths are usually at a low altitude and tend to run on flatter terrain. They also go through villages where it is possible to buy food and drink, so one can hike with a lighter backpack.

Among the most interesting *Mare e Monti* hikes is the one that goes from Cargèse to Calenzana, in Balagne, via Evisa and Galéria.

Besides these long routes, there are many areas that are of interest to hikers. Among these are the Vallée de l'Asco (*see p150*), at the foot of Monte Cinto, the Calacuccia zone (*see p151*), the upper Vallée de la Restonica (*see p139*), the Col de Vizzavona (*see p142*) and the splendid Col de Bavella area (*see pp122–3*).

There are many useful hiking guide books, such as *Trekking in Corsica*, by David Abram, published by Trailblazer Guides, which covers all the island's best routes (including the GR20), or Robin G Collomb's *Corsica Mountains*, published by West Co, UK. The *Guide de la Randonnée en Corse* ("Guide to Long Hikes in Corsica"), published by Didier Richard, provides many hiking suggestions, as does *Corse*, a guide published by the Institut Géographique National. The topographical maps produced by the same institute are vitally important for difficult hikes.

Before setting off with your backpack, bear in mind that, although the Corsican mountains in summer seem to be hiker-friendly and sunny, bad weather and storms are

An exciting canoeing experience on a rushing torrent

quite common at high altitudes and may easily cause sudden sharp drops in temperature. Furthermore, remember that the food- and water-supply stations are not always well-stocked.

CLIMBING

ALTHOUGH THERE ARE no internationally famous rock-climbing areas in Corsica, there are plenty of challenging cliffs and walls.

There are basically two types of rock – granite and limestone – and they require different climbing techniques and styles.

Among the climbers' favourite sites are Ponte Leccia and Solenzara, the Nebbio region, with the cliffs of Caporalino and Pietralba, the Col de Bavella (see pp122–3), with routes of varying difficulty, and the longest routes in the Teghje Liscie and Balagne areas.

RAFTING

ONE OF THE MAIN features of Corsica consists of the watercourses, both large and small, in the valleys of the interior. Rafters love these rivers because of the wild scenery they pass through. Rafting is a very technical sport for experts only, and in Corsica there are agencies and specialized guides that organize the descents down the rivers, from the easiest to the most difficult. The easiest gorges are along the course of the Vecchio, Aïtone and Tavignano rivers. More difficult routes are some stretches of the Taravo and the Vacca (near Bavella) rivers, and the long descents of torrents such as the Negretto (near Ponte Leccia), the Sportellu (Porto) and the Polischello.

CANOEING AND KAYAKING

CORSICA HAS a lot of rainfall, and in the mountains this becomes rather heavy snow-fall, sometimes as much as 2 m (6ft). Consequently, in spring, when the temperatures rise and the thawing season begins, the island welcomes many canoeists who come from all over Europe, eager to take advantage of the abundance of water.

Corsican rivers tend to be technical and spectacular. The Taravo, Rizzanese and Fium'Orbo rivers offer splendid descents. The most famous and difficult are the Tavignano, Golo and Prunelli rivers, as well as the Liamone.

HORSE RIDING

Riding on the beach

CORSICA OFFERS many opportunities for horse riding. The most interesting areas for this activity are the green hills of the Castagniccia area, the divide between the Bozio and Corte regions, the Tavignano river as far as the plateaus of Lac de Nino, the Désert des Agriates, the Sartène region, with its many prehistoric monuments, and the mountainous region of Cagna.

You can also ride on the sandy shores of the east coast or on the grassy top of the white cliffs of Bonifacio.

A departure point for canoe or kayak excursions

SAILING

WITH ITS RUGGED coasts, small rocky islands and the Scandola and Lavezzi marine reserves, Corsica is a favourite with yachting buffs from all over the world. This appeal is compounded by the constant presence of wind.

The voyage from the ports in southern France is rather long (Cap Corse is 119 nautical miles from St-Tropez, 100 from Nice and 83 from Menton), but it sails over a zone famous for frequent sightings of fin whales. The stretch of the sea 45 nautical miles north-west of Calvi is where you are most likely to find these marvellous sea mammals.

Departing from the Italian coast, the crossing to Corsica is shorter and one can make a stopover at the islands of the Tuscan archipelago. Cap Corse is 49 nautical miles from Livorno, while the distance from Bastia to the island of Elba is 40 nautical miles.

The circumnavigation of Corsica is also popular with yachtsmen *(see p198)*. This route passes by various types of coastline: sandy and filled with pools on the eastern sides; craggy and indented at Cap Corse; and varied, with tall rock faces on the west side. The strongest wind is around the Straits

Sailing lessons at Marina de Meria, Cap Corse

of Bonifacio, between Corsica and Sardinia. Be careful when sailing here, because the wind is often violent and there are numerous large ships that navigate this part of the sea.

If you do not have a boat of your own, it is possible to hire one in all the ports and tourist resorts, where there are also agencies that offer boat tours of the coast with the skipper and crew included in the price.

Navigating along the coasts of Corsica, you will come across two very important marine reserves: the Scandola Nature Reserve *(see pp104–5)* and the Réserve de Lavezzi *(see p117)*, which, in turn, is part of the Parc Marin de Bonifacio *(see p113)*, an

initiative of the French and Italian governments that has succeeded in protecting and improving this major stretch of sea, where numerous regattas are held.

THE DISTANCE IN NAUTICAL MILES BETWEEN PORTS

Bastia–St-Florent	48
St-Florent–Calvi	30
Calvi–Girolata	21
Girolata–Porto	6
Porto–Cargèse	12
Cargèse–Ajaccio	21
Ajaccio–Propriano	22
Propriano–Roccapina	15
Roccapina–Bonifacio	12
Bonifacio–Lavezzi	6
Lavezzi–Porto-Vecchio	18
Porto-Vecchio–Bastia	67

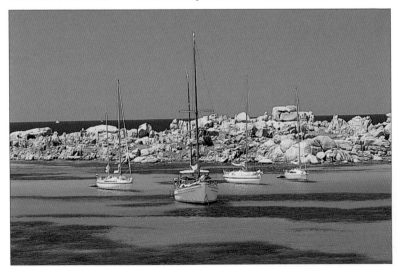

Boats anchored at one of the many fabulous coves on Îles Lavezzi

WINDSURFING

THE AREAS AND resorts where sailing is common and nautical clubs are based also tend to have facilities for windsurfing. All the tourist towns along the coast offer the possibility to practise this sport, which is an exciting combination of surfing and sailing. There are many small schools that rent windsurfing equipment and offer courses at different levels of ability.

Corsica, like most islands, is blessed with good breezes, especially along the west coast and the cliffs in the south. However, in the south the wind is perhaps too strong and potentially dangerous, so windsurfing in this area should be practised by experts only.

A windsurfer in search of wind at Îles Lavezzi

DIVING

THE SEA FLOORS in Corsica are rich in fauna and natural beauty. There are about 60 clubs on the island that have ideal sites for diving. Among these, the **Station Recherches Sousmarines et Océanographiques**, which is situated at the Pointe Revellata promontory, not far from Calvi, offers courses for beginners and short courses on marine biology. It is also possible to stay here and organize your own dives.

Among the most famous diving sites are the beautiful Mérouville zone, northeast of Îles Lavezzi, and the islet

A diver about to surface with a fine day's catch

of Sperduto, which is part of the Réserve de Lavezzi. As is the case with all protected areas, diving here is subject to strict regulations and limits, so it is best to make enquiries at the Réserve offices or in one of the diving clubs in the area beforehand.

In southeast Corsica, not far from the Golfe de Porto-Vecchio, the small Îles Cerbicale have interesting diving sites in the Île du Toro area, where there are many shipwrecks.

In southwest Corsica, in the Golfe de Valinco, facing Propriano, the most popular sites are those around the rocks of the so-called *cathédrales* ("cathedrals"), off the coast of Porto-Pollo, and the Secche di Belvedere. Near the Pointe de la Parata, which, together with the Îles Sanguinaires, closes off the Golfe d'Ajaccio to the north, is a diving site called Tabernacle, while in the southern part of the gulf is the shipwreck of the *Meulère*.

Further north, in the Golfe de Sagone are the sandbanks of the Provençale and the wreck of a Canadair aeroplane. In the Golfe de Porto, the Punta Mucchilina sand bar offers a great variety of fauna and flora, as well as the wreck of a coal ship.

Divers in the Calvi area often visit the Pointe Revellata canyon, at the northernmost confines of the Scandola Nature Reserve *(see pp104–5)*, and the wreck of a Boeing B-17 bomber that lies 28 m (90 ft) below sea level.

Further north, in the Golfe de St-Florent, there are the sea floors of Punta Vecchiara and the sand bar of Saleccia, while the Île de Giraglia, at the northern tip of Cap Corse, is famous for a wonderful dive west of the lighthouse.

CYCLING

CORSICA OFFERS several opportunities for cyclists. Many routes follow paths on the hills through the central mountain range, and they are generally located in very beautiful forest areas.

In spring and summer, there is an abundance of cyclists at the Col de Vizzavona, Col de Verghio, Col de Verde and Col de Bavella. The coastal roads are also lovely, but be aware that they tend to be very windy and congested.

Whatever your choice, bear in mind that the roads are narrow, mostly on hills with steep rises, and have many curves. There are few places for food and drinks along the way. Furthermore, the road surface is not always good, so it is advisable to bring along a spare inner tube and the tools needed for repairs.

Cycling fans normally have their own bicycles, but there are agencies that offer bicycle tours of a week or more. The advantage of these tours is that a van is available to carry your luggage from one stop to another. In case of fatigue, cyclists are taken into the van or to a doctor.

Consulting a map for the next leg of a bicycle journey

MOUNTAIN BIKING

ONE OF THE MOST ecologically friendly ways to discover the interior of Corsica is by mountain bike. The rises are generally steep and the paths quite rough, so make sure you are well equipped and that you take plenty of water with you.

Among the areas suggested by experts for their beauty are the forests of Ospédale, Bavella and Cagna, and the entire central Alta Rocca zone. Except for the summer months, the paths through the maquis in the Désert des Agriates, in the northern part of the island, are splendid, as are some stretches of the *Mare a Mare* and *Mare e Monti (see p25)* paths and the long route from Propriano to Ajaccio.

It is easy to find a bike for hire in the summer.

GOLF

THE ULTIMATE golf course in Corsica is without a doubt the one at Pointe de Sperone *(see p117)*, a short distance from Capo Pertusato. The course lies on the soft hills bordered by maquis facing the Îles Lavezzi and Cavallo. This 18-hole, par-72 golf course is more than 6 km (4 miles) long.

The other golf courses and golf schools on the island are at Ajaccio (school), Bastia (9 holes), Lezza (6 holes) and Reginu (6 holes).

Information concerning the golf courses and the various tournaments held on the island is available upon request at the **Ligue Corse du Golf** in Borgo.

WINTER SPORTS

THE TOURISTS WHO throng to Corsica in the summer may find it hard to believe, but in winter there is a considerable amount of snow on the mountain peaks of the central range. So, from December to March, four small ski resorts inland offer fine downhill runs and even circular cross-country courses to skiing aficionados.

Snow-capped peaks in the Monte Cinto region

But the real attraction of Corsica, which does not have many ski-lift facilities, are the routes for alpine cross-country skiing (*ski de randonnée*), for which there are various possibilities in spring as well. First of all, there is the difficult route that follows the central divide and runs more or less along the routes marked out in summer by the GR20 long-distance path. There are also many other possible routes starting off from the locality of Ghisoni (towards Monte Renoso), from the upper Vallée de la Restonica, from Haut-Asco and from the Campotile plateau.

Between Quenza and Zicavo, on the Coscione plateau, there are several courses for those who love adventurous cross-country skiing or long walks with snowshoes. Here the utmost caution is necessary, since the weather can be treacherous. Be sure to have plenty of supplies with you, because supply stations are few and far between. Spring alpine skiing requires the same precautions adopted on other mountains.

Alpine cross-country skiing

The prestigious golf club on the Pointe de Sperone, near Bonifacio

DIRECTORY

HIKING

Compagnie Régionale des Guides et Accompagnateurs de Montagne de Corse
04 95 48 10 43.
www.guidesmontagnes corses.com

Corse Odyssée
Quenza.
04 95 78 64 05.

Corsica Raid Aventure (race)
www.corsicaraid.com

In Liberta Association Montagne Corse
2 Avenue de la Garde Armée, Ajaccio.
04 95 20 53 14.
www.montagne-corse.com
mcl@montagne-corse.com

Interlacs (race)
Associazione A Rinascita, Corte.
04 95 46 12 48.
www.inter-lacs.com

In Terra Corsa
Boite Postale 39, Ponte Leccia.
04 95 47 69 48.
www.interracorsa.fr

Move en Balagne
04 95 61 51 46.

Parc Naturel Régional de la Corse
Ajaccio.
04 95 51 79 00.
www.parc-naturel-corse.com

CLIMBING AND MOUNTAINEERING

Corsica Madness
(alpine guides).
06 83 26 95 15.

Jean-Paul Quilici
(alpine guides).
04 95 78 64 33.

Marc Gambotti
(alpine guides).
06 20 90 18 05.

Pierre Griscelli
(alpine guides).
04 95 30 82 51.

Pierre Pietri
(alpine guides).
04 95 32 62 76.

René Eymerie
(alpine guides).
04 95 31 68 86.

RAFTING

Corse Aventure
Route de Sartène, Corri Bianchi, Eccica-Suarella.
04 95 25 91 19.
www.corse-aventure.com

In Terra Corsa
Boite Postale 39, Ponte Leccia.
04 95 47 69 48.
www.interracorsa.fr

CANOEING AND KAYAKING

Altore
St-Florent.
04 95 37 19 30.
www.altore.com
info@altore.com

Commission Nager en Eau Vive
Bastia.
c/o Jean Pierre Vergnon.
04 95 30 85 35.
perso.wanadoo.fr/gjl/crc/nev.html

HORSE RIDING

Association Régionale pour le Tourisme Equestre en Corse (ARTE)
04 95 20 60 86,
04 95 04 04 95 46.

SAILING AND WINDSURFING

Calvi Marine
Calvi.
04 95 65 01 12.

Calvi Nautique Club
Calvi.
04 95 65 10 65.

Centre Nautique des Fauvettes
Porto-Vecchio.
04 95 70 93 00.

Centre Nautique des Glénans
Bonifacio.
04 95 73 03 85.

Centre Nautique de Porticcio
Porticcio.
04 95 25 01 06.

Corsica Voile
Macinaggio.
04 95 35 48 20.

L'Île Bleue – Mer et Nautisme
Bonifacio.
04 95 73 04 12.

Moorings Sail-Med
Ajaccio.
04 95 51 40 12.

Multi Service Plaisance
Porto-Vecchio.
04 95 70 29 13.

Soleil Rouge Yachting
Ajaccio.
04 95 21 89 21.

USBTP
Favone.
04 95 73 20 37.

DIVING

Fédération Française Études et Sports Sousmarins
Solenzara.
(list of 83 Corsican clubs)
04 95 57 48 31.
04 95 57 48 32.
perso.wanadoo.fr/gjl/crc

Station Recherches Sousmarines et Océanographiques
Pointe Revellata, Calvi.
04 95 65 06 18.
04 95 65 01 34.
stareso@stareso.com
www.stareso.com

CYCLING AND MOUNTAIN BIKES

Corsica Moto Rent
Ajaccio.
04 95 51 34 45.
Calvi.
04 95 60 08 07.
Porto-Vecchio.
04 95 70 03 40.

Cyclisme en Corse
perso.wanadoo.fr/cyclisme-en-corse

Garage d'Angeli
Place Christophe Colomb, Calvi.
04 95 65 02 13.

Loca Corse
Ajaccio.
04 95 20 71 20.

Rout'evasion
Ajaccio.
04 95 22 72 87.

TTC Moto
Propriano.
04 95 76 15 32.

GOLF

Golf Club Sperone
Domaine de Sperone, Bonifacio.
04 95 73 17 13.
04 95 73 17 85.
golf@sperone.net

Ligue Corse du Golf
Castellarese, Borgo.
04 95 38 33 99.
04 95 36 38 06.

WINTER SPORTS

Bergerie de Catanelle
Ghisoni.
04 95 57 01 81.

Calacuccia Skiing Resort (cross-country skiing)
Calacuccia tourist office.
04 95 48 05 22.

Col de Verghio Skiing Resort
04 95 48 00 01.

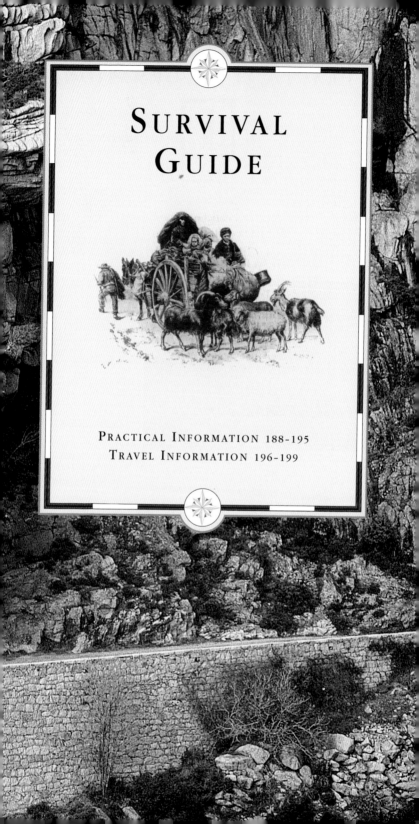

SURVIVAL
GUIDE

PRACTICAL INFORMATION

I N CORSICA, TOURISM is an important industry – and not only in summer, when visitors come to enjoy the sea. Spring and autumn are ideal for tours inland, for hikes in the mountains and visits to the archaeological sites. Travelling within Corsica is easy: the hotels, restaurants and camp sites are of a high quality and visitors can rely on the wide-ranging network of assistance from the Agence de Tourisme de la

Sign for tourist information

Corse and the local tourist offices. When planning a trip to Corsica, it is best not to have a heavy schedule, and to avoid long trips, despite the apparently short distances: the roads may be extremely scenic, but they are not very fast because of the numerous bends and the sometimes rough surfaces. Furthermore, each village has surprises in store, be they historic, scenic or gastronomic, and it would be a pity to miss them.

The Corsican coastline in the spring

In the tourist offices you may find brochures and maps of the area, lists of the local hotels and restaurants, and information on the museums and archaeological sites.

The larger cities, such as Ajaccio and Bastia, also print pamphlets every year concerning festivals and other cultural activities, including music, dance, cinema and theatre.

If you want to plan your vacation from home, make enquiries at a French tourist organization, such as the **Maison de la France**, which has much material on Corsica and can also provide information over the telephone.

WHEN TO GO

C ORSICA OFFERS varied natural scenery and many different environments.

July and August are the best months for seaside holidays, but beware: the resorts will be crowded and it will be very warm.

The best period for hiking and climbing is from May to September, but even October can be quite pleasant if you limit your hikes to the foothills.

In order to enjoy the tranquil beauty of the island to the full, it is advisable not to visit Corsica between mid-July and mid-August.

VISAS AND PASSPORTS

C ORSICA IS A region of France and follows the same laws and regulations. European Union citizens are not subject to customs controls, but it is a good idea to have your documents handy.

For stays of three months or less, no visa is required for citizens of other European countries and for US, Canada and New Zealand nationals. However, visitors from other parts of the world, including Australia, must have a visa, which can be obtained from a French consulate in the country of departure.

TOURIST INFORMATION

A LL THE MAIN CITIES on the island have a tourist office, which may be called either Office de Tourisme or Syndicat d'Initiative. Smaller Corsican towns have centres that provide information on that particular area, including nearby villages. Sometimes the town hall itself (*mairie*) is used as a visitors' centre.

TICKETS AND OPENING HOURS

A S A GENERAL RULE, archaeological sites and museums in Corsica charge an admission fee. Most of them, however, have reduced prices for visitors under 18 and over 60. In some cases, discounted tickets are available for students with international student cards.

The opening hours of museums and archaeological sites vary: generally speaking, the main museums stay open all day, while digs are closed one day a week (either Sunday or Monday). If you want to visit churches and chapels, it is best to find out the opening hours from the town

Logo of Bastia tourist office

◁ **One of the most fascinating stretches of the D81 highway, cut out of the marvellous Calanques de Piana**

CUCURUZZU
Site Archéologique

A road sign indicating an historic monument

halls or tourist offices before embarking on your trip. Likewise, if you are planning to take a special tour to minor localities, it is advisable to contact the relevant tourist offices first.

Bear in mind that opening hours differ in high and low season. Detailed information is provided in the central section of this guide, which has the individual descriptions of the resorts, as well as in this section and the *Travellers' Needs* section (*see pp152–85*).

Cover of the catalogue of the Musée Fesch art collection

DISABLED TRAVELLERS

Iᴺ ᴛᴇʀᴍs ᴏꜰ ᴘʀᴏᴠɪᴅɪɴɢ for the disabled, Corsica is still a long way behind mainland France. Only a relatively small number of establishments – bars, restaurants, hotels and pensions – supply adequate facilities for wheelchair access.

The French guidebook *Guide Rousseau H comme Handicapés*, published by La Route Robert, contains detailed lists of the places with wheelchair access and other facilities. **Holiday Care** publishes an English-language brochure with information on all the establishments in France and Corsica in which architectural barriers have been eliminated to allow for easier access for the disabled.

SERVICES FOR STUDENTS

Fᴜʟʟ-ᴛɪᴍᴇ sᴛᴜᴅᴇɴᴛs who own an **International Student Identity Card** (ISIC) are entitled to reductions in the price of tickets and for numerous tourist initiatives. The ISIC card is an internationally recognized document that can be purchased from student travel agents or via the ISIC website.

LANGUAGES

Aʟᴛʜᴏᴜɢʜ the official language in Corsica is French, the local language has also always been in use there, making the island a bilingual area.

In 1974 Corsican was officially recognized as a regional tongue. After the reopening of the University of Corte in 1981, written Corsican was codified and old literary texts re-evaluated (*see pp30–31*).

Corsican is more like Italian than French – it is reminiscent of Ligurian dialect spoken with a Sardinian accent. As a result, many Corsicans understand and speak Italian. Road signs are in Corsican and French, although the French is often obscured by nationalist graffiti.

FRENCH TIME

Cᴏʀsɪᴄᴀ ɪs ᴏɴᴇ ʜᴏᴜʀ ahead of Greenwich Mean Time (GMT) and summer (daylight saving) time operates from spring to early autumn. Postmeridian time is indicated in two ways: either "8pm" or "20:00" (20 heures), for example.

ELECTRICAL ADAPTORS

Eʟᴇᴄᴛʀɪᴄᴀʟ ᴄᴜʀʀᴇɴᴛ in Corsica is 220v AC. Except for some small villages inland, the central hole of the sockets is generally earthed. It is wise to purchase an adaptor before leaving for Corsica.

DIRECTORY

EMBASSIES & CONSULATES

Australian Consulate
Paris. ☎ 01 40 59 33 00.

British Consulate
Marseille. ☎ 04 91 15 72 10.

Canadian Consulate
Paris. ☎ 01 44 43 29 02.

Irish Embassy
Paris. ☎ 01 44 17 67 00.

US Consulate
Marseille. ☎ 04 91 54 92 00.

TOURIST ORGANIZATIONS

Agence de Tourisme de la Corse
17 Blvd du Roi Jérôme, Ajaccio.
☎ 04 95 51 00 00.
ᴡ www.visit-corsica.com

Maison de la France
☎ 09068 244 123 (UK only).
ᴡ www.franceguide.com
ᴡ www.francetourism.com
(US-based)

TOURIST OFFICES

Bastia
Place St-Nicolas.
☎ 04 95 54 20 40.

Bonifacio
2 Rue Fred Scamaroni.
☎ 04 95 73 11 88.

Calvi
97 Port de Plaisance.
☎ 04 95 65 16 67.

Corte
☎ 04 95 46 26 70.

USEFUL NUMBERS

Holiday Care
7th Floor, Sunley House,
Croydon, Surrey, CRO 2AP.
☎ 01293 774 535.
ᴡ www.holidaycare.org.uk

International Student Identity Card (ISIC)
ᴡ www.isiccard.com

Parc Naturel Régional de la Corse
2 Rue Major Lambroschini, Ajaccio.
☎ 04 95 51 79 10.
ᴡ www.parc-naturel-corse.com

Personal Security and Health

Fire Brigade insignia

Corsica is a tranquil and safe region for travellers. The locals welcome foreign visitors, being well aware that they are a positive factor for the island's life and economy. Generally speaking, personal security is not really a problem, for either men or women. The disorders that sometimes make the news are the work of a handful of extremists of the Corsican independence movement and do not represent a danger for foreign visitors. Health standards on the island are high: as well as the hospitals in the main cities, there are physicians on 24-hour duty and medical facilities in all the resorts, especially those popular with tourists.

PERSONAL SECURITY

On the whole, dangerous or harmful incidents in Corsica rarely take place. Visitors, including lone women travellers, are unlikely to come across any problems of personal security.

Anyone walking along the streets on the island cannot help noticing the large amount of graffiti everywhere calling for Corsican independence from France. In recent years, some violent incidents have been linked to the independence movement. But even though the extremist fringe of this movement has sometimes made recourse to acts of terrorism, this tension is on the wane, and tourists have never been targeted by these factions. It is, however, a good rule to avoid entering into heated arguments or taking part in public demonstrations while in Corsica, as they might have unpleasant consequences.

CORSICAN POLICE

In France there is a police corps called *Gendarmerie Nationale*, which deals with major crimes and operates mainly outside the large cities, although it might intervene should serious incidents occur.

In the cities, those responsible for maintaining law and order act both as traffic wardens and as policemen, also taking care of minor problems. In case of need, go to the nearest police station *(gendarmerie)*. If you are in a small, isolated village, you can go to the local town hall *(mairie)* during office hours.

A gendarme in uniform

ROAD HAZARDS

The roads in Corsica are not the best maintained in Europe. The road surface is not always in good condition, the lanes are often narrow and there are a great many bends, especially in the mountainous interior. When travelling by car *(see p197)*, it is therefore a good idea to bring along a spare tyre and tools for minor repairs or problems.

FIRE HAZARDS

Since a large part of the island is covered with luxuriant forests, Corsica appears as a verdant paradise compared to other islands in the Mediterranean.

In the extensive woods in the interior and in the coastal areas with thick maquis vegetation, fire prevention is of vital importance. In these areas the wind blows almost constantly, the climate is hot and there is abundant vegetation – all factors that favour outbreaks of fire. Furthermore, because of the many steep ridges, canyons and rough terrain on the island, fires can be hard to control and put out. A case in point is the huge fire in the Vallée de la Restonica, which occurred in the summer of 2000.

Firemen intervene both on the ground, and, as soon as possible, with firefighting aeroplanes known as Canadair, and smaller, more manageable helicopters that get their water supply from the artificial lakes inland.

Not only is common sense called for, but European regulations must be obeyed as well. It is strictly forbidden to light fires outdoors, except in rigorously controlled areas. Smokers must never throw lighted cigarette butts on the roads or in the brush. You must also keep an eye out for any fire or smoke and make sure you report it to the fire brigade as soon as possible.

A vehicle used by the fire brigade suitable for rough terrain

A Canadair dumping tons of water on to a brush fire

If you are planning to take a long hike on terrain that is a potential fire risk, it is best to inform the local authorities of this before you start off. This way they will know how many people may be in danger should a fire break out in that area.

LEGAL ASSISTANCE

AS WITH ANY DESTINATION, for your own security take out a travel insurance policy.

In case of particular difficulties or serious incidents that require police intervention, the best thing to do is to contact your consulate (see p189) as soon as possible, since it will be able to provide all the necessary assistance in your language.

Pharmacy sign

PERSONAL BELONGINGS

ALTHOUGH CORSICA, like so many other tourist areas, is a peaceful region, travellers should take all the necessary precautions dictated by common sense.

Always take out insurance on your personal belongings, do not leave your luggage unattended and visible in a car, and do not travel with a lot of cash.

All cases of theft should be reported at the nearest police station immediately. Should you lose your documents, it is best to ask for help at your country's consulate in France (see p189).

MEDICAL TREATMENT

WHEN VISITING CORSICA, citizens of European Union countries who are entitled to medical treatment from their own national health service have the right to the same assistance they would receive in their own country. Before leaving the UK, British tourists must get a copy of the E111 health service form, which, when properly filled in, allows complete medical treatment and reimbursement of most of the expenses (which have to be paid on the spot) on the part of the Caisse Primarie d'Assurance-Maladie.

Non-EU citizens must obtain medical insurance from their own countries prior to departure. The number to call for the emergency service is 15.

HOSPITALS AND PHARMACIES

HOSPITALS IN Corsica are well organized and efficient. They are situated in the four main cities and in the largest tourist resorts, where there are also 24-hour duty physicians for foreign visitors.

Almost all the towns have pharmacies. They can be recognized by the neon sign in the form of a green cross outside. If a pharmacy is closed, the address of the nearest open one is always listed outside, as are the opening hours.

DIRECTORY

EMERGENCY NUMBERS

Police
(17.

Fire Brigade
(18.

Ambulance
(15.

Night-duty Physician
(17.

24-hour Pharmacies
(17.

Road Emergencies
Touring Club **(** 08 00 08 92 22.
AA Europe **(** 04 72 17 12 00.
AA (non-members) **(** 00800 33
22 88 77 (freephone).

HOSPITALS

Hôpital d'Ajaccio
27 Avenue Impératrice Eugénie.
(04 95 29 90 90.

Hôpital de Bastia
Route Royale.
(04 95 59 11 11.

Hôpital de Bonifacio
Route Santa Manza.
(04 95 73 95 73.

Hôpital de Corte
Avenue 9 Septembre.
(04 95 45 05 00.

Hôpital "Cacciabello"
D48 outside Sartène.
(04 95 77 95 00.

MINOR RISKS

TAKE PRECAUTIONS to avoid sunburn, which is as much a risk for those hiking in the mountains as for those holidaying on the coast.

If you suffer from allergies, take along insect repellent.

Sign for a Corsican hospital with the building in the background

Banking and Local Currency

SINCE 2002, MOST EUROPEAN tourists in Corsica no longer have to deal with the issue of currency exchange, since France is a member of the European Monetary Union and the currency in circulation within the Union is the euro. For visitors from other countries, however, exchanging currency is an easy and rapid procedure, both in banks and at the reception desks of hotels and pensions. The exchange rate of the euro and other non-European Union currencies is established daily and the rates can be found in all newspapers.

A cash dispenser (ATM) outside a bank

BANKS

BANKS IN CORSICA have the same opening hours as those in the south of France (8.30am to noon; 1:30 to 4:30pm) and are closed on Saturday and Sunday. Over public holidays, they are often closed from Friday noon to Tuesday morning.

Most European visitors no longer need to exchange currency, since the euro became the common currency of many EU countries in January 2002.

Although documents are not normally necessary when exchanging currency, your identification card or passport may sometimes be requested.

The main foreign currencies can be exchanged in banks, as can travellers' cheques, the rates of which are slightly different (they tend to be less advantageous). Banks also offer other services for foreign visitors; relevant information is provided on the spot.

For security reasons, many banks have double electronically operated doors. You must first push the button outside to open the door leading off the street. Once you are in the area between the two doors, you must wait for the green light to come on (which it

does when the outside door is closed) and then the inside door opens automatically.

CASH DISPENSERS (ATMS)

CASH DISPENSERS (ATMs) can be found in and outside of almost all the banks in Corsica and they operate around the clock. Cash withdrawals can be made by means of bank cash-dispenser cards or credit cards, such as Visa, MasterCard, Diners Club and American Express.

Be aware of your surroundings and make sure that no one sees your personal identity number (PIN) when you withdraw cash from an ATM.

CREDIT CARDS

EVEN IF THE AMOUNT is small, payment with credit or debit cards in all kinds of shop and in hotels and restaurants is quite widespread and normal in Corsica. However, be aware that small shops and eateries inland might prefer cash.

The most widely accepted cards in Corsica are Visa and MasterCard. You may find it difficult at times to use American Express and Diners Club credit cards.

An alternative to credit cards is Visa TravelMoney, which works as a pre-paid ATM card. This service can be arranged with Visa or Travelex before your departure, creating an account that will hold your pre-determined holiday funds. The Visa TravelMoney card can then be used to withdraw cash from any Visa ATM by means of a PIN number.

DIRECTORY

BANKS

Banque de France
8 Rue Sergent Casalonga, Ajaccio.
C 04 95 51 72 40.

Crédit Lyonnais
22 Rue César Campinchi, Bastia.
C 04 95 55 01 41.

Travelex
W www.travelex.com

LOST CREDIT CARDS

American Express
C 01 47 77 72 00 (Paris).

Visa/MasterCard
C 0892 705 705.

When the funds in the holiday account are exhausted, the card can be thrown away.

BUREAUX DE CHANGE

THE LARGEST tourist resorts have exchange offices where the exchange rates are quite close to the official ones. Before you exchange your money, check the official rate that day and the commissions charged for every single currency-exchange operation.

Many hotels also have currency-exchange services for their clients. Again, it is best to know what the rates and commissions are beforehand, since these operations are usually expensive. There is no limit to the amount of money you may take into France, but if you bring more than €7,500 into the UK you need to declare it on arrival.

One of the many bureaux de change in Corsica

LOCAL CURRENCY

THE OFFICIAL CURRENCY in Corsica is the euro, which is used in 12 of the 25 European Union member countries: Austria, Belgium, Finland, France, Germany, Greece, Ireland, Italy, Luxem-bourg, Holland, Portugal and Spain. The UK, Denmark and Sweden have for the present chosen not to take the euro.

The front of all euro notes shows windows or doorways to represent the new spirit of openness within the EU; the back of the notes portrays a bridge, which symbolizes communication. The 12 stars of the European Union are also shown on all notes.

Citizens of non-euro and non-European countries need to get their currency exchanged before travelling or during their stay in Corsica.

Bank Notes
Euro bank notes are the same in all the European Monetary Union countries. The €5 note (grey) is the smallest, followed by the €10 note (pink), €20 note (blue), €50 note (orange), €100 note (green), €200 note (yellow) and €500 note (purple).

5 euros

10 euros

20 euros

50 euros

100 euros

200 euros

500 euros

2 euros

1 euro

50 cents

20 cents

10 cents

Coins
The euro has eight coin denominations: the €2 and €1 coins are silver and gold in colour; the 50-, 20- and 10-cent coins are gold, and the 5-, 2- and 1-cent coins are bronze. One side is the same for all nations, while the back has an image chosen by each national mint.

5 cents

2 cents

1 cent

Communications

Public telephone sign

THE FRENCH NATIONAL telephone company is called *France Telecom*, while the postal service is called *La Poste*. Both are quite efficient and there are phone booths and post offices throughout Corsica. Internet access is less widespread, even though all the public offices and tourist bureaus have e-mail and there are various websites for visitors looking for information on the island. There are also two networks for mobile phones. In the summer, some foreign newspapers can be found in the main towns, but they usually arrive a day after publication.

Two examples of telephone cards used in France and Corsica

POSTAL SERVICE

THE FRENCH postal service is efficient and punctual. In the post office *(bureau de poste)* it is possible to purchase stamps *(timbres)*, either singly or in sheets *(carnets)* with ten stamps, and to post letters and parcels in various ways (priority, special delivery and so on). Here you can also consult telephone directories *(annuaires)*, purchase pre-paid telephone cards *(télécartes)*, receive or send money by means of postal money orders *(mandats)*, and cash postal giros. The main post office of every city or town also offers *poste restante*, or a post-office box service. In addition, French post offices feature a variety of financial services.

The main post offices are open from 8am to 7pm, sometimes with an hour's break for lunch. In smaller towns, and everywhere on Saturday, they are open only in the morning.

There are eight different postal rates for international post. The least expensive is for items for European Union countries, which is the same as the domestic rate. The

Corsican postbox

most expensive is for items to Asia and Australia. Sending bulky parcels is usually rather expensive.

Corsican postboxes are yellow, with the blue logo of *La Poste* on them, and they may have different holes for local post, post for another *département* and international post.

THE DÉPARTEMENTS

THE ADMINISTRATIVE system in France dates back to the time of the French Revolution, when the nation was divided into administrative units with equal authority and value. These were the 96 *départements* that are still operative; they are grouped into *régions* and subdivided into 35,000 local *communes*.

Corsica is a region with two *départements*: 2A Corse-du-Sud and 2B Haute-Corse, which correspond more or less to the old separation into the *Delà des monts* and *Deça des monts* areas *(see p40)*.

Addresses in France always have a five-digit postcode. The first two digits correspond to the *département*, the third indicates the city, and the last two are for the quarters or minor localities.

PUBLIC TELEPHONES

MOST PUBLIC TELEPHONES in Corsica are touch-tone and function with pre-paid telephone cards, which come in various denominations, measured in units *(unités)*. For local calls, a *unité* lasts about six minutes; this time progressively decreases as the distance increases (for example, for a call to Australia a unit lasts four seconds).

Bars and restaurants have a different type of phone, coin- or token-operated, while post offices have booths where you pay after the call.

The international-calls service is called *pays direct*. With this system you call the operator and then pay either with your credit card or by making a collect call.

PHONING IN CORSICA

ALL PHONE NUMBERS in France now have ten digits and they include the former area codes. The first two figures indicate the four zones into which France is divided – in Corsica these digits are 04, which stand for the southeast zone. The next two figures, which, in the case of Corsica, are 95, indicate the *région*. For local directory enquiries, dial 12; for police emergencies, dial 17.

INTERNATIONAL CALLS

IF YOU WANT to make an international call, you must dial 00 and then the inter-national number for the country you're phoning (44 in the case of the UK), followed by the area code and the number you want to reach. Other country codes are 1 for Canada and the

Logo of the French postal and telecommunications service

USA, 353 for Ireland, 61 for Australia, and 64 for New Zealand.

To call Corsica from abroad, dial 0033 followed by the number of the person or business you want to contact, leaving out the initial 0.

If you want the operator, dial 13, while for information on international numbers you should dial 12 for Germany, 13 for all other European countries, and 14 for the rest of the world.

A telephone booth with the logo of France Telecom

MOBILE PHONES AND INTERNATIONAL CALLS

Corsica has two companies that manage mobile-phone services: *Orange* and *SFR*. Mobile phones from all European countries work perfectly well along the coast of the island, but less so in the interior, where both coverage and reception can be patchy.

It is also worth bearing in mind that, should you make a call from Corsica to a foreign country, added to the cost of the call is the price of the international portion. Likewise, when you receive a call, the price of the international part of the call is charged to the mobile phone that was called. For more detailed information on the fees charged by the various mobile-phone companies and the best rates available,

contact your mobile-phone company in your own country. For long phone calls it is usually cheaper to use one of the many telephone booths throughout the island.

RADIO AND TV

As well as the national television networks, Corsica has local TV and radio stations, some of which broadcast in Corsican.

Due to the proximity to Sardinia and Tuscany, many private homes and hotels in Corsica also receive the main Italian TV channels.

Hotels tend to offer the leading European and American satellite channels, such as Sky News, BBC World and CNN.

The France Arte channel shows foreign films in their original language every night.

NEWSPAPERS

As in the other regions in France, there are two kinds of newspapers in Corsica: those distributed on a nationwide scale, such as *Le Monde*, *Le Figaro* and *Libération*, and the local, regional ones, such as *Corse-Matin*. Local papers provide useful information regarding cultural events, cinema, theatre and sports, but they do not leave much space for foreign news.

In the summer, in the main cities it is easy to find foreign newspapers, which usually arrive one day late.

The daily newspaper *Corse-Matin*, with its weekly insert

DIRECTORY

POST OFFICES

Ajaccio
13 Cours Napoléon.
☏ 04 95 51 84 75.

Aléria
Cateraggio.
☏ 04 95 56 55 00.

Bastia
Avenue Maréchal Sebastiani.
☏ 04 95 32 80 70.

Bonifacio
Place Carrega, Rue St Dominique.
☏ 04 95 73 73 73.

Calvi
1 Boulevard Wilson.
☏ 04 95 65 90 90.

Cargèse
Traverse Stéphanopoli de Comène.
☏ 04 95 26 41 97.

Corte
Avenue Baron Mariani.
☏ 04 95 46 80 00.

Porto-Vecchio
Route Nationale 198.
☏ 04 95 70 95 00.

Zonza
Au Bourg.
☏ 04 95 78 67 67.

INTERNET

In the main cities, there are Internet cafés where customers can surf the Web.

The website of the central Agence de Tourisme is **www.visit-corsica.com**. Among the most useful websites are **www.corsica-guide.com**, with information on local events, geography, culture and museums; and **www.corsica-online.com**, for hotels, restaurants and tours. For accommodation, you can also visit **www.ilotel.com**.

The site of the Parc Naturel Régional de la Corse is **www.parc-naturel-corse.com**; and if you are interested in the local wineries, the website is **www.vinsdecorse.com**.

Information on current events in Corsica is at **www.corsica-info.com**, while **www.u-corsu.com** is a good search engine for all things Corsican.

TRAVEL INFORMATION

CORSICA HAS excellent connections with the rest of Europe and there are regularly scheduled flights linking the airports in Ajaccio, Bastia, Figari Sud Corse (near Bonifacio) and Calvi with others in Provence and southern France, as well as Paris. There are also several charter flights in the high season. Another popular means of transport to the island from both southern France and Italy is the ferry. To get

Bus for tourist excursions

around the island there are few alternatives to a car. The only railway line connects Bastia to Ajaccio and Calvi. There is a network of public buses, but they do not go to all the inland resorts and you may have to wait a long time for connections. When driving, bear in mind that the roads are often winding and panoramic, and the average speed limit is rather low; be very careful when the traffic is heavy, especially if the weather is bad.

ARRIVING BY AIR

IN THE SUMMER Corsica is well served by charter flights departing from Gatwick (Calvi, Ajaccio, Figari and Bastia), Heathrow (Ajaccio), Stansted and Manchester (Figari and Calvi), Birmingham (Bastia) and Edinburgh (Calvi). **Holiday Options** offers flights at good prices, as well as package holidays.

GB Airways offers direct scheduled flights from the UK to Corsica. **British Airways** and **Air France** go there via Paris, Marseille or Nice, where a change of plane is required.

US visitors have to go via France, which is served by Air France, **United Airlines** and **Delta** among others. From Corsica can be reached with a regional carrier (such as **Nouvelles Frontières/Corse Air International** or **Air Lib**).

Logo of the French national airline Air France

AIR FARES

GENERALLY SPEAKING, air fares to Corsica are fairly expensive during the summer season. However, for those willing to shop around, there are also good-value last-minute deals to be had, as well as various combinations, with a minimum and maximum number of days,

One of the large car ferries serving Corsica

that allow you to stay in Corsica without spending too much. In the low season the offers are cheaper.

PACKAGE HOLIDAYS

THERE ARE SEVERAL package-tour operators dealing with Corsica. A package holiday includes at the very least air fare and accommodation; some also include food, car rental and activities.

One of the most reputable package-tour operators is **Club Med**. Renowned for the high level of service and excellent facilities, Club Med has a holiday village (see p155) near Cargèse. Childcare and all activities are included in the price.

Package tours are also handled by **Simply Corsica**, the UK's largest operator on the island, and **Voyages Ilena**, both of which offer hotel rooms and a variety of self-catering accommodation.

ARRIVING BY FERRY

FERRIES are a popular means of transportation for visitors travelling to Corsica from France or Italy. Because of the large number of visitors, if you plan to go to the island by car in the summer it is best to book well ahead, especially if you are towing a caravan or travelling in a camper.

In the summer there are fast car ferries that save you a lot of time in the crossing, but they cost more than the normal ferries.

The port of Bastia has many routes, with links to Marseille, Nice, Toulon, Genoa and Savona, La Spezia, Livorno, and Piombino. Ajaccio is accessed via regular ferries departing from southern France and from Genoa, and there is also a line that goes from Ajaccio to Porto Torres, in Sardinia. Bonifacio can be reached by ferry only from Sardinia.

On the train from Ajaccio to Bastia

The **Société Nationale Maritime Corse Mediterranée** (SNCM) and **Compagnie Méridionale de Navigation** (CMN) are the French shipping lines. If you leave from Italy, **Corsica Ferries** offers several links with the island, including departures from Civitavecchia (only in summer) and Livorno and Savona (all year round). **Moby Lines** connects Bastia and Piombino (July and August), Livorno and Genoa for about the same price.

In the summer there is also a frequent ferry service from France and Italy to Calvi, L'Île Rousse and Porto-Vecchio.

FERRY FARES

THE HIGHEST FARE for two people and a car 4–5 m (13–16 ft) long on the Livorno–Bastia ferry is about €260 return, but there are special rates and discount tickets (up to a minimum of €105).

TRAVELLING BY TRAIN

ON THE narrow-gauge Bastia–Corte–Ajaccio railway – which is worth travelling, especially for the magnificent views it affords – there are four trains per day in each direction.

One of the most frequented train stations is Vizzavona, which many visitors use as a departure point for the remarkable GR20 long-distance hiking path (*see pp20–25*).

To get to Calvi by train from Ajaccio (and vice versa), change trains at the small station of Ponte Leccia.

Information about timetables can be found at the main railway stations, especially Bastia and Ajaccio.

TRAVELLING BY BUS

THE BUS LINE that offers service in the area around Corte is the **Société des Autocars Cortenais**. Another company covering the central-north area of Corsica is **Autocars Santini**. Ajaccio, Sartène and Bonifacio are served by bus lines such as **Eurocorse**.

Because of the seasonal variation in the schedules, it is always a good idea to make enquiries at the local tourist offices before setting off on a bus journey.

TRAVELLING BY CAR

A REGULAR DRIVER'S licence is the only document required to travel by car in Corsica. Naturally, the great number of minor roads is an invitation to explore the lesser-known areas on the island; these require a much lower speed and particular attention and caution. When planning a tour or excursion, you should base it on an average speed of 40–50 km/h (25–30 mph). There may be animals on the road or, in summer, large caravans and campers that go slowly on the hairpin turns, so you must reduce your speed.

You can travel faster only on the Routes Nationales (Bastia–Calvi, Bastia–Corte–Ajaccio, Bastia–Porto-Vecchio and Ajaccio-Bonifacio).

There are more petrol stations along the coast than inland, and in the tourist resorts near the sea it is easy to find automatic petrol pumps that will accept bank notes or credit cards.

CAR RENTAL

THE OFFICES of the main car-rental companies are in airports and port passenger terminals. These include **Avis**, **Hertz**, **Europcar** and **Budget Rent a Car**, as well as local companies such as **Ada**, which offers very different rates according to the season. By paying a small surcharge, you can pick up your car in one place and return it in another.

TRAVELLING BY MOTORCYCLE

CORSICA IS A paradise for motorcyclists. The roads are difficult but rewarding, and the dry summers are favourable for this means of transportation. Motorcycles are also advantageous in avoiding traffic jams, especially along the coast.

As is the case with cars, you must be extremely careful, especially on the mountain roads.

Motorcycles can be hired from most main cities in Corsica (Ajaccio, Porto-Vecchio, Bastia, Calvi, Porto and Propriano). You will also find centres that hire motorcycles and offer assistance for those arriving with their own bikes.

Travelling by camper in Corsica – a simple way to enjoy the scenery

TRAVELLING BY BOAT

BOATS OF ALL KINDS can be found in Corsican waters during the summer months. You can use your boat to travel from one resort to another within Corsica or for making the crossing from a port in Italy or France *(see p182)*. Obviously, this voyage should be made only by expert navigators whose boats are able to withstand the hazards of the open sea. Even the shortest crossing, from Sardinia in the Straits of Bonifacio *(see p113)*, is not without its pitfalls due to the strong winds that often blow in this part of the sea.

Sailing remains undoubtedly one of the best ways to explore the coasts of Corsica. Even a simple dinghy or a small sailboat, rented or brought along with your car in a ferry, are ideal for leaving in the morning and returning in the evening after a fine day's boating.

BOAT HIRE

THERE ARE many possibilities for hiring boats in Corsica. The boat-hire companies

The harbour at Cargèse, one of the stages on a tour of the coast

have all types of craft to offer their clients, and they also provide assistance and maintenance. The rates can be by the hour or by the day, and there are even weekly rates for those who decide to make long trips. In such cases the agencies offer boats with a skipper or even a crew.

Naturally, the price varies according to the type of boat you hire, the duration of the trip and whether a skipper or crew are provided. The period of rental is also a factor, the highest rates being in July and August.

CIRCUMNAVIGATING THE ISLAND

A CLASSIC CHOICE of trip for experienced yachtsmen is a tour around the island. This is a fascinating adventure because the coast of Corsica is spectacular and has many secluded coves that cannot be reached by car or even on foot.

The chart below lists the ports on the island and their facilities. Although temporary berths are added in summer, ports are likely to be crowded, so phone beforehand or arrive in the early afternoon.

PORTS	INFORMATION	BOAT BERTHS TOTAL	TEMPORARY	FUEL STATION	MAINTENANCE AND REPAIR
Ajaccio, Ornano	04 95 22 31 98	856	130	●	●
Ajaccio, Tino Rossi	04 95 21 93 28	260	40	●	●
Bastia, Port de Toga	04 95 34 90 70	357	50	●	●
Bastia, Vieux Port	04 95 31 31 10	260	40	●	●
Bonifacio	04 95 73 10 07	220	120	●	●
Calvi	04 95 65 10 60	550	200	●	●
Campoloro	04 95 38 07 61	465	100	●	●
Cargèse	04 95 26 47 24	235	25	●	●
Lumio	04 95 60 70 88	250	0	●	●
Macinaggio	04 95 35 42 57	585	240	●	●
Pianottoli Caldarello	04 95 71 83 57	160	80	●	
Porto-Vecchio	04 95 70 17 93	450	150	●	●
Propriano	04 95 76 10 40	420	50	●	●
St-Florent	04 95 37 00 79	750	150	●	●
Solenzara	04 95 57 46 42	450	100	●	●

DIRECTORY

AIRPORTS

Ajaccio
Campo dell'Oro.
[04 95 23 56 56.

Bastia
Poretta.
[04 95 54 54 54.

Calvi
Ste-Catherine.
[04 95 65 88 88.

Figari-Sud-Corse
[04 95 71 10 10.

AIRLINES

Air France
France. [0820 820 820.
UK. [0845 0845 111.
W www.airfrance.com

British Airways
[0845 773 3377.
W www.british
airways.com

**Corse-Méditerranée
(CCM)**
Marseille, Nice, Lyon.
[0820 820 820.
W www.ccm-airlines.com

Delta Air Lines
[(800) 241 4141.
W www.delta.com

GB Airways
[0870 850 9850.
W www.gbairways.com

Holiday Options
49 The Martlets,
Burgess Hill,
West Sussex RH15 9NJ.
[0870 013 0450.
W www.holiday
options.co.uk

**Nouvelles
Frontières/Corse
Air International**
*Paris, Marseille, Bordeaux,
Strasbourg, Lyon, Lille,
Nice, Toulouse, Brussels.*
Ajaccio.
[04 95 21 55 55.
Bastia.
[04 95 32 01 62.
W www.nouvelles-
frontieres.fr

United Airlines
[(800) 241 6522.
W www.ual.com

PACKAGE HOLIDAYS

Club Med
[0845 367 6767.
W www.clubmed.co.uk

Simply Corsica
[020 8541 2205.
W www.simply-travel.com

Voyages Ilena
[020 7924 4440.
W www.voyagesilena.
co.uk

FERRY PORTS

Ajaccio
[04 95 51 21 80.

Bastia [04 95 55 25 00.

Bonifacio
[04 95 73 06 75.

Calvi [04 95 65 05 21.

L'Île Rousse
[04 95 60 45 54.

Porto-Vecchio
[04 95 70 43 08.

Propriano
[04 95 76 04 36.

FERRIES

**Compagnie
Méridionale
de Navigation**
Ajaccio. [04 95 11 01
00. W www.cmn.fr

Corsica Ferries
*Livorno, Savona, Toulon,
Nice.*
Bastia. [04 95 32 95 95.
W www.corsicaferries.com

Moby Lines
Genoa, Livorno, Piombino.
Bastia. [04 95 34 84 94.
Bonifacio.
[04 95 73 00 29.
W www.mobylines.it

**Societé Nationale
Maritime Corse
Mediterranée
(SNCM)**
*Marseille, Toulon, Livorno,
Nice.*
Ajaccio.
[04 95 29 66 99.
Bastia. [04 95 54 66 99.
Calvi. [04 95 65 01 38.
L'Île Rousse.
[04 95 60 09 56.

Livorno. [0586 21 05 07.
W www.sncm.fr

RAILWAY STATIONS

Ajaccio
[04 95 23 11 03.

Bastia [04 95 32 80 61.

Calvi [04 95 65 00 61.

Corte [04 95 46 00 97.

L'Île Rousse
[04 95 60 00 50.

Ponte-Novo
[04 95 38 60 72.

Vizzavona
[04 95 47 21 22.

BUS COMPANIES

Autocars Santini
[04 95 37 04 01.

Eurocorse
[04 95 21 06 30.

**Société des
Autocars Cortenais**
[04 95 46 02 12.

CAR RENTAL

Ada
Ajaccio.
[04 95 23 56 57.
Bastia.
[04 95 54 55 44.

Avis
Ajaccio.
[04 95 23 56 90.
Bastia. [04 95 54 55 46.
Calvi. [04 95 65 88 38.
Figari. [04 95 71 00 01.
W www.avis.com

Budget Rent a Car
Ajaccio.
[04 95 23 57 21.
Bastia. [04 95 30 05 04.
Calvi. [04 95 65 88 34.
W www.budget
rentacar.com.

Europcar
Ajaccio.
[04 95 23 57 01.
Bastia. [04 95 30 09 50.
Bonifacio.
[04 95 73 10 99.
Calvi. [04 95 65 10 19.
Corte. [04 95 46 06 02.
W www.europcar.co.uk

Hertz
Ajaccio. [04 95 52 20 22.
Bastia. [04 95 30 05 00.
W www.hertz.com

MOTORCYCLE HIRE

Corse Motos Service
U Centru, Porto-Vecchio.
[04 95 70 12 88.

Rout'Evasion
2 Avenue Franchini, Ajaccio.
[04 95 22 72 87.

BOAT HIRE

Aubert Gaston
Route Cala Rossa,
Porto-Vecchio.
[04 95 70 23 97.

Balagne Sports
Rue Napoléon, L'Île Rousse.
[04 95 60 05 17.

Cap Evasion
Macinaggio.
[04 95 35 47 90.

Centre Nautique
Porticcio.
[04 95 25 01 06.

Corsica Voile
Macinaggio.
[04 95 35 48 20.

**Dominique
Plaisance**
St-Florent.
[04 95 37 07 08.

Evasion Valinco
Propriano.
[04 95 76 04 26.

Marine Location
Porto-Vecchio.
[04 95 70 58 92.

Multi-Service
Santa Giulia, Porto-Vecchio.
[04 95 70 29 13.

Panzani Nautique
Quai Paoli, Porto-Vecchio.
[04 95 70 29 32.

Plaisance Location
Port de Toga, Bastia.
[04 95 34 14 14.

Tra Mare e Monti
Port de Plaisance, Calvi.
[04 95 65 21 26.

**Union Nautique
Insulaire**
Port de l'Amirautée,
Ajaccio. [04 95 20 66 31.

Index

Acknowledgments

FABIO RATTI EDITORIA would like to thank the following staff at DORLING KINDERSLEY:

PUBLISHING MANAGER
Anna Streiffert.

SENIOR ART EDITOR
Marisa Renzullo.

PUBLISHER
Douglas Amrine.

SENIOR DTP DESIGNER
Jason Little.

CARTOGRAPHERS
Casper Morris, Dave Pugh.

DORLING KINDERSLEY would also like to thank all those whose contribution and assistance have made the preparation of this book possible.

MAIN CONTRIBUTORS
FABRIZIO ARDITO, a journalist and photographer born in Rome in 1957. Among his publications are several books on hiking. In the Dorling Kindersley Eyewitness Travel Guides series he has contributed to *Sardinia*, *Sicily* and *Jerusalem & the Holy Land*, as well as the following (so far published in Italian only, by Guide Visuali Mondadori): *The Dolomites*, *Northeast Italy*, *Central Italy*, *South Italy*. He has written texts and articles for various Italian publishers, periodicals and newpapers on the environment, geography and travelling in general. These include *Nuova Ecologia*, *Espresso*, Gambero Rosso-De Agostini, Touring Club, Giorgio Mondadori and *Unità*. He has also worked for the Italian State Television (RAI), producing various films and documentaries on nature, sports and the subterranean areas of cities.

CRISTINA GAMBARO is a journalist who has contributed articles to the leading Italian periodicals. For Gambero Rosso-De Agostini she wrote *Guide to Italian Hotels*; for Clupguide she wrote *Sardinia* and *Pakistan*; for Airplane, *Scotland* and *Ireland*; for White Star, *The Castles of Scotland*. She was also a main contributor to the following Dorling Kindersley Eyewitness Travel Guides: *Sardinia*, *Sicily* and *Jerusalem & the Holy Land*, as well as *Northeast Italy*, *Central Italy*, *South Italy* and *The Dolomites* (published in Italian by Guide Visuali Mondadori).

EDITORIAL ASSISTANCE
Cayetana Muriel Aguado, Thierry Combret, Géraldine Gonard, Marina Dragoni.
For Dorling Kindersley: Karen Villabona.

EDITORS, UK EDITION
Sylvia and David Tombesi-Walton at Sands Publishing Solutions, Lauren Robertson.

FACTCHECKER
Irina Zarb.

CONSULTANT
David Abram.

PROOF-READER
Jane Simmonds.

INDEXER
Helen Peters.

SPECIAL THANKS
We would like to thank the following persons for their contribution to this guide:
Messieurs Xavier Olivieri and Jean-Philippe di Grazia, Agence de Tourisme de la Corse, Ajaccio; Madame Marie-Eugénie Poli-Mordiconi, Musée de la Corse, Corte; Monsieur Pascal Rinaldi, Parc Naturel Régional de Corse, Ajaccio; Madame Viviane Gentile, Domaine Gentile, St-Florent; Monsieur Jean-Noël Luigi, Clos Nicrosi, Rogliano; Ms Marina della Rosa, expert sailor; the chef Carlo Romito and his assistants Giorgio Brignone and Marco Fanti, of the Palazzo Granaio restaurant in Settimo Milanese, specializing in cuisine of the upper

Tyrrhenian Sea; Mrs Delphine Jaillot, Sopexa Italia, Milan; Ms Charlotte Grant, Christie's, London; Dr Biondi, Scientific Committee, Palazzo Ducale, Genoa; Dr Campodonico, curator, Museo Navale di Pegli, Genoa; Dr Alessandro Avanzino, Palazzo San Giorgio, Genoa; the Associazione Amici di Palazzo Ducale, Genoa; the Museo di Sant'Agostino, Genoa; Gabriele Reina and Roberto Bosi, Franco Maria Ricci Publishers, Milan; all the Stations Touristiques in Corsica; the Musée Fesch, Ajaccio; the French Tourist Board, Milan.

PHOTOGRAPHY PERMISSIONS

The Publisher would like to thank the local bodies, associations and firms for the authorization to take photographs, in particular Archivio Electa, Milano; Musée de la Corse, Corte; Musée d'Antropologie de la Corse, Corte; Sopexa Italia, Milan. The Publisher would also like to thank the cathedrals, churches, museums, galleries, restaurants, hotels, shops and all those who furnished material – too numerous to be mentioned here individually – for their kind assistance and valuable contribution.

Every effort has been made to trace the copyright holders. The Publisher apologizes for any unintentional omissions and would be pleased, in such cases, to add an acknowledgment in future editions.

KEY TO PICTURE CREDITS

t = top; tl = top left; tlc = top left centre; tc = top centre; trc = top right centre; tr = top right; tra = top right above; cla = centre left above; ca = centre above; cra = centre right above; cl = centre left; c = centre; cr = centre right; cla = centre left above; crb = centre right below; cb = centre below; bl = bottom left; br = bottom right; b = bottom; bc = bottom centre; bcl = bottom centre left; bcr = bottom centre right; (d) = detail.

PICTURE CREDITS

AGENCE DE TOURISME DE LA CORSE, Ajaccio: 15bcr, 31 (all photos), 33cb, 34 (all photos), 35cra, 37ca, 38tl, 40cb, 40crb, 41cr, 41 br, 45bc, 49bc, 87tl, 90tl, 99tc, 123br, 148tc, 162br, 163br, 174br, 176cla, 181cr, 184cl, 189cl.

CHRISTIAN ANDREANI, Ajaccio: 99br.

ARCHIVIO FABIO RATTI EDITORIA, Milan: 113cra, 113crb, 113clb.

ARCHIVIO MONDADORI, Milan: 16clb, 16crb, 16bcl, 17clb, 17tr, 17bl, 17bc, 17crb, 18tl, 40cla, 40bl, 42–3c, 42tl, 42br, 43tl, 43cr, 47cra, 48tc, 49tl, 69ca, 73tc, 96cla, 102c, 122tl, 122cl, 139cr, 142cl, 153 (box), 166crb, 167tr, 167br, 183br, 184 (box), 191c, 196clb.

ARCHIVIO SCALA, Florence: 36.

ARDEA LONDON LTD: Stefan Meyers 24cla.

ADRIANO BACCHELLA, Turin: 1c; 13ca, 14tl, 16cla, 16cra, 17cla, 17cra, 18tr, 18clb, 18bcr, 19tc, 19bcl, 20crb, 21tc, 26tl, 28tl, 32bcr, 52trc, 52clb, 52bl, 53cr, 53br, 56cl, 61br, 66bc, 68bc, 69br, 73clb, 73crb, 78clb, 79crb, 85trc, 93bcl, 99cla, 99crb, 99bl, 101tl, 102bcr, 108trc, 108clb, 109cra, 109bcd, 115tl, 115cb, 115bcl, 117tlc, 117cra, 117bcr, 125bcr, 126tlc, 127ca, 132clb, 133br, 151tlc, 156b, 181tlc, 184b, 186–7, 188cla.

ENRICO BANFI, Milan: 105tl.

CONTRASTO, Milan: 49cb, 81cla, 81clb, 97tc, 113cl, 113bcr, 165clb, 165cb, 166cla, 166ca, 176tc, 183tc, 184tr.

LOUIS DOAZAN, Corsica: 99cl.

XIAOYANG GALAS: *Sea, Sunshine and Village* 8–9.

GETTY IMAGES: Michelle Bussellle 118–19.

GÎTES DE FRANCE: 154t.

GRONCHI FOTOARTE, Pisa: 43tr.

RMN, Paris: 90tr, 90cl, 90bl, 90br, 91tl, 91cra.

ANNA SERRANO, Barcelona: 16bcr.
SOPEXA, Italiy: 167 crb.

STUDIO AQUILINI, Milan: 94–5, 100tl, 100clb, 100bcl, 101cra, 114tr, 114bcr, 180cra, 181b.

SYNDICAT D'INITIATIVE DE PIANA: 100tr.

JACKET
Front – DK PICTURE LIBRARY: Fabrizio Ardito bl; Cristina Gambaro bc, br; LONELY PLANET IMAGES: David Tomlinson main image. Back – DK PICTURE LIBRARY: Cristina Gambaro t; LONELY PLANET IMAGES: Oliver Cirendini t. Spine – LONELY PLANET IMAGES: David Tomlinson.

All other images © Dorling Kindersley.
For further information:
www.dkimages.com

SPECIAL EDITIONS OF DK TRAVEL GUIDES

DK Travel Guides can be purchased in bulk quantities at discounted prices for use in promotions or as premiums. We are also able to offer special editions and personalized jackets, corporate imprints, and excerpts from all of our books, tailored specifically to meet your own needs.

To find out more, please contact:
(in the United States) **SpecialSales@dk.com**
(in the UK) **Sarah.Burgess@dk.com**
(in Canada) DK Special Sales at **general@tourmaline.ca**
(in Australia) **business.development@pearson.com.au**

Corsican Words and Phrases

Although French is spoken everywhere, a few Corsican phrases can come in handy. Coriscan is closer to Italian, in fact to Medieval Tuscan, both in its vocabulary and its pronounciation, but also shows a few other Mediterranean influences. Geographical terms appear in many sight names, and on the bilingual signs.

BASICS

A'ringraziavvi: Thank you
Fate u piacè: Please
Ié: Yes
Nò: No
Và bé: OK
Induve: Where
Quandu: When
Chì: What, who, which
A'vedeci: Goodbye
A dopu: See you
Buona notte: Goodnight
Buona sera: Good evening
Buonghjornu: Hello
Cumu sì?: How are you?
Me dispiace: Sorry
(Nò) Capiscu: I (don't) understand
Parla inglese?: Do you speak English?

GEOGRAPHICAL TERMS

a marina: beach
anse/cala: cove
boca/foce/col: mountain pass
calanca: gorge, ravine
casa: house
casatorre: stronghold
castellu/casteddu: fortified settlement
fiume: river
fiumicellu: stream
lau/lavu: lake
licettu: oak forest
muntagna: mountain
orriu: shelter under a large stone or boulder, sometimes bricked in
pianu: plateau
piscia: waterfall
ponte: bridge
stagnu: pool or pond
torre: tower
u paese: village
vignale/vignetu: vineyard

DIRECTIONS

dritta: right
sempredrittu: straight on
sinistra: left
Induv'é...?: Where is...?

SHOPPING

aperta/apertu: open
Avetene...?: Do you have...?
basta: enough
buonu mercatu: cheap
chiusu: closed
grande/maio: big
Hè troppu caru: It is too much.
menu: less
nulla/nunda/nudda: nothing
piccola/chjucu: small
pui: more
Quantu costa/Quanto hè?: How much does it cost/is it?
Vogliu...: I want...

TIME, DAYS AND MONTHS

Chi ora hè?: What is the time?
oghje: today
ieri: yesterday
dumane: tomorrow
ghjurnu: day
simana: week
meze: month

Monday:	**luni**
Tuesday:	**marti**
Wednesday:	**mercuri**
Thursday:	**ghjovi**
Friday:	**venneri**
Saturday:	**sabatu**
Sunday:	**dumenica**
January:	**Ghjennaghju**
February:	**Febbraghju**
March:	**Marzu**
April:	**Aprile**
May:	**Maghjiu**
June:	**Ghjiugnu**
July:	**Ghjugliu**
August:	**Aostu**
September:	**Sittembre**
October:	**Ottobre**
November:	**Novembre**
December:	**Dicembre**

SEASONS

auturnu: autumn
estate: summer
imbernu/ingnernu: winter
veranu: spring

French Phrase Book

IN EMERGENCY

Help!	**Au secours!**	oh se**koor**
Stop!	**Arrêtez!**	aret-**ay**
Call a doctor!	**Appelez un médecin!**	apuh-**lay** uñ medsañ
Call an ambulance!	**Appelez une ambulance!**	apuh-**lay** oon oñboo-**loñs**
Call the police!	**Appelez la police!**	apuh-**lay** lah poh-**lees**
Call the fire brigade!	**Appelez les pompiers!**	apuh-lay leh poñ-**peeyay**
Where is the nearest telephone?	**Où est le téléphone le plus proche?**	oo ay luh tehleh**fon** luh ploo **prosh**
Where is the nearest hospital?	**Où est l'hôpital le plus proche?**	oo ay l'**opee**tal luh ploo **prosh**

COMMUNICATION ESSENTIALS

Yes	**Oui**	wee
No	**Non**	noñ
Please	**S'il vous plaît**	seel voo **play**
Thank you	**Merci**	mer-**see**
Excuse me	**Excusez-moi**	exkoo-**zay** mwah
Hello	**Bonjour**	boñ**zhoor**
Goodbye	**Au revoir**	oh ruh-**vwar**
Good night	**Bonsoir**	boñ-**swar**
Morning	**Le matin**	matañ
Afternoon	**L'après-midi**	l'apreh-**meedee**
Evening	**Le soir**	swar
Yesterday	**Hier**	eey**ehr**
Today	**Aujourd'hui**	oh-zhoor-**dwee**
Tomorrow	**Demain**	duh**mañ**
Here	**Ici**	ee-**see**
There	**Là**	lah
What?	**Quel, quelle?**	kel, kel
When?	**Quand?**	koñ
Why?	**Pourquoi?**	poor-**kwah**
Where?	**Où?**	oo

USEFUL PHRASES

How are you?	**Comment allez-vous?**	kom-moñ tal**ay** voo
Very well, thank you.	**Très bien, merci.**	treh byañ, mer-**see**
Pleased to meet you.	**Enchanté de faire votre connaissance.**	oñshoñ-**tay** duh fehr votr kon-ay-**sans**
See you soon.	**A bientôt.**	abyañ-**toh**
That's fine.	**Voilà qui est parfait.**	vwalah kee ay par**fay**
Where is/are...?	**Où est/sont...?**	oo ay/soñ
How far is it to...?	**Combien de kilomètres d'ici à...?**	kom-**byañ** duh is keelo-**metr** d'ee-**see** ah
Which way to...?	**Quelle est la direction pour...?**	kel ay lah d**eer**-ek-**syoñ** poor
Do you speak English?	**Parlez-vous anglais?**	par-**lay** voo oñg-**lay**
I don't understand.	**Je ne comprends pas.**	zhuh nuh kom-**proñ** pah

Could you / I'm sorry.

Could you speak slowly, please?	**Pouvez-vous parler moins vite, s'il vous plaît?**	poo-**vay** voo par-**lay** mw**añ** veet seel voo play
I'm sorry.	**Excusez-moi.**	exkoo-**zay** mwah

USEFUL WORDS

big	**grand**	groñ
small	**petit**	puh-**tee**
hot	**chaud**	show
cold	**froid**	frwah
good	**bon**	boñ
bad	**mauvais**	moh-**veh**
enough	**assez**	as**say**
well	**bien**	byañ
open	**ouvert**	oo-**ver**
closed	**fermé**	fer-**meh**
left	**gauche**	gohsh
right	**droit**	drwah
straight on	**tout droit**	too drwah
near	**près**	preh
far	**loin**	lwañ
up	**en haut**	oñ **oh**
down	**en bas**	oñ **bah**
early	**de bonne heure**	duh bon **urr**
late	**en retard**	oñ ruh-**tar**
entrance	**l'entrée**	l'on-**tray**
exit	**la sortie**	sor-**tee**
toilet	**les toilettes, les WC**	**twah**-let, vay-**see**
unoccupied	**libre**	leebr
no charge	**gratuit**	grah-**twee**

MAKING A TELEPHONE CALL

I'd like to place a long-distance call.	**Je voudrais faire un interurbain.**	zhuh voo-dreh fehr uñ añter-oorbañ
I'd like to make a reverse-charge call.	**Je voudrais faire une communication PCV.**	zhuh voo**dreh** fehr oon kom-oonikah-**syoñ** peh-seh-veh
I'll try again later.	**Je rappelerai plus tard.**	zhuh rapel**eray** ploo tar
Can I leave a message?	**Est-ce que je peux laisser un message?**	es-**keh** zhuh puh leh-**say** uñ mehsazh
Hold on.	**Ne quittez pas, s'il vous plaît.**	nuh kee-**tay** pah seel voo play.
Could you speak up a little please?	**Pouvez-vous parler un peu plus fort?**	poo-**vay** voo par-**lay** uñ puh ploo for
local call	**la communication locale**	komoonikah-**syoñ** low-**kal**

SHOPPING

How much does this cost?	**C'est combien s'il vous plaît?**	say kom-**byañ** seel voo play
Do you take credit cards?	**Est-ce que vous acceptez les cartes de crédit?**	es-**kuh** voo zaksept-**ay** leh kart duh kreh-**dee**

Do you take travellers' cheques?	Est-ce que vous acceptez les chèques de voyage?	es-**kuh** voo zaksept-**ay** leh shek duh vwa**yazh**
I would like ...	Je voudrais...	zhuh voo-**dray**
Do you have?	Est-ce que vous avez?	es-**kuh** voo zav**ay**
I'm just looking.	Je regarde seulement.	zhuh ruh**gar** suhl**moñ**
What time do you open?	A quelle heure vous êtes ouvert?	ah kel urr voo zet oo-**ver**
What time do you close?	A quelle heure vous êtes fermé?	ah kel urr voo zet fer-**may**
This one	Celui-ci	suhl-wee-**see**
That one	Celui-là	suhl-wee-**lah**
expensive	cher	shehr
cheap	pas cher, bon marché	pah shehr, boñ mar-**shay**
size, clothes	la taille	tye
size, shoes	la pointure	pwañ-**tur**
white	blanc	bloñ
black	noir	nwahr
red	rouge	roozh
yellow	jaune	zhohwn
green	vert	vehr
blue	bleu	bluh

TYPES OF SHOP

antique shop	le magasin d'antiquités	maga-**zañ** d'oñteekee-**tay**
bakery	la boulangerie	booloñ-**zhuree**
bank	la banque	boñk
book shop	la librairie	lee-**brehree**
butcher	la boucherie	boo-**shehree**
cake shop	la pâtisserie	patee-**sree**
cheese shop	la fromagerie	fromazh-**ree**
chemist	la pharmacie	farmah-**see**
dairy	la crémerie	krem-**ree**
department store	le grand magasin	groñ maga-**zañ**
delicatessen	la charcuterie	sharkoot-**ree**
fishmonger	la poissonnerie	pwasson-**ree**
gift shop	le magasin de cadeaux	maga-**zañ** duh ka**doh**
greengrocer	le marchand de légumes	mar-**shoñ** duh lay-**goom**
grocery	l'alimentation	alee-moñta-**syoñ**
hairdresser	le coiffeur	kwa**fuhr**
market	le marché	marsh-**ay**
newsagent	le magasin de journaux	maga-**zañ** duh zhoor-**no**
post office	la poste, le bureau de poste, les PTT	pohst, booroh duh pohst, peh-teh-teh
shoe shop	le magasin de chaussures	maga-**zañ** duh show-**soor**
supermarket	le super-marché	soo pehr-**marshay**
tobacconist	le tabac	tabah
travel agent	l'agence de voyages	l'azhoñs duh vwayazh

MENU DECODER

l'agneau	l'an**yoh**	lamb
l'ail	l'eye	garlic
la banane	ba**nan**	banana
le beurre	burr	butter
la bière	bee-**yehr**	beer
le bifteck, le steack	beef-**tek**, stek	steak
le boeuf	buhf	beef
bouilli	boo-**yee**	boiled
le café	kah-**fay**	coffee
le canard	kanar	duck
le citron pressé	see-**troñ** press-**eh**	fresh lemon juice
les crevettes	kruh-**vet**	prawns
les crustacés	**kroos**-ta-say	shellfish
cuit au four	kweet oh foor	baked
le dessert	deh-**ser**	dessert
l'eau minérale	l'oh **meeney**-ral	mineral water
les escargots	leh zes-kar-**goh**	snails
les frites	freet	chips
le fromage	from-**azh**	cheese
les fruits frais	frwee freh	fresh fruit
les fruits de mer	frwee duh mer	seafood
le gâteau	gah-**toh**	cake
la glace	glas	ice, ice cream
grillé	gree-**yay**	grilled
le homard	omahr	lobster
l'huile	l'weel	oil
le jambon	zhoñ-**boñ**	ham
le lait	leh	milk
les légumes	lay-**goom**	vegetables
la moutarde	moo-**tard**	mustard
l'oeuf	l'uf	egg
les oignons	leh zon**yoñ**	onions
les olives	leh zo**leev**	olives
l'orange pressée	l'oroñzh press-**eh**	fresh orange juice
le pain	pan	bread
le petit pain	puh-**tee** pañ	roll
poché	posh-**ay**	poached
le poisson	pwah-**ssoñ**	fish
le poivre	pwavr	pepper
la pomme	pom	apple
les pommes de terre	pom-duh tehr	potatoes
le porc	por	pork
le potage	poh-**tazh**	soup
le poulet	poo-**lay**	chicken
le riz	ree	rice
rôti	row-**tee**	roast
la sauce	sohs	sauce
la saucisse	soh**sees**	sausage, fresh
sec	sek	dry
le sel	sel	salt
le sucre	sookr	sugar
le thé	tay	tea
le toast	toast	toast
la viande	vee-**yand**	meat
le vin blanc	vañ **bloñ**	white wine
le vin rouge	vañ **roozh**	red wine
le vinaigre	vee**naygr**	vinegar

EATING OUT

Have you got a table?	**Avez-vous une table libre?**	avay-**voo** oon tahbl leebr
I want to reserve a table.	**Je voudrais réserver une table.**	zhuh voo-**dray** rayzehr-**vay** oon tahbl
The bill, please.	**L'addition, s'il vous plaît.**	l'adee-**syoñ** seel voo **play**
I am a vegetarian.	**Je suis végétarien.**	zhuh swee vezhay-**tehryañ**
Waitress/ waiter	**Madame, Mademoiselle/ Monsieur**	mah-**dam**, mah-dem wah zel/muh-**syuh**
menu	**le menu, la carte**	men-**oo**, kart
fixed-price menu	**le menu à prix fixe**	men-**oo** ah pree feeks
cover charge	**le couvert**	koo-**vehr**
wine list	**la carte des vins**	kart-deh vañ
glass	**le verre**	vehr
bottle	**la bouteille**	boo-**tay**
knife	**le couteau**	koo-**toh**
fork	**la fourchette**	for-**shet**
spoon	**la cuillère**	kwee-**yehr**
breakfast	**le petit déjeuner**	puh-**tee** deh-**zhuh-nay**
lunch	**le déjeuner**	deh-**zhuh-nay**
dinner	**le dîner**	dee-**nay**
main course	**le plat principal**	plah prañsee-**pal**
starter, first course	**l'entrée, le hors d'oeuvre**	l'oñ-**tray**, or-duhvr
dish of the day	**le plat du jour**	plah doo zhoor
wine bar	**le bar à vin**	bar ah vañ
café	**le café**	ka-**fay**
rare	**saignant**	say-noñ
medium	**à point**	ah **pwañ**
well done	**bien cuit**	byañ **kwee**

STAYING IN A HOTEL

Do you have a vacant room?	**Est-ce que vous avez une chambre?**	es-kuh voo-**zavay** oon shambr
double room	**la chambre pour deux personnes, avec un grand lit**	shambr ah duh pehr-**son**, avek un groñn lee
twin room	**la chambre à deux lits**	shambr ah duh lee
single room	**la chambre pour une personne**	shambr ah oon pehr-**son**
room with a bath, shower	**la chambre avec salle de bains, une douche**	shambr avek sal duh bañ, oon doosh
porter	**le garçon**	gar-**soñ**
key	**la clef**	klay
I have a reservation.	**J'ai fait une réservation.**	zhay fay oon rayzehrva-**syoñ**

SIGHTSEEING

abbey	**l'abbaye**	l'abay-**ee**
art gallery	**la galerie d'art**	galer-**ree** dart
cathedral	**la cathédrale**	katay-**dral**
church	**l'église**	l'ay**gleez**
garden	**le jardin**	zhar-**dañ**
library	**la bibliothèque**	beebleeo-tek
museum	**le musée**	moo-**zay**
railway station	**la gare (SNCF)**	gahr (es-en-say-ef)
bus station	**la gare routière**	gahr roo-tee-**yehr**
tourist information office	**les renseignements touristiques, le syndicat d'initiative**	roñsayn-**moñ** too-rees-**teck**, sandee-ka d'eenee-syat**eev**
town hall	**l'hôtel de ville**	l'ohtel duh veel
private mansion	**l'hôtel particulier**	l'ohtel partikoo-**lyay**
closed for public holiday	**fermeture jour férié**	fehrmeh-**tur** zhoor fehree-**ay**

NUMBERS

00	**zéro**	zeh-**roh**
01	**un, une**	uñ, oon
02	**deux**	duh
03	**trois**	trwah
04	**quatre**	katr
05	**cinq**	sañk
06	**six**	sees
07	**sept**	set
08	**huit**	weet
09	**neuf**	nerf
10	**dix**	dees
11	**onze**	oñz
12	**douze**	dooz
13	**treize**	trehz
14	**quatorze**	ka**torz**
15	**quinze**	kañz
16	**seize**	sehz
17	**dix-sept**	dees-**set**
18	**dix-huit**	dees-**weet**
19	**dix-neuf**	dees-**nerf**
20	**vingt**	vañ
30	**trente**	tront
40	**quarante**	karo**ñt**
50	**cinquante**	sañko**ñt**
60	**soixante**	swaso**ñt**
70	**soixante-dix**	swasoñt-**dees**
80	**quatre-vingts**	katr-**vañ**
90	**quatre-vingts-dix**	katr-vañ-**dees**
100	**cent**	soñ
1,000	**mille**	meel

TIME

one minute	**une minute**	oon mee-**noot**
one hour	**une heure**	oon urr
half an hour	**une demi-heure**	oon **duh-mee** urr
Monday	**lundi**	luñ-**dee**
Tuesday	**mardi**	mar-**dee**
Wednesday	**mercredi**	mehrkruh-**dee**
Thursday	**jeudi**	zhuh-**dee**
Friday	**vendredi**	voñdruh-**dee**
Saturday	**samedi**	sam-**dee**
Sunday	**dimanche**	dee-**moñsh**

EYEWITNESS TRAVEL INSURANCE

FOR PEACE OF MIND ABROAD,
WE'VE GOT IT COVERED

DK INSURANCE PROVIDES YOU
WITH QUALITY WORLDWIDE
INSURANCE COVER

For an instant quote
go to **www.dk.com/travel-insurance**

Organised by Columbus Travel Insurance Services Ltd, 17 Devonshire Square, London EC2M 4SQ, UK.
Underwritten by certain underwriters at Lloyd's and Professional Travel Insurance Company Ltd.

Road Map of Corsica